In Praise of Wisdom

Kim Paffenroth

In Praise of Wisdom

Literary and Theological Reflections on Faith and Reason

continuum
NEW YORK • LONDON

Copyright © 2004 by Kim Paffenroth

The Continuum International Publishing Group, 15 East 26th Street, New York, NY 10010

The Continuum International Publishing Group Ltd, The Tower Building, 11 York Road, London SE1 7NX

All rights reserved. No part of this book may be reproduced, stored in a retrieval system, or transmitted in any form or by any means, electronic, mechanical, including photocopying, recording, or otherwise, without the written permission of the publishers.

Unless otherwise indicated, Scripture quotations are taken from the New Revised Standard Version of the Bible, copyright 1989 by the Division of Christian Education of the National Council of the Churches of Christ in the USA. Used by permission. All rights reserved.

Cover art: William Blake, "Job Rebuked by His Friends." The Pierpont Morgan Library / Art Resource, NY.

Cover design: Corey Kent

Library of Congress Cataloging-in-Publication Data

Paffenroth, Kim, 1966–
  In praise of wisdom : literary and theological reflections on faith and reason / Kim Paffenroth.
    p. cm.
  Includes bibliographical references and index.
  ISBN 0-8264-1603-9 (hardcover)
  1. Faith and reason—History of doctrines. I. Title.
  BT50.P34 2004
  231'.042—dc22
                                    2003021665

04 05 06 07 08 09 10 9 8 7 6 5 4 3 2 1

For Charles and Sophia

You are the only [ones] of all [people] whom
I would wish to surpass me in all things.

—Cicero

Thou shouldst not have been old till thou hadst been wise.
King Lear (1.5.38)

You don't have to be old to be wise.
—Judas Priest

Contents

Preface	xi
1. The Sins of the Father: Evil and Folly in the Old Testament and Dostoevsky	1
2. "The Eternal Feminine Draws Us Upward": Feminine Wisdom in the Old Testament, Augustine, and Goethe's *Faust*	33
3. "Reason in Madness": The Wisdom of Folly in the New Testament and *King Lear*	53
4. The Inadequacy of Reason in Ecclesiastes and *Pensées*	85
5. The Meaning of Suffering in Job and *Moby Dick*	101
Conclusion: Life and Love with Wisdom of the Heart	135
Bibliography	143
Index	153

Preface

In this work I examine the many nuances and developments of the biblical concept of wisdom. The special perspective of this work lies in how it examines wisdom in theological works—the Bible, Augustine, and Pascal—and at the same time shows how these theological concepts of wisdom are taken over and elaborated by some of the most important literary figures of the sixteenth through nineteenth centuries—Shakespeare, Goethe, Melville, and Dostoevsky. All of these thinkers finally think of wisdom as an expression of the positive interaction of faith and reason as mutually dependent ways of human knowing, as well as fundamental elements of human fulfillment. Although they sometimes toy with the more modern idea of faith versus reason, they all depict this conflict as false and falsifying, an unnecessary and unhealthy fracturing of human experience, one doomed to cause unhappiness and emptiness.

My hope is that this study will move Christian readers beyond this modern dichotomy by showing the variety and profundity of Christian teaching on the mutually constructive relation between reason and faith, and the rich scriptural, theological, and literary traditions that have expressed this relation. And as much as I want to consider the theological and psychological helpfulness of *Christian* literature, I also want to stress the importance of reading and discussing Christian *literature*. While I find the foundation of my theological reflections in Scripture, I usually find the fullest elaboration or the most helpful illustration of that foundation in later literature. When I first read about Lady Wisdom in Proverbs, I found the image beautiful and intriguing, but I don't think I really knew what it meant until I met Gretchen in Goethe's *Faust* or Monica in Augustine's *Confessions*. And to be quite honest, I had always found the description of folly in Proverbs rather unbelievable and unlikely, a straw man or bogey man one could never meet, at least until I met Fyodor Karamazov and the narrator of *Notes from Underground,* two utterly believable characters who show us how far we will go to perpetuate our foolishness and lose ourselves and our pain in our folly. And as compelling and true as I found Job's suffering, Lear and Ahab are a good deal more complex and rounded, and they have helped me understand the original story in light of them, while at the same time Job has helped me to understand and frame their trials. This learning and connecting need not be confined to great literature (though I will always advocate that as the best place to start). Consider the quotations I have paired at the beginning of this book: There is no denying the similarity and truth of both, even though it is quite unlikely that the lads of Judas Priest had the Bard of Avon in mind when they penned their own immortal lyrics. When we put old ideas and the texts that express them into dialogue with new books and ideas, and, more important, when we put ourselves into dialogue with both—questioning them and being questioned by them—the outcome is a deeper understanding of their ideas and of our own lives. The world becomes for us a richer place that speaks to us more often and more eloquently.

There are further advantages and challenges to this consideration of literature as opposed to more narrowly theological works. First, most people, even the churched, have had much greater exposure to literary than to theological works. I will be honest at the beginning: Seven years of graduate school, and I have read only a few pages of Bultmann and Barth, and none of Troeltsch or Tillich. And from the hours I spent on what I did read, I am in no special hurry to read more, for while I respect and value their insights, the authors just make you work too hard to understand them; the return on investment is far too low, for me at least. On the other hand, year after year I turn back to plays, poems, and novels and find more and more beauty and truth therein, while enjoying every minute I spend reading. I can only assume that my readers have just as little exposure to or patience for narrowly theological works. Even the theologians I have chosen—Augustine and Pascal—are among the few I would consider lyrical or literary in their writing; they appreciate the texture, tone, or beauty of ideas as much as they appreciate the logic of them.

But just because we all have more exposure to literature, it is a true cliché that familiarity breeds contempt. Just as many of my students who have been through twelve years of Catholic school are quite bored and fed up with theology, many of my students are quite bored with Shakespeare and Sophocles, feeling that they have heard quite enough of all that fate and tragic flaw and hubris stuff. Surprisingly, many who scoff at literature are voracious readers; most will read pulp fiction (romance, spy thrillers, sci-fi) insatiably on the subway or bus ride to and from school, but they are sure that reading (like watching movies or television) is for pure entertainment, not enlightenment or improvement. It is indeed an enormous irony that I myself am writing on literature: Twenty years ago I assumed I knew everything there was to know about literature, and I had little interest in learning more. Partly this was typical teenage arrogance and immaturity, but partly I think it is that we are all taught very badly in high school to read literature. We are trained in the most boring and formulaic of practices—to find the various devices of writing, to look for meter, rhyme, parallelism, foreshadowing, irony—but almost never to ask what a book *means,* and even more, whether that meaning might be *true.* We are taught to analyze, or more accurately, to dissect, not to understand or *enjoy*—to feel some deep, joyful change in us at something we have read. So my goal in this work is not so much to give information or analysis as to whet readers' appetites for more great religious literature by showing them some of the joy it has brought me. If some of my readers begin to think of reading literature as a way to inform their faith as well as to be entertained, I think this will be a valuable volume indeed.

Wisdom is a hugely important concept in both Testaments. It is found in some of the oldest surviving works of the Old Testament (Proverbs 10–29), in some of the more recent Old Testament writings (Ecclesiastes), and in the New Testament, thereby showing that it was an important category in Israelite thought for well over a millennium. Nor was it the exclusive property of Israel, but it was a point of view and a movement that Israelite sages shared with other seekers from all over the Near East: "Hebrew Wisdom was by no means a unique phenomenon in the ancient world. On the contrary, its literature has been found to have much in common with similar records from contemporary and older cultures, notably those of Egypt and Mesopotamia."[1] In later centuries, it would be a point of contact between Greek and Hebrew thought, though scholars still debate the degree and type of influence.[2] Wisdom offered all its followers simple yet profound guidance in their relations with God and with other people. Though it changed over time, the tradition's reliance on experiential knowledge remained consistent, and believers still turn to the wisdom books for their frankness, practicality, and beauty.[3]

In this work I examine biblical wisdom under five broad categories and show connections between its concepts and later theological and literary works that elaborate and expand on these ideas: the destructiveness of folly, the feminine side of wisdom, the folly of Christ as the Wisdom of God, the inadequacy of reason, and the problem of suffering. The destructiveness of folly will be examined in Proverbs and Sirach, and then in Dostoevsky, who goes so far as to make folly and evil the necessary foundations of life, goodness, and freedom. Proverbs, Sirach, the Book of Wisdom, Augustine's writings, and Goethe's *Faust* provide examples of the feminine side of wisdom. Both Augustine's writings and *Faust* contain powerful and problematic relationships with women, and both Augustine and the character Faust are ultimately self-deprecating and appreciative of something they lack that the women in their lives have—the soothing, healthful ability to integrate their reason and faith and live whole and peaceful lives, not the conflicted, fractured lives of strife that these two men suffered. The New Testament and Shakespeare's *King Lear* contain examples of the folly of Christ and the wisdom of God. Such moments can be seen in the Christlikeness of Cordelia and in the redemption that Lear finds when he abandons the worldly wisdom of appearance and power for the divine wisdom of truth, love, and sacrifice. We will look at the inadequacy of reason in Ecclesiastes and in Pascal's *Pensées*. Finally, Job and Melville's *Moby-Dick* vividly illustrate the problem of innocent suffering and the redemptive reaction to it. These later authors allude directly to the biblical tradition, even as their works carry us far beyond their biblical bases. Pascal's relentless reason and Ahab's relentless rage take us to places the biblical texts hint at but never fully explore.

The truth, beauty, and pain of all these works capture fully what it is to be human and give us a glimpse of what the divine and our relationship to it might be like. Their art makes their theology much closer to practice than to theory, and it affects us more deeply. All of the later authors anchor their theology in human experience, just as the biblical wisdom tradition did, and they also constantly return to the same primal themes as the biblical writers—love and death. Whether it is Augustine and Monica, Lear and Cordelia, Faust and Gretchen, the Man from Underground and Liza, the sordid lives of the Karamazov family, the sickly Pascal ruminating on human mortality, Queequeg and Ishmael, or Ahab's obsession with the White Whale/God—they all try to make sense of human life, death, and love in a world that usually seems devoid of meaning and full of pain. And in their different ways, they reiterate the lessons from Proverbs on down: The human mind and heart can never understand each other, but they can live, love, and learn together meaningfully, sometimes even beautifully.

This work was begun at my former institution, Villanova University, where the constant harping of my boss Jack Doody about transcendence and a life of the mind has left an indelible impression on my analyses of these literary and theological texts. I have continued the work at my present position at Iona College, where the encouragement of my colleagues in the Religious Studies Department—Brian Brown, Kathleen Deignan, Robert Durning, Elena Procario-Foley, and Barbara Srozenski—has allowed me to continue and even expand my eclectic tastes. Especially generous was how they and Dean Alex Eodice allowed me to teach these works in a course on evil and suffering. This final journey through these works with my students was just the finishing touch I needed on thoughts I have mulled over for years.

At both of these schools and the others at which I have taught, it is my interaction with students that has most shaped my thinking about these books. As I have said on many other occasions in other writings, the ideas in this book come directly from my classroom experience. The comparisons and connections between these works never would have occurred to me if I had not read them together with such insightful and perceptive students, from whom I have learned much more than they from me. I would especially single out Amy Barone, Erica DePalo, and Colleen O'Boyle; their essays on Dostoevsky and Melville still awe me with their sublime beauty, and garnered me the highest honor I have experienced in my professional life—the honor of presenting them with much deserved writing awards at Villanova University. Among my students at Iona College, for the last year Christine Casino and Angela Harris have posed persistent and thoughtful questions that have focused my thought on these works and made my analysis of them more precise. The section on *King Lear* owes much to Joe Sachs, the sensitive and patient teacher with whom I first read the play, and to the women and men of the Shakespeare discussion group at Borders Books and Music in Bryn Mawr, Pennsylvania, from whom I learned so much about Shakespeare in the two and a half years we read him together. Special thanks also go to my friends and colleagues Tom Bertonneau, Rick Bolles, Todd Breyfogle, Mary Lu Hill, Bob Jarrell, Robert Kennedy, Jon Levenson, Bob McCutcheon, Bob McMahon, Dan Morehead, Dave Schindler Jr., and Brian Weimer for their comments as this work progressed: They have brought to the material much deeper literary and religious sensitivity than I could offer. And to Glenn, K. K., Ian, Scott, and Tim—your music continues to inspire me (however strange that may seem to many), and it makes me smile when my children dance around to it.

The staff at Ryan Library of Iona College has been most accommodating in letting me check out more than the allowable limit of books and in their leniency toward late returns. Jenna Freedman has rendered exceptional service both to my research and to the Iona community by her acquisition of new books for the Ryan collection. Also, Susan Robinson and Lina Poidomani have been very helpful and efficient at obtaining difficult-to-find items from other libraries.

Thanks go to my editor, Henry Carrigan. His support of this project made it possible and his ideas have improved it. I am lucky and grateful for finding such a sympathetic and intelligent reader.

Financial support for this project has come from two extremely generous grants from the Earhart Foundation that have allowed me the time to pursue this topic of research.

Finally, I thank my wife, Marlis, for all her support and encouragement, and especially for the most precious gift of our two children, Charles and (the appropriately named) Sophia, to whom this book is dedicated, and who I am sure will always exceed me in wisdom and faith throughout their lives.

KIM PAFFENROTH
Cornwall on Hudson, NY
August 28, 2002, Feast Day of St. Augustine

Notes

1. R. B. Y. Scott, *The Way of Wisdom in the Old Testament* (New York: Macmillan, 1971), 23.

2. See R. E. Murphy, *The Tree of Life: An Exploration of Biblical Wisdom Literature* (2d ed.; Grand Rapids: Eerdmans, 1990), 171–75.

3. Although the subject has been treated thoroughly by experts in Hebrew history and theology, there still remain some oversimplifications that I think obscure and hinder a regular Christian's understanding of the tradition. For example, it is generally portrayed as evolving from this-worldly to other-worldly, and from a naive acceptance of ethical norms to a pessimistic questioning of them. The tradition seems more consistent to me: I cannot imagine books that are more profoundly this-worldly than Ecclesiastes and Job, supposedly examples of late Wisdom. True, there is a tendency in later Wisdom to ask more specifically God-oriented questions—to talk about theology in addition to anthropology or ethics—but it remains true to the tradition by rooting its theology in human experience: Job is so powerful precisely because it will not accept a simplistic theology that flies in the face of human experience. And although the later tradition does not assume that overt physical harm will result from bad behavior, it seems that attitudes of self-sufficiency and self-absorption remain as dangerous and damaging as ever to human beings, whether they result in sickness and shame as in Proverbs, boredom and sadness as in Ecclesiastes, or smugness versus despair as in Job. Human attitudes, not our physical state, are always what determine whether our lives are wretched or blessed.

1. The Sins of the Father:
Evil and Folly in the Old Testament and Dostoevsky

Introduction

Consider for a moment what you say to your children before they leave the house to go to the playground alone, or to your teenagers when they take the car. In English we would automatically shout after them the vaguely concerned "Be careful!" while in French it is the more philosophical-sounding *"Soyez prudent!"* ("Be wise!") and in German the more panic-stricken *"Pass auf!"* ("Watch out!"). If examined closely, common speech often has a way of revealing underlying assumptions and connections that we may have overlooked. Why are the mundane-sounding "careful" and the much more elevated "wise" closely related in our minds and speech? And how do both relate to being worried or scared about something against which we are supposed to be on our guard, something for which we are to "watch out"? What are we afraid of, and what do we want?

Wisdom in its most basic sense relates to the ideas of prudence, care, and caution. In very small children it relates strictly to physical well-being: Don't run while carrying scissors, wear your galoshes in the rain, wash your hands before you eat. When you see a three-year-old running with scissors in his hand, you exclaim, "Watch out!" followed by a stern lecture about the reasons for this prohibition: Your first response is the immediate, reflexive expression of wisdom or common sense, while your follow-up lecture is the fuller explanation of the same perspective. Both demonstrate that you are wiser than the three-year-old. Running with scissors is not immoral or evil; it is just dangerous and imprudent. As these basic habits of prudence are acquired and more complicated and dangerous behaviors are taken up, the same idea of wisdom would be applied to control them, still primarily focused on physical well-being: Don't drive the car too fast, don't drink and drive, don't smoke, don't be promiscuous. When you examine your teenagers' friends, this is the kind of wisdom you are looking for in them, much more than whether they are intelligent or enlightened people. (Your teenager would surely have no friends if such elevated criteria were applied.) The answer to my earlier question about what we are afraid of is that we are afraid of being unhappy, and having your eye poked out with scissors or being crippled in a car accident would make you unhappy (or at least much less happy than you might have been), so part of wisdom is learning to avoid the behaviors that tend to produce those injuries.

It is precisely in its application to interpersonal dealings—to the friends you have and how you treat them—that wisdom begins to take on a higher, moral sense, even before the teenage years. Unlike running with scissors, being cruel or inconsiderate is immoral, and avoiding both kinds of behavior is part of growing up and growing wise. When I tell my small children to be careful with other children, my exhortation includes prohibitions against pushing, hitting, and breaking other children's toys, but I give this advice not primarily out of concern for their physical safety but because such behavior would result in my children being disliked and excluded, causing them much more social and emotional, rather than physical, harm. At a further level of abstraction, such behavior is forbidden because it is immoral and damaging to their souls, but such reasoning is usually way beyond adults, let alone children; a great advantage of an appeal to wisdom is that it shows the advantageousness of morality in less abstract and much more concrete and immediate terms. Even in the very young, we expect that care and consideration in their relationships will include kindness, honesty, and generosity. We have these expectations to a large extent because it is in their best interest to act this way. Eventually in life, this moral and personal sense of wisdom comes to predominate: One does not call an eighty-year-old man wise because he drives slowly (most all old people would be wise in that case), but rather because a lifetime of dealing with other people has given him a broader perspective and more insight into other people and into himself. A lifetime of observing what motivates people has made him a better judge of character and values and, just as importantly, has made him honest about his own needs and limitations. The answer to my earlier question about what we want is that we want to be happy, and learning what really makes us happy—our relations with other people and with God—and how best to pursue such happiness is the real goal and measure of a person's wisdom.

The biblical wisdom tradition gives ample expression to both of the senses of wisdom and the close connection between them. The Old Testament texts repeatedly praise the common sense that we should learn and practice in order to maintain our physical well-being, but at the same time we are mastering that, we should be looking to the higher sense of wisdom as a moral and spiritual improvement slowly achieved over a long life of practice, devotion, and reflection.

Worldly Wisdom for a Successful Life: Proverbs and Sirach

The book of Proverbs has been one of the more popular biblical books, often invoked for the simple but timely truths it contains.[1] These are conveyed in pithier form than Aesop's fables and often have more direct, everyday applications than Confucius' sayings.[2] The book of Sirach (or Ecclesiasticus or the Wisdom of Ben Sira) is less well known, preserved only in the Apocrypha, which comprises books of the Old Testament not usually considered authoritative by Protestants or Jews but considered worthy of study by all who seek to understand ancient Israelite thought.[3] Together these books show us the transmission and development of the wisdom tradition over the course of eight centuries. Proverbs itself probably took centuries to accumulate as we now have it (900–200 B.C.E.),[4] and Sirach (ca. 180 B.C.E.)[5] shows us a glimpse of the wisdom tradition in the second century B.C.E.

Biblical wisdom is most often synonymous with what we would term common sense.[6] It is enlightened self-interest or self-interested enlightenment in its clearest, oldest form: "To get wisdom is to love oneself; to keep understanding is to prosper" (Prov 19:8). The sayings are rooted in and confirmed by experience: "Practical, or experiential, wisdom was an elementary ordering of life in all its dimensions. It entailed close study of human behavior in every conceivable situation, from which certain basic principles for successful behavior were formulated."[7] Such sayings are numerous and cover a wide variety of topics: "A soft answer turns away wrath, but a harsh word stirs up anger" (Prov 15:1); "My child, eat honey, for it is good" (Prov 24:13); "For sickness alights on overeating" (Sir 37:30).[8] The speaker has often seen people provoked by harsh words, he has discovered that the sticky liquid produced by bees is not as inedible as it looks, and he has often seen people who eat too much get sick. He has then drawn generalized conclusions from these observations for his audience so that they will not have to experience these setbacks personally before they learn to avoid them. Implicit in such advice is the idea that the audience could see such generalizations confirmed if they too observed life as long as the sage has done; furthermore, since the conclusion is based on experience, if enough contrary observations are made, then the saying would have to be modified or discarded. We will see an even more radical reformulation of the wisdom tradition in Ecclesiastes and Job as the biblical authors consider how the world does not match up with what is expected according to the wisdom tradition of their time.

But one needn't believe in God to believe that experience can teach us to avoid certain self-destructive behaviors and to describe general patterns in life. This fact has led some to question whether the Wisdom books are religious or theological in any specific sense.[9] Perhaps they are compatible with Judaism (or Christianity) but not really a part of it. I think it would be more accurate to turn this view around and say that the sayings of the wise are mostly compatible with atheism or agnosticism (a few specifically mention God, but the vast majority do not), but their underlying assumption is the same as that of the rest of the Bible: A loving, caring God has made and governs all creation according to his rules and purposes. If anything, the Wisdom books are an important look at some areas of God's activity that are otherwise neglected in the Bible:

> In the smaller concrete details of life one found innumerable situations that called for attitudes, actions, and decisions that ultimately had a profound effect on the individual. This sphere was not felt to be withdrawn from the Lord and his activity; God was as much at work here as in the heady experiences of Israel's history and liturgical worship. The Lord's dominion over the created world is at the core of wisdom's effort to help one live in the world.[10]

Wisdom theology is everyday theology. It is not concerned with the crucial but unrepeatable events of salvation—for Jews, the Exodus and Covenant; for Christians, the Passion, death, and resurrection of Christ—but with helping believers understand and enjoy God's creation while they seek him in it.

Perhaps God's presence in creation can be shown by considering how the sages thought God would punish folly. Here is how the writer of Proverbs 5:1–14 exhorts a man to avoid the folly of promiscuity:

> My child, be attentive to my wisdom; incline your ear to my understanding, so that you may hold on to prudence, and your lips may guard knowledge. For the lips of a loose woman drip honey, and her speech is smoother than oil; but in the end she is bitter as wormwood, sharp as a two-edged sword. Her feet go down to death; her steps follow the path to Sheol. She does not keep straight to the path of life; her ways wander, and she does not know it.
>
> And now, my child, listen to me, and do not depart from the words of my mouth. Keep your way far from her, and do not go near the door of her house; or you will give your honor to others, and your years to the merciless, and strangers will take their fill of your wealth, and your labors will go to the house of an alien; and at the end of your life you will groan, when

your flesh and body are consumed, and you say, "Oh, how I hated discipline, and my heart despised reproof! I did not listen to the voice of my teachers or incline my ear to my instructors. Now I am at the point of utter ruin in the public assembly."

No thunderbolts smite the sinner this time, for God has constructed the world in such a way that sins often carry their own punishment within them: "The iniquities of the wicked ensnare them" (Prov 5:22). God has built this punishment into several parts of creation: in the case of promiscuity, it can assert itself in the physical realm in the form of disease ("flesh and body are consumed"); in the legal realm by the enforcement of the rights of the illegitimate children ("strangers will take their fill of your wealth"); and in the social realm by the shame that accompanies the behavior ("the point of utter ruin in the public assembly"). God's construction of the world around observable, repeated phenomena can also have a positive aspect, for just as God has built punishment for sin into the creation, he has given people the wisdom to understand, help, and heal: "Make friends with the physician, for he is essential to you; him also God has established in his profession. From God the doctor has his wisdom" (Sir 38:1–2). God's creation is full of signs that make folly unattractive and that show the advantageousness of wisdom.

Of course, not every form of folly fits the model so well, which is why the sages constantly return to those that usually do—promiscuity (e.g., Prov 7:1–27; 23:26–28; Sir 9:1–9; 22:18–26), drunkenness (e.g., Prov 23:29–35; Sir 31:25–31), and laziness (e.g., Prov 20:13; 24:30–34; 26:13–16; Sir 22:1–2). In our world we can trace all sorts of ailments to activities that are usually thought of as morally neutral—working in a coal mine, typing fast on a computer, talking on a cell phone. Here wisdom would probably counsel us to modify our behavior if we are to enjoy life, or to use our own wisdom to find solutions. It doesn't seem evil to have an appliance plugged in right next to the bathtub, but it does seem profoundly foolish once one understands some basic properties of electricity, conductivity, and water; and since one cannot change how God has chosen to make electricity behave, one had better move the appliance. God does not want to punish people who don't understand electricity, so God has given them the ability to figure it out, and God expects them to do so. On the other hand, even the ancient sages must have noticed that there is no equivalent of syphilis or cirrhosis to strike down those who lie, cheat, steal, dishonor their father and mother, or take the Lord's name in vain; here the social networks that produce shame and punishment would have to do all the work of showing God's disapproval. But since society itself is part of God's order, this is no surprise to the ancient sages, and they constantly counsel honesty and generosity toward other people, lest one suffer reproach and ostracization from not acting so:[10]

> Whoever betrays a secret destroys confidence; he will never find an intimate friend. (Sir 27:16)
> Like a maniac who shoots deadly firebrands and arrows, so is one who deceives a neighbor and says, "I am only joking!" (Prov 26:18–19)
> A good name is to be chosen rather than great riches, and favor is better than silver or gold. (Prov 22:1)
> A slanderer besmirches himself, and is hated by his neighbors. (Sir 21:28)
> Whoever is miserly with food is denounced in public, and this testimony to his stinginess is lasting. (Sir 31:24)

When we have learned to be wise in our dealings with other people, we have learned not just to be wary or careful (though that may well be a large part of one's dealings with strangers, enemies, or superiors) but to be "trustworthy, patient, generous, modest, peaceable, and self-controlled."[12] In short, we learn that goodness is a part of wisdom, for we learn that benefiting others is the best way to benefit ourselves.

And as we learn how much our happiness and well-being depend on others, we also learn how dependent we are on God. The wisdom tradition uses the phrase "fear of the Lord" to express this sense of dependence, respect, and awe before our Creator and makes it the epitome or foundation of wisdom: "The fear of the LORD is the beginning of wisdom" (Prov 9:10; cf. 1:7; 8:13; 15:33); "The whole of wisdom is fear of the Lord" (Sir 19:20; cf. 1:11–30). As negative as "fear" sounds to us, the Bible nonetheless relates it to love: "Those who fear the Lord do not disobey his words; those who love him keep his ways" (Sir 2:15).[13] We obey those we fear (kings, bosses), as well as those we love (parents), and our obedience to God includes both these elements. The wisdom writers stress fear as something very positive: "Fear of the Lord is glory and exultation, gladness and a festive crown" (Sir 1:11). To fear the Lord is not the same as saying, "I'm scared of the Lord"; the right kind of fear makes us happy, not frightened, and it makes us secure by acknowledging our vulnerability. Fear of the Lord brings this joy because it acknowledges what is most true about human beings: that we are limited, imperfect, and need help. Denying these human characteristics would not make people happy but only more unhappy. An essential part of being wise or happy is understanding our limitations and reliance on others, especially God: "Do not be wise in your own eyes; fear the LORD" (Prov 3:7). The people and things in our lives that bring us joy come to us only from God, to whom we can be either grateful or ungrateful, but the latter does not give us any greater enjoyment or independence: "Wisdom stands and falls according to the right attitude of man to God."[14] A large part of the appeal and profundity of biblical wisdom is that it unites the extremes of simple self-interest and total submission to God throughout its expression. It is in our self-interest to submit to God, for the loving God to whom we submit has our best interests at heart.

The Necessity of Folly and Evil: Dostoevsky's *Notes from Underground*

Even more than other authors, Fyodor Dostoevsky (1821–81) reflects his personal experiences of suffering and of the search for meaning and redemption in pain. His life seemed full of more than the usual number of mishaps and tragedies.[15] Both his parents died when he was young, the burden of his father's death worsened by its circumstances, for he was murdered by his own serfs in retaliation for his cruelty. Dostoevsky began writing in 1846 and was arrested in 1849 for alleged political crimes. Sentenced to death, he had to endure the terrifying ordeal of the guards going through with the preparations for the execution to the last possible moment, a cruel charade designed to torment and break the prisoners, for the guards knew that they had already been granted a reprieve. Dostoevsky then suffered four years of hard labor in Siberia, followed by four years of compulsory military service; during this time, his periodic epileptic seizures began. Dostoevsky's wife and brother both died in 1864, leaving him with considerable debts from his brother, which he proceeded to compound through compulsive gambling. But that year also saw the publication of his first great work, *Notes from Underground*. A second very happy and successful marriage brought a measure of stability to his troubled life, but even this brought Dostoevsky anguish by the deaths of two of their children, to whom he was very loving and attached by all accounts. Although he intended to write a sequel to his masterpiece *The Brothers Karamazov* (1879–80), it now stands as his final statement on the themes of suffering and redemption that both haunted and elevated his life and his writing.

Notes from Underground is divided into two parts; in both parts the fictitious narrator tells us about his life, alternating between being guarded and open or frank and deceitful. The first part is the narrator's theoretical account of his life and philosophy. Here Dostoevsky creates one of the great anti-heroes of all time in a disarmingly honest first-person narrative that begins, "I am a sick man . . . I am a spiteful man."[16] The narrator, whose name is never revealed, is neither a villain nor a hero; he is just barely a protagonist, as he doesn't do much of anything, nor is he capable of much, as he admits early on: "It was not only that I could not become spiteful, I did not know how to become anything; neither spiteful nor kind, neither a rascal nor an honest man, neither a hero nor an insect."[17] He may have a disease, or he may be imagining it, but the effect would be the same: to paralyze him with thinking about it. He imagines himself living a loathsome life in a dirty, stinking, damp "underground," for which he names his memoirs, when in fact we learn from his description that his apartment is on the second floor.[18] He claims extreme intelligence but evinces none even to us, his private audience, and of course none to the other characters in the book, whom he despises and yet desperately needs: He would not deign to act intelligently in front of them, for they don't deserve to see intelligence and could not understand it, according to him. He claims he is "too conscious,"[19] which causes him to become obsessed with and then overanalyze every situation: Every gibe is a crushing, mortal insult to his very being, every offhand remark must really have been carefully thought out to inflict the maximum damage on him, every triviality is fraught with meaning and malice directed at him. He is the most neurotic, narcissistic character ever conceived, a loathsome precursor to George Costanza of television's *Seinfeld*, but unlike George, there is nothing funny about the Underground Man. Instead there is only despair at the seemingly insurmountable abyss between his aspirations and his reality, between a fantasy life of the "sublime and beautiful"[20] and a real life of the pettiest vindictiveness, in which he imagines himself as

> the man of acute consciousness, who has come, of course, not out of the lap of nature but out of a retort (this is almost mysticism, gentlemen, but I suspect this, too), this retort-made man is sometimes so nonplussed in the presence of his antithesis that with all his exaggerated consciousness he genuinely thinks of himself as a mouse and not a man.... There in its nasty, stinking, underground home our insulted, crushed and ridiculed mouse promptly becomes absorbed in cold, malignant and, above all, everlasting spite. For forty years together it will remember its injury down to the smallest, most ignominious details, and every time will add, of itself, details still more ignominious, spitefully teasing and tormenting itself with its own imagination.... On its deathbed it will recall it all over again, with interest accumulated over all the years.[21]

The image would vie with Dante for sheer hellishness and hopelessness. The Underground Man's paranoid fantasies do not end with a laugh at his own expense or someone else's; they don't even end with violent rage, but only with a moan of pain, or a stifled wheeze of suffocation, and this pain and suffocation can and do go on forever in his self-created hell.

So the Underground Man is a masterpiece of characterization; we believe in him and we are fascinated by his ugliness. Like George Costanza, he is more extreme than anyone we know, but he is completely believable, as we all would acknowledge that we can hold grudges and petty insecurities just like he does, just not as extremely or neurotically: "All of us would speak this way, if we had the courage to do so, and if the barriers, the conventions . . . and certain norms of humanity did not prevent us from doing so."[22] His life is like a hellish version of the movie *Groundhog Day:* Just imagine the worst day of your life played over and over, and you know it will be played over, but you can't bring yourself to change it. But what is the point of this character? We believe that such a person could exist, and we sympathize with him to some small degree as we acknowledge our limited similarity to him, but what are we to learn from this most deranged and untrustworthy of narrators?

As the Underground Man rants to us in this first part of the novella, he reveals what are to Dostoevsky fundamental truths of human existence, fundamental questions that Dostoevsky is beginning to formulate and that will recur throughout his great works, finding more complete answers than they do here.[23] These questions come down to stripping away everything until we can consider the essence of being human and the purpose of human life. Human nature and human purpose are first laid bare by the Underground Man as they will be later by Ivan in *The Brothers Karamazov.* One of the fundamental parts of human nature that both characters question is the role of reason in our lives. The constitutive importance of reason, of our ability and need to figure out the world around us and ourselves, is a basic assumption of the biblical wisdom tradition or of Western thought in general with which they take issue:

> As soon as they prove to you, for instance, that you are descended from a monkey, then it is no use scowling, accept it for a fact. When they prove to you that in reality one drop of your own fat must be dearer to you than a hundred thousand of your fellow-creatures, and that this conclusion is the final solution of all so-called virtues and duties and all such prejudices and fancies, then you have just to accept it, there is no help for it, for twice two is a law of mathematics. Just try refuting it.
>
> "Upon my word," they will shout at you, "it is no use protesting: it is a case of twice two makes four! Nature does not ask your permission, she has nothing to do with your wishes, and whether you like her laws or dislike them, you are bound to accept her as she is, and consequently all her conclusions. A wall, you see, is a wall. . . . and so on, and so on." Merciful Heavens! but what do I care for the laws of nature and arithmetic, when, for some reason I dislike those laws and the fact that twice two makes four? Of course I cannot break through the wall by battering my head against it if I really have not the strength to knock it down, but I am not going to be reconciled to it simply because it is a stone wall and I have not the strength.[24]

In George Orwell's *1984* it is one of the ultimate, dehumanizing tyrannies of the state that they can mandate that two plus two is five, that they can finally use sheer terror and force to overturn reason. But here Dostoevsky is asking us to consider whether the tyranny of our reason is any less dehumanizing: If reason tells us that we are not made in the image of God, that there is no such thing as an altruistic act, and that we are not really responsible for anything we do, then reason has destroyed both human dignity and responsibility and reduced us to animals or machines much more thoroughly than any police state ever could. But Dostoevsky's pillorying of the idolatrous and dehumanizing glorification of reason goes an extra step in the twisted mind of his narrator, for he leaps from the one dehumanizing extreme of never questioning reason (being an automaton) to the other dehumanizing extreme of always denying it (being a madman). This makes the Underground Man insane and unhappy, but it does not make him wrong; he has seen clearly that human purpose does not—cannot—lie only in the right exercise of reason, and that understanding the human person cannot consist only in dissecting an animal, psychoanalyzing a mind, or disassembling a machine.

Having blasted the ideal of humans as only or primarily reasoning animals, Dostoevsky's mad spokesman now takes on another related fetish of the Western mind, one that is strongly rooted in common sense or wisdom. He questions whether people must pursue their self-interest, to what extent self-interest can be equated with the good, and how we would even determine our self-interest:

> In all these thousands of years has there been a time when man has acted only from his own interest? What is to be done with the millions of facts that bear witness that men, *consciously,* that is fully understanding their real interests, have left them in the background and have rushed headlong on another path, to meet peril and danger, compelled to this course by nobody and by nothing, but, as it were, simply disliking the beaten track, and have obstinately, wilfully, struck out another difficult, absurd way, seeking it almost in the darkness. So, I suppose, this obstinacy and perversity were pleasanter to them than any advantage. . . .
>
> Advantage! What is advantage? And will you take it upon yourself to define with perfect accuracy in what the advantage of man consists? And what if it so happens that a man's advantage, *sometimes,* not only may, but even must, consist in his desiring in certain cases what is harmful to himself and not advantageous. And if so, if there can be such a case, the whole principle falls into dust. . . . Have man's advantages been reckoned up with perfect certainty? Are there not some which not only have not been included but cannot possibly be included under any classification?[25]

The Underground Man's thought has broadened: Now not only is reason to be denied, but so too is anything positive or beneficial, whether arrived at by reason or pursued using reason. As with the total abandonment of reason, the insane aspect of his thought is also clear on this point. He has gone from the dehumanizing extreme of asserting that all human behavior stems from self-interest to the personal rule that all his behavior must be against self-interest, so he must make himself as self-destructive and despicable as possible all the time. And again, the element of truth in the narrator's madness is clear: If humans pursue only their own calculable self-interest, then there is nothing left in them that is mysterious, nothing that could be called good or evil, beautiful or ugly, true or false, any more than such terms would be appropriate to a functioning machine. Dostoevsky is profoundly Augustinian here. Augustine repeatedly insists that his youthful theft of pears—which he describes in his *Confessions*—was done with full knowledge of the evil of the act and with no desire for gain. Augustine's act perfectly fits the Underground Man's hypothetical action that would be "harmful . . . and not advantageous." But the narrator is defending not only Christianity but humanity: "The mouse speaks for the dignity of the whole human species."[26] If self-interest is the explanation for all human behavior, then people are incapable not just of being Christian but of being human in any distinct, nonanimal, nonmechanistic way; they are reduced to formulae or machines.

The Underground Man has again seen the truth that humans are not machines, but he also sees the terrible truth that it might be possible to convince them that they are machines and they will thereby increasingly resemble them:

> That is not all; then, you say, science itself will teach man (though to my mind it's a superfluous luxury) that he never has really had any caprice or will of his own, and that he himself is something of the nature of a piano-key or the stop of an organ, and that there are, besides, things called the laws of nature; so that everything he does is not done by his willing it, but is done of itself, by the laws of nature.[27]

In his climactic tirade against the dehumanizing forces of the modern world, the Underground Man makes his mad stand:

> One's own free unfettered choice, one's own caprice, however wild it may be, one's own fancy worked up at times to frenzy—is that very "most advantageous advantage" which we have overlooked, which comes under no classification and against which all systems and theories are continually being shattered to atoms. And how do these wiseacres know that man wants a normal, a virtuous choice? What has made them conceive that

> man must want a rationally advantageous choice? What man wants is simply *independent* choice, whatever that independence may cost and wherever it may lead.[28]
>
> It preserves for us what is most precious and most important—that is, our personality, our individuality. Some, you see, maintain that this really is the most precious thing for mankind.[29]

Again, his stand is surely mad, but it is not wrong, for he has stripped away the distractions of reason and advantage and gotten to the essential core that is human. What is most essential for human beings is not that they reason, nor that they feel, but that they *will*, and their will trumps any claims made by reason or the emotions. To be what it is, the will need not decide between right and wrong, pleasant and unpleasant; it just has to be *able* to will *anything*,[30] for unless it is free and limitless, it is not human will but just the limited, prescribed directives of a machine's programming or the unconscious instincts of an animal. Humans are only human if they are free: "All the meaning and all the joy of human life lie precisely in man's freedom, in the freedom of his mind, of his will, of his actions. All the values of human existence presuppose freedom."[31]

By the end of the first half of *Notes from Underground*, the narrator has formulated the truth of what human beings are: Humans find their dignity and meaning—or their shame and damnation—in what they will, not what they think or feel. Where his deranged mind has jumped the tracks is in his further conclusion that everything he wills must therefore go against what he thinks and feels. The second half of the novella describes a series of incidents in the narrator's life in which he shows how he has lived according to his philosophy. It consists of three incidents of increasing intensity and depth. First, he tells of how he once felt insulted by some unknown man. He proceeded to stalk this man for years, looking for the opportunity to gain back his self-respect. He finally decided he could accomplish his goal through a game of pedestrian "chicken": He would walk down the sidewalk straight at this man, not swerving the least bit to either side, and the man would have to step aside for him. He tries this several times unsuccessfully, since every time it is he himself who steps aside and not the man who supposedly insulted him. But finally he gets it right, plowing straight ahead until they collide, the other man of course not even knowing that he had insulted the Underground Man in the first place, nor that he had just now been chastened by this strange collision. But the victory can provide no real consolation or self-respect to the Underground Man, for even he sees when it is all over that the whole scene was merely ridiculous and pathetic, and then he crawls back into his "underground" to nurse the wounds of more imagined hurts and to hatch more plans for their reprisals. More important, the event offers no real freedom, for the Underground Man has been a slave to this obsession and others like it his whole life: "Far from being a master of his fate, the Underground Man in his very efforts to declare his independence from the laws of nature demonstrates his enslavement to them."[32]

One gets the impression that a scene such as this was repeated numerous times in the Underground Man's life. But the second two scenes seem to hold a special fascination for him—they were unique and definitive in his life. First, he recalls a time when he invited himself to a dinner party with four acquaintances whom he despised and who likewise despised him. In what is perhaps the most painful part of the book, he insults them, then goes to the other side of the room and sulks for three hours, as if this will hurt their feelings, but all the while knowing that he is only hurting and humiliating himself:

> At times, with an intense, acute pang I was stabbed to the heart by the thought that ten years, twenty years, forty years would pass, and that even in forty years I would remember with loathing and humiliation those filthiest, most ludicrous, and most awful moments of my life. No one could have gone out of his way to degrade himself more shamelessly, and I fully realised it, fully, and yet I went on pacing up and down from the table to the stove.[33]

The Underground Man despises others yet intensely needs them around. He has no inner resources yet holds the resources of others in contempt. Again, his neurotic extreme still displays some truth about human relationships: Most of the time, it really is not much fun being by ourselves, but if each of us has an infinite will that strives to go beyond all limits, then it is very difficult to be around others in a meaningful and healthful way, because the temptation will always be either to subjugate and tyrannize other people or, at the other extreme, to give in and be bullied by them. It is a constant temptation to treat others as objects or to let oneself be treated as one, because it is just easier and more consistent: Being a tyrant or a doormat requires less thought and effort than being a real friend or partner. But the complicated and frustrating truth, which the Underground Man understands in the abstract but cannot apply to reality, is that human beings are not objects. The Underground Man's acquaintances are happy because they are vain and shallow, and these qualities allow them to be either a rather casual, undemanding bully like Zverkov, the leader of the group, or satisfied toadies like the other three. But the Underground Man is both vain and deep, a horrible combination, for it means that he is absurdly ineffective at either bullying or toadying and instead wildly oscillates between the two extremes of behavior, challenging men to duels one minute, then throwing himself in tears at their feet and offering them his undying loyalty and friendship the next.

The final climactic incident begins immediately following the scene at the dinner party, and the painful memory of it has haunted the narrator for fifteen years.[34] The four acquaintances go to a brothel and the Underground Man follows them, further humiliating himself by having to ask to borrow money to do so. His mood swings back in the direction of grandiosity and he imagines challenging Zverkov to a duel, but of course, when he gets to the brothel, everyone has gone off to separate rooms, and nothing comes of his dramatic plans. Instead he has sex with one of the prostitutes, Liza, and then a long conversation with her. He tries to shame and frighten her with what he thinks are insightful and vivid images of the shamefulness of prostitution and the beauty of real love. But her first reaction surprises him: "'Why, you . . . speak somehow like a book,' she said, and again there was a note of irony in her voice. That remark sent a pang to my heart. It was not what I was expecting."[35] Again, he tries to treat her as an object whose feelings can be predicted and manipulated, but as a real human being she does not play her role as expected; she sees his sentimentality for the shallow imitation of real life that it is and has no reaction to such fakery. So he tries a different tactic—he talks about things that he knows very intimately and that he really can describe with great honesty and real feeling: despair, loneliness, death. The sincerity of this tirade finally does get through to Liza, and it reduces her to tears. But as perverse as the Underground Man is, he really doesn't have the heart for cruelty. When he succeeds at making her cry, it disturbs him even more than her: "But now, having attained my effect, I was suddenly panic-stricken."[36] Or perhaps it is not just niceness on his part; seeing his own pain reflected in another person makes him realize and cringe at exactly how miserable he himself is—his sadistic attempt to hurt her has backfired into a "self-laceration."[37]

The Underground Man runs off, but Liza looks him up a few days later and forces him to confront her and himself one last time. He doesn't know what to do, so he seeks to drive her away by humiliating her to the point at which (he thinks) she could never forgive him and would desert him. He tells her that the whole previous scene was a lie and that he just wanted to make her cry: "Power, power was what I wanted then, sport was what I wanted, I wanted to wring out your tears, your humiliation, your hysteria—that was what I wanted then!"[38] But rather than running off, Liza does something different, surprising, simple, and, most of all, beautiful:

> What happened was this: Liza, insulted and crushed by me, understood a great deal more than I imagined. She understood from all this what a woman understands first of all, if she feels genuine love, that is, that I was

myself unhappy. . . . She came close to me, put her arms round me and stayed motionless in that position. But the trouble was that the hysterics could not go on for ever, and (I am writing the loathsome truth) lying face downwards on the sofa with my face thrust into my nasty leather pillow, I began by degrees to be aware of a far-away, involuntary but irresistible feeling that it would be awkward now for me to raise my head and look Liza straight in the face. Why was I ashamed? I don't know, but I was ashamed. The thought, too, came into my overwrought brain that our parts now were completely changed, that she was now the heroine, while I was just a crushed and humiliated creature as she had been before me that night, four days before. . . .

I am convinced to this day that it was just because I was ashamed to look at her that another feeling was suddenly kindled and flamed up in my heart . . . a feeling of mastery and possession.[39]

His shame, which is another way to say his absurd and self-destructive sense of self-worth, is so great that he can never face her in a healing, positive way, never let her forgive him, never let himself be vulnerable to her again; he can only twist his shame into a destructive loathing of her and of himself. For me it is a scene more tragic than anything from Sophocles or Shakespeare, even if it is not so bloody and violent, because the protagonist has goodness and beauty right in his grasp and knowingly, deliberately casts it away. Letting ourselves be forgiven or loved makes us more humbled and vulnerable than feeling shame, for it puts us completely in the other's power. Although we feel shame usually in front of other people, they do not have complete control over whether we feel or do not feel shame—we can will to ignore them; but the other person does have total control over whether we are forgiven or loved, as the other can refuse to give us these things. And it is sometimes just too painful and frightening to let another have this power. The pain of shame and loneliness might be preferable to the risk and vulnerability of asking for forgiveness or love. The Underground Man drives Liza away and lives the rest of his miserable life haunted by the terrible memory of how he once almost let another human being touch him, change him, love him, save him.

What, finally, is Dostoevsky trying to tell us in this story of a deranged, willfully evil narrator and protagonist? In a way, Dostoevsky is showing us a life that is a lie based on the truth. The Underground Man has seen a truth of human nature, that humans must be completely free, and their freedom necessitates or is made possible by the presence of evil and folly in the world. If we were hardwired or programmed (like machines) to be good and wise, or if we were so automatically by instinct (like animals), we would not be fully human. Possessing perfect mental and moral health (normalcy is more like it), we would lack all of the inconvenient, embarrassing little idiosyncrasies that make us individuals, that give us personalities—in short, that make us fun or interesting to be around. Nothing we did could be considered noble or meaningful, any more than one would apply such labels to a bee gathering honey or to a supermarket door opening when someone approaches it: Such actions are merely data in an unconscious world, not a sign or a hope that points to something more. All human worth, purpose, and dignity come from living a life that includes freely chosen acts (within fairly formidable limitations, to be sure), and with such freedom will necessarily come ugliness and pain.

But Dostoevsky is also deeply critical of his narrator, as much as he agrees with him: "It is certainly true that both Dostoevsky and Kierkegaard are critical of totalising rational systems and bourgeois complacency—but they are equally critical of the kind of arbitrary, capricious and individualistic protest that Dostoevsky portrays in the Underground Man."[40] The Underground Man builds a cowardly and false life on this foundation of truth, a life that is as ugly and inhuman as any that he sees in the dehumanizing modern world around him, one that embraces only a self-destructive "abyssal freedom."[41] He has correctly asserted the ultimate value of the will and freedom, but when he sees the embodiment of these ideals in Liza, all he can do is deny it, degrade it, try to destroy it. Her act of loving him is as free and as willful as any act he has ever attempted, but it is beautiful rather than ugly, redemptive rather than damning:

> This moment . . . points the way out of the underground. In the embrace of the Underground Man and Liza, all walls of ego and pride are dissolved. It is a moment of revelation of higher truth, an epiphany, a pietà. The fundamental problem of freedom posed in *Notes from the Underground* is not resolved here; it is dissolved. It is not twice two is four, not twice two is five, but reciprocal love that is the way out of the underground.[42]

It is exactly the kind of irrational act the narrator so passionately defends in the first half of the book, as Liza chooses to love him and forgive him, no matter how unreasonable and disadvantageous this response might seem at the moment.[43] All he has to do is something similar: will himself to accept her and give himself to her, rather than try to dominate and abuse her. But he lacks the courage to live up to his theories and convictions, and the novella ends with him knowing the truth but being unable to believe in it, will it, or live it. In all this, of course, there is no need for us to feel superior to our narrator; how many of us achieve the level of introspection and honesty that he possesses, let alone the courage and will to act upon those insights? The Underground Man's disease is one that can show us our own, and Liza was the beginning of Dostoevsky's thoughts on the cure to human sin and folly. Years later his thoughts would come together in *The Brothers Karamazov*, in another world of ugliness and brutality, but one that contained many more of the glimmers of hope and love that Liza had first shown.

Folly, Family, and Freedom: Dostoevsky's *The Brothers Karamazov*

The interplay—sometimes terrible, sometimes beautiful—between free will as the essence of human nature, and love and redemption as the ultimate goals of human life, continues in *The Brothers Karamazov*. Three (possibly four) half brothers enact a terrible drama among themselves in which one of them kills their father, and all of them wanted him dead.[44] The ambiguity of what has happened is reflected in the vague ending of the novel, in which one of the brothers is dead, another may be dying, and another is to be exiled, though plans are being made for him to escape. And although Alyosha, the most pious and sane of the brothers, is relatively unscathed and gets three cheers (literally) at the end, it is unclear what he has learned or whether he will be happy.

As ambiguous as Alyosha's redemption may be at the end,[45] the negative side of humanity seems much clearer in the novel. While Alyosha is quiet and honest, his father, Fyodor, is boisterous and constantly lying. The wise monk Zossima at least momentarily subdues him by diagnosing his problem: "Above all, don't lie to yourself. The man who lies to himself and listens to his own lies comes to such a point that he cannot distinguish the truth within him, or around him, and so loses all respect for himself and for others."[46] Fyodor is the picture of Old Testament folly: drunken, lustful, deceitful out of habit and for no reason, and completely incapable of caring for his family, as well as totally disinterested in doing so. If real, higher wisdom is shown in how we deal with others, then Fyodor shows himself completely inept and destructive in his relationships with other people. Fyodor is so self-absorbed that he doesn't even hate people so much as he simply forgets they exist: "He completely abandoned the child of his marriage with Adelaide, not from spite nor because of his matrimonial grievances, but simply because he forgot him."[47] This is in sharp contrast to Alyosha and Father Zossima, whose detailed memories of past goodness serve to perpetuate and extend that goodness, while Fyodor's obliviousness is like a black hole, sucking goodness and life into its own dead emptiness.[48] Exactly as Father Zossima warns him, he respects no one, not even himself, and so no one respects or cares for him. Dostoevsky repeatedly describes him as a "buffoon"[49] and as "senseless," and he is careful to show how this quality can coexist with "intelligent."[50] Fyodor in fact seems quite shrewd, but he lacks all sense of order, balance, and value in his life; he can use his cunning only to pursue his self-destructive appetites, and even these fail to satisfy him for more than a moment. Perhaps his perverted outlook is best given in the semi-oxymoronic description "He was sentimental. He was evil and sentimental."[51] One can easily imagine Fyodor blubbering over some broken knickknack because it has sentimental value, without recalling in any way the person who gave it to him, a person he probably treated badly all the time. His priorities are so absurdly unbalanced and foolish that they would be comical in a different book.

But as much as Fyodor is the epitome of foolish self-indulgence, he is not cruel or malicious. Dostoevsky shows us there are far greater depths of evil than mere folly in the character of Smerdyakov, rumored to be Fyodor's illegitimate son. The most evil of the brothers, his disordered being goes far beyond Fyodor's excessive appetites into much more disturbing contradictions or negations: Physically repulsive, he is described as both smelling bad and smelling too good; an excellent cook, he himself does not enjoy food; spiritually apathetic, nonphysical things are as unattractive to him as the delicious food he prepares but cannot enjoy; physically sick, he doesn't even excite our sympathy, because he seems to have a diabolical power to make himself ill on command; emotionally dead, "devoid of moral sense and human affections,"[52] he is the only one in the family who lacks the passion that is so characteristic of the Karamazovs and that makes them fascinating to us; a moral invertebrate or vacuum, he doesn't even have the attraction that real evil might hold; he lives in a state of "lackeydom . . . spiritual spinelessness, a lack of autonomy accompanied by the remarkable ability to look after one's own material interests,"[53] epitomized in his cowardly but shrewd act of laying all suspicion on his brother Dmitri and all blame on his brother Ivan. His father values very foolish things, while Smerdyakov seems to value nothing. His final frame of mind is vividly described:

> But why, why, asks the prosecutor, did Smerdyakov not confess in his last letter? Why did his conscience prompt him to one step and not to both? But, excuse me, conscience implies penitence, and the suicide may not have felt penitence, but only despair. Despair and penitence are two very different things. Despair may be vindictive and irreconcilable, and the suicide, laying his hands on himself, may well have felt redoubled hatred for those whom he had envied all his life.[54]

Even worse than the Underground Man or even Judas, both of whom at least regretted the things over which they despaired, Smerdyakov is completely lost, feeling despair without remorse.

If despair without remorse is the most negative twisting of human feeling, then remorse without despair might logically be the spiritual ideal. Some idea of this is given in the middle of the novel, in the chapters around Alyosha's meeting with his brother Ivan and then his reflections on the life of Father Zossima. Ivan is the intellectual of the family and the literary descendant of the Underground Man.[55] His painful objections and doubts are similar to what we will see in other books we will examine, and they are also part of what makes *The Brothers Karamazov* so powerful, for they are Dostoevsky's own doubts, as well as our own: "The would-be prophet [Dostoevsky] had attained his 'hosanna', his faith, 'through a great *furnace of doubt.*' Yet the doubt had not been left behind. It informs the arguments of Ivan, it gives Zosima's counterweight, that Western monk, the Grand Inquisitor, his haunting and lasting power."[56] So compelling are Ivan's doubts that some have thought they remain, to the end, Dostoevsky's own, as he struggles like his hero, "an agnostic thirsty for God."[57] Dostoevsky himself described such doubts in a much earlier letter: "I will tell you regarding myself that I am a child of the age, a child of non-belief and doubt up till now and even (I know it) until my coffin closes."[58] But to be "an agnostic thirsty for God" is to be considerably closer to God than a "Christian" who is sated with his or her idea of God: "His very atheism was itself a vivid experience of the Holy, and this atheist had an appreciation for the Numinous far more profound than much conventional moralistic piety."[59] Like any relationship with another person, one's relation with God derives all its power from longing, being unsure, wondering, hoping: "It is our great arrogance to believe that any revelation is complete; but it is our worst humility to think that revelation is always at hand; in both cases we regard it as our possession."[60] It is wrong to think one can possess God or any human being in the way one possesses an object or a piece of knowledge: One should long and thirst for God and people always.

Speaking to Alyosha, Ivan first describes his own agony at how he sees people behave. He recounts numerous horrible stories that he masochistically gathers from the newspapers about the abuse, torture, and murder of children. His point goes beyond theodicy, though, beyond merely questioning God's justice, to questioning how it would be possible to achieve happiness or "harmony" in a world where such misery, such screaming disharmony, occurs. At both ends, Ivan attacks the easy answers that Christianity sometimes gives. To the idea that there is a hell in which abusers would be eternally punished, Ivan responds:

> It's not worth it, because those tears are unatoned for. They must be atoned for, or there can be no harmony. But how? How are you going to atone for them? Is it possible? By their being avenged? But what do I care for avenging them? What do I care for a hell for oppressors? What good can hell

do, since those children have already been tortured? And what becomes of harmony, if there is hell? I want to forgive, I want to embrace.[61]

But just a few lines later, Ivan also rejects the idea of forgiveness: "I don't want harmony. From love for humanity I don't want it. I would rather be left with unavenged suffering. I would rather remain with my unavenged suffering and unsatisfied indignation, *even if I were wrong.*"[62] Neither punishment nor forgiveness can be enough for Ivan, for neither really repairs the damage that has been done to the creation of God (in whom Ivan here expresses belief, despite his supposed atheism); the one just increases the amount of suffering in the universe and the other just overlooks it. Ivan longs for and even demands something that will fix what is wrong with human beings, but he can see no possibility of it.

It is at this point that Alyosha offers another Christian answer that goes far beyond mere punishment: Christ's sacrifice makes possible the fixing of what is wrong with human beings. Ivan enthusiastically jumps at the chance to bring Christ into the discussion: "Ah! The One without sin and His blood! No, I have not forgotten Him. On the contrary I've been wondering all the time how it was you did not bring Him in before."[63] Ivan then tells the story of the Grand Inquisitor. In the story, the Grand Inquisitor runs sixteenth-century Seville with complete, unswerving brutality and certainty. People are burned every day, and those who remain live in fear, obedience, and peace. Christ returns to earth and heals some people in Seville, and the Grand Inquisitor has him arrested. The Grand Inquisitor then harangues Christ, blaming him for the terrible freedom he gave people:

> Instead of taking men's freedom from them, Thou didst make it greater than ever! Didst thou forget that man prefers peace, and even death, to freedom of choice in the knowledge of good and evil? . . . We have corrected thy work and have founded it upon *miracle, mystery,* and *authority*. And men rejoiced that they were again led like sheep, and that the terrible gift that had brought them such suffering, was, at last, lifted from their hearts. Were we right teaching them this? Speak! Did we not love mankind, so meekly acknowledging their feebleness, lovingly lightening their burden, and permitting their weak nature even sin with our sanction?[64]

People do not even appreciate the freedom Christ has given them, because it seems rather like a terrible burden. To be responsible for our own lives is simply too much for us to bear, too risky, too frightening.

According to the Grand Inquisitor, humans are pathetic and evil, a view not very different from *Notes from Underground*. But unlike the Underground Man, who tries to maximize his freedom and evil, the Grand

Inquisitor has taken away people's freedom, so as to render them merely pathetic and to give them a life that is at least happy and harmless: "The Grand Inquisitor, descending further than the Underground Man in his pessimistic analysis of the human creature, renders man infantile and denies him the status of an adult."[65] Nor are even the Grand Inquisitor and his minions free, for they are just as enslaved to their enormous, "selfless" task of keeping everyone else blissfully ignorant and in line: "And all will be happy, all the millions of creatures except the hundred thousand who rule over them. For only we, we who guard the mystery, shall be unhappy."[66] The Grand Inquisitor perversely models himself after Christ, for now he has taken away the sins of the world, but only by committing the greatest and most essential sin—making himself God: "Sin, therefore, was not the violation of some precept or prohibition, it was the assumption: I am God."[67] At the same time he models himself after Satan, ensnaring humans with a love that destroys them in a more profound way than even their own self-destructive actions (made possible by the freedom that Christ brought): "Even if . . . he is really moved by compassion for the frail and the weak, the love which fails to respect freedom and is ready to eliminate it for human love is a demonic counterfeit."[68] The Grand Inquisitor has made the world as "good" as it can be by making it as unfree and unholy as it can be: "It may be easier to identify the Holy and the Good, it may be more practical, it may even be more rational and normal to do so. But the Christian faith does not pretend to be easy or rational or normal."[69] Christ speaks not a word of defense or accusation to the Grand Inquisitor, but only kisses him silently before being banished, so that the old man can continue to run his ecclesiastical police state for the "betterment" of humanity. Christ confirms the Grand Inquisitor's depiction of the absurd freedom he brings, for he will not limit even the freedom of the man who burns people in his name: "Christ seals with a kiss the freedom he has brought. . . . Man's freedom is absolute and cannot be evaded; even misguided, it is sealed by God."[70] While the Grand Inquisitor abolishes human freedom and usurps divine power, Christ establishes human freedom and completely pours out his divine power.

So Alyosha's pious answer turns out not to answer things as neatly as he would have liked. Christ's sacrifice, which people are totally free to believe, disbelieve, ignore, or reject, only armed this race of "impotent rebels"[71] with the terrible weapon of freedom, with which they have been considerably less impotent but infinitely more evil, destructive, and miserable. Incapable of achieving happiness, they are terrifyingly capable of making each other very unhappy. It should not be thought that Ivan, much less Dostoevsky, completely identifies with the Grand Inquisitor, for he has also created the Christ of his story: "With his Grand Inquisitor, Ivan grips the world in the cold rings of despair. With his Christ, before whom the doors to the dungeon open, Ivan creates a breath of hope."[72] Rather, Dostoevsky, through Ivan, has eloquently and painfully painted two hellish, inhuman worlds. In the one we live in, there is complete freedom, and as beautiful as the love of Christ and a few of his followers such as Alyosha may be, the horrifying truth is that this freedom is bought at the expense of the screams of millions of children as they are raped, tortured, and murdered, day after day, year after year, from one end of the globe to the other, from the dawn of time until the final judgment day.[73] He then imagines a "perfect" world in which such atrocities are suppressed, but only at the expense of all freedom, so that people live the harmless lives of sheep, cowed into obedience and rewarded occasionally by having their minor, sinful whims indulged as long as they meekly ask for permission. Because he relies completely on reason, Ivan is as incapable of answering his own questions as was the Underground Man: "One thing is clear: those who pursue the truth rationally, confident of their human reason, are led into error."[74] Relying on limited, inadequate human reason, Ivan has caught himself in a maddening dilemma, in which he refuses to accept either scenario but cannot see any alternative: Freedom and goodness are incompatible in his mind.[75] Both he and the Underground Man have made the existence of freedom and evil intolerable and maddening, because they have thought of both in entirely individualistic terms, when the essence of these ideas, as well as the resolution of their difficulties, lies in their social dimension.[76] To separate oneself as they do is a kind of self-mutilation or suicide, for humans are by nature "social . . . meant for communal life."[77] As the extent of his responsibility for his father's murder dawns on him, Ivan also finds that his reason and isolation are completely powerless against evil, which can even turn his own remorse against him: "The strength of autonomous will, of all-destroying arbitrary wilfulness, turns out to be helpless in a conflict with evil. . . . and the truth of repentance becomes a demonic farce."[78]

After this, as Alyosha remembers the life and teachings of his beloved teacher, Father Zossima, Dostoevsky's paradoxical answer to the questions of the Underground Man and Ivan begins to emerge by denying the necessity of the two hellish alternatives.[79] Father Zossima remembers that as his brother was dying, he began to say strange things:

> "Mother darling," he would say, "there must be servants and masters, but if so I will be the servant of my servants. And another thing, mother, every one of us has sinned against all men, and I more than any." . . . "You take too many sins on yourself," mother used to say, weeping. "Mother darling, it's for joy, not for grief I am crying. Though I can't explain it to you, I like to humble myself, for I don't know how to love enough. If I have sinned

against everyone, yet all forgive me, too, and that's heaven. Am I not in heaven now?"[80]

Universal guilt, omnipresent but freely taken upon oneself, mysteriously becomes the answer to individual guilt and unhappiness. It has been called kenotic, not in the Western sense of a theological discussion of Christ's human and divine nature(s), but as a means of spiritual improvement widely practiced by Russian monks who imitated Christ's humility and self-abnegation, practicing "unceasing humiliation as a means of transcendence."[81] A small child is not guilty of much of anything, but as Father Zossima's brother *makes* himself feel more responsible for more and more things that he has not done, over which he has no control, he experiences increasing happiness and well-being, even as his physical life is slipping away.

The lesson his brother learned as he was dying gets repeated in episodes throughout Father Zossima's life, and he summarizes it in his final exhortation to his friends and students at his deathbed:

> My friends, pray to God for gladness. Be glad as children, as the birds of heaven. And let not the sin of men confound you in your doings. Fear not that it will wear away your work and hinder its being accomplished. Do not say, "Sin is mighty, wickedness is mighty, evil environment is mighty, and we are lonely and helpless. Evil environment is wearing us away and hindering our good work from being done." Fly from that dejection! There is only one means of salvation. Make yourself responsible for all men's sins. As soon as you sincerely make yourself responsible for everything and for all men, you will see at once that you have found salvation. On the other hand by throwing your indolence and impotence on others you will end by sharing the pride of Satan and murmuring against God.[82]

We all have the falsifying and deadening freedom (of which we all too often avail ourselves) to deny responsibility for the things we have done. But what Dostoevsky does through Father Zossima is suggest the possibility that at the opposite extreme there is a true and life-giving freedom, the freedom to take responsibility for the things we have not done, but without falling into despair. Paradoxically, the more things one feels responsible for, the less despair one feels, for it is the community and connectedness that we have among ourselves, and between ourselves and God, that makes this thought liberating and not oppressive.

The true freedom offered here is nothing less than the human ability to be like God, to imitate him in the right, affirmative way, rather than the negating, (self-)destructive way of Satan: "What remains of the image of God in man after the Fall is freedom—human freedom. . . . Freedom is the essence of the spiritual existence of man and the reflection in him of the Divine Archetype."[83] By bringing God and other people into the relation, Dostoevsky gives a radical and profound reformulation of freedom and responsibility, seeing that "personal freedom is not by definition self-seeking . . . and does not, therefore, need to be set aside in a more co-operative order. . . . The only way out of the impasse is for people to belong together (not merely co-operate) by their own commitment."[84] Finally freed from the Underground Man's dungeon and the Grand Inquisitor's infantilizing totalitarian state, people can live lives of real freedom and purpose together and with God, as a "communion . . . a pooling of spiritual resources in a common adoration."[85] By focusing on our own sins individually, we destroy ourselves with despair, and by focusing on the sins of others, we destroy ourselves with pride and self-righteousness. Ivan tragically manages to do both, for although he believes finally in universal guilt, he believes that it entails the "possibility to lighten, or perhaps to remove altogether, his *personal* guilt and responsibility,"[86] while his awareness of his own guilt entraps him in despair: "The absence in his spiritual make-up of authentic inner freedom hinders him from breaking through to Alyosha's simplicity and clarity."[87] Both his despair and his pride trap him within himself: "Ivan's pride strengthens his ego and thus cuts him off from God. His concern for others is false, being grounded in self-love. . . . Ivan cherishes his hatred for God more than he cherishes truth."[88]

In contrast to Ivan's self-destructive worldview, Father Zossima's convictions powerfully lead him to be the least judgmental man imaginable, as well as one of the most happy and carefree. He is "saintly and utterly uncensorious,"[89] a man who believes we are all awful sinners yet is nonjudgmental, a man who takes upon himself the sins of the entire world yet is carefree. When a woman approaches him for advice and explains that she has been unable to stop grieving the death of her son, he tells her that enough time has passed and she should stop weeping. She tells him that she cannot stop, that she just cannot bring herself to do it, to which he responds, "Weep and be not consoled, but weep. . . . A long while yet will you keep that great mother's grief, but it will turn in the end into quiet joy."[90] While tears for the deaths of children drove Ivan to despair, they give Father Zossima another chance to love, forgive, and heal.[91] Shortly afterwards, another woman tells him that she killed her abusive husband, to which he replies, "Can there be a sin which could exceed the love of God? . . . If I, a sinner even as you are, am tender with you and have pity on you, how much more will God have pity upon you."[92] Here is a complete acceptance of human weakness, but it is through this acceptance, not judgment or despair, that sin and misery are undone. And together with this acceptance is a profound belief in God's omnipotent love, so that the healing of misery is first begun imperfectly by us and later completed perfectly by God. But even in our earthbound, imperfect expression of it, love transforms the world from the hell Ivan experiences into an earthly paradise that is a foretaste of the heavenly one: "Zosima's paradise is predominantly a terrestrial condition. . . . Zosima speaks less specifically of man's love for God, more of love for man (however sinful he may be) and—insistently and poignantly—of love for all Creation."[93] Father Zossima is "not oblivious of the evil in the world, but utterly convinced that it is a good place to live in,"[94] because he can find so much joy and peace by beginning to heal the world's ills. It is only by focusing on the power of God's forgiveness, as well as the connection and even the identification between the sins of others and our own, that we can be forgiven, liberated, loved, and saved.

The idea that human life and purpose are found in the will and not in the mind or the emotions is deeply biblical; we are commanded to love and trust God, not just believe in him, and certainly not necessarily to like him. That the will and freedom are the most fundamental aspects of being human is beautifully elaborated by Dostoevsky, who shows how reason becomes a self-destructive extreme in Ivan, while human passions overcome and destroy his father, both men having enslaved their wills to what should be lesser faculties. In his depiction of Fyodor, Dostoevsky has followed closely the Old Testament image of the fool, someone who is unrestrained in his appetites, oblivious to others, and ultimately self-destructive. But the saving alternative to Fyodor's folly is not just restraint or prudence. Rather, it turns into something like the reversal of the situation in *Notes from Underground*. Whereas the Underground Man lived a lie based on the truth, Father Zossima counsels that one should live a life of truth and love based on what is fundamentally untrue,[95] or at least an absurdity, the absurd statement that one is responsible for the sins of the whole human race. Clearly at some level this is not an accurate statement, but it can be willed to be a statement by which one lives. Father Zossima stresses that this responsibility is not only a fact but a willful action: "*Make* yourself responsible for all men's sins." Responsibility, like love or trust, is not thought, proven, or even felt; it is willed. Even with a direct, mystical experience of God, it is the command to love that makes the experience real, ongoing, and salvific: "Though active love is buttressed by mystery, it is realized only through struggle. If there is any salvation it is not at the moment of the mystical experience at all, but in the actual performance of the commandment that is revealed through it."[96] Obedience to the love commandment connects us to others and to God, and at the same time it frees us from our limitations: "Faith is not reason, or paradox . . . but active love. Faith follows from a spontaneous awakening to the other. . . . As soon as one commits the act of love and recognizes the quality and freedom of the other in oneself, one believes in Christ, because then one has acted out the truth of His vision of humanity."[97] Love, trust, and responsibility become the basis of all human meaning and happiness for Dostoevsky, and they can overcome all that is ugly, brutal, and false.

Conclusion: Different Kinds of Wisdom and Happiness

I began this chapter with a consideration of how the concepts of prudence, fear, and wisdom are related, suggesting that they all have to do with our pursuit of happiness. We fear being unhappy, and so we try to be careful, because being injured, sick, poor, or addicted to substances tend to make us unhappy. A deeper sense of fear is seen in the Bible, where some of the right kind of fear is a positive thing and a part of wisdom, because it reminds us of our creatureliness and dependence on others and so keeps us from falling prey to other bad habits and attitudes that bring unhappiness—pride, arrogance, selfishness, stinginess. Such habits tend to make us unhappy in a different way, because they don't harm our bodies, but they harm our relations with other people. This I suggested was the beginning of a higher sense of wisdom, a moral and religious sense that values relationships over physical well-being.

Having considered Dostoevsky's work, we are perhaps in a position to say a little more about why exactly one should value one's relationships with people and God over physical well-being. There is no point in saying that relationships bring us more pleasure than other pursuits—they are often very painful and require great sacrifice: "And if Dostoevsky still believed in the power of love, it was the love of Christ that he was preaching, the Crucified Love."[98] You might get a little further by claiming that relationships tend to last longer than the pleasures gained from drugs or food or money, but even this is not always the case. I think that Dostoevsky has shown us that love, trust, and responsibility are the only endeavors that render us truly free, breaking the limitations of reason, self-interest, appetites, and sin, and ending our enslavement to them. To pursue anything else may well bring happiness in some limited sense, but happiness to whom? To an addict, to an "omnivorous . . . private self,"[99] or to a machine or an animal, but not to a woman or man. Happiness as the satisfaction of desires is rightly labeled by Father Zossima as "slavery and self-destruction . . . isolation and spiritual suicide."[100] Love, trust, and responsibility also ironically bring us greater power, for they let us draw on the resources of others, but at an enormous risk—the risk of vulnerability, betrayal, abandonment. As human beings, we can buy the very costly, risky freedom and happiness of attaching ourselves to others, rather than sell ourselves to the other kinds of happiness that enslave and own us. Indeed, to achieve or earn real humanity, we must do so.

Notes

1. Cf. R. E. Murphy, *The Tree of Life: An Exploration of Biblical Wisdom Literature* (2d ed.; Grand Rapids: Eerdmans, 1990), 15: "The book has been very popular in Western culture, both for the picturesque language and for the timely truths it is seen to convey. It is quoted freely, and many times not exactly, and it has received greater authority than many another book of Holy Writ."

2. Cf. J. L. Crenshaw, *Old Testament Wisdom: An Introduction* (Atlanta: John Knox Press, 1981), 13–14, for a comparison with African proverbs.

3. Briefly, the early church used a Greek translation of the Hebrew Bible called the Septuagint (which was, however, produced before Christianity, ca. 250 B.C.E.). The Septuagint included some books written in Greek, for which there is no Hebrew original extant: Judith, Tobit, Baruch, 1 and 2 Maccabees, Sirach, and the book of Wisdom. Protestant reformers later rejected these books, insisting that everything in the Old Testament must have a Hebrew original, and they are usually labeled the Apocrypha (confusing, since many other books are also considered "apocryphal"). See the discussion in L. Boadt, *Reading the Old Testament: An Introduction* (New York: Paulist Press, 1984), 15–19. A discussion of the problem of how to refer to the Old Testament or Hebrew Bible will be given when we turn to the New Testament in chapter 3.

4. See the discussion of the vagaries of dating in Murphy, *Tree of Life*, 19. Throughout I will be using the newer convention of B.C.E./C.E. (before the common era/common era), rather than the older convention of B.C./A.D. All numbers remain the same.

5. For the date, see G. von Rad, *Wisdom in Israel* (trans. J. D. Martin; Nashville: Abingdon Press, 1972), 240; P. W. Skehan and A. A. Di Lella, *The Wisdom of Ben Sira: A New Translation with Notes* (New York: Doubleday, 1987), 8–10; Murphy, *Tree of Life*, 65.

6. See von Rad, *Wisdom in Israel*, 3–5.

7. Crenshaw, *Old Testament Wisdom*, 93.

8. All quotations from Sirach are from Skehan and Di Lella, *Wisdom of Ben Sira*.

9. See the discussion of such doubts in Murphy, *Tree of Life*, 121–22. Cf. the fairly simplistic development from practical to theological wisdom given by Crenshaw, *Old Testament Wisdom*, 93–96.

10. Murphy, *Tree of Life*, 124.

11. See the discussion in von Rad, *Wisdom in Israel*, 74–96.

12. R. B. Y. Scott, *The Way of Wisdom in the Old Testament* (New York: Macmillan, 1971), 9–10.

13. See the discussion in Murphy, *Tree of Life*, 78–79.

14. Von Rad, *Wisdom in Israel*, 69.

15. The facts of Dostoevsky's life are taken from the excellent website at Dartmouth: http://www.dartmouth.edu/~karamazo/dostoevsky.html (visited 5 July 2002). See also the summary in D. A. Webb, "Dostoevsky and Christian Agnosticism," *The Iliff Review* 27 (1970): 31–39, esp. 31; L. Hegedus, "Jesus and Dostoevsky," *European Journal of Theology* 1 (1992): 49–62, esp. 51–53.

16. F. Dostoevsky, *Notes from Underground* (trans. C. Garnett; New York: Dover Publications, 1992), "Underground," I, p. 1. All my thanks to Ms. Alexandra Matthews of the University of Notre Dame for letting me advise her senior essay, "Beyond Reason: Dostoevsky's Journey from the Underground to God," which started my thinking on *Notes from Underground*.

17. Dostoevsky, *Notes from Underground*, "Underground," I, p. 2.

18. Ibid., "On the Occasion of Wet Snow," X, p. 89.

19. Ibid., "Underground," II, p. 3.
20. Ibid., VI, p. 13.
21. Ibid., III, pp. 6–7.
22. Hegedus, "Jesus and Dostoevsky," 54.
23. Cf. A. B. Gibson, *The Religion of Dostoevsky* (Philadelphia: Westminster, 1973), 82–83: "His anti-rationalism, his antipathy to scientific and particularly mathematical paradigms, his sense of freedom as unlimited opportunity for good and for evil, his emphasis on the evil which in the absence of some antidote to humiliation is certain to prevail—all this is pure Dostoevsky."
24. Dostoevsky, *Notes from Underground,* "Underground," III, p. 8.
25. Ibid., VII, p. 14, emphasis in this translation as well as in that of M. Ginsburg (New York: Bantam, 1974).
26. Gibson, *Religion of Dostoevsky,* 81.
27. Dostoevsky, *Notes from Underground,* "Underground," VII, pp. 16–17.
28. Ibid., pp. 17–18.
29. Ibid., VIII, p. 20.
30. Cf. Descartes' description of the infinite will in *Meditations on First Philosophy,* meditation 4 (trans. D. A. Cress; 3rd ed; Indianapolis: Hackett Publishing, 1993).
31. G. Florovsky, "The Quest for Religion in 19th Century Russian Literature," *Epiphany* 10/11 (1990): 43–58; quote from p. 50.
32. R. L. Jackson, "Aristotelian Movement and Design in Part Two of *Notes from the Underground,*" in *Dostoevsky: New Perspectives* (ed. R. L. Jackson; Englewood Cliffs, N.J.: Prentice-Hall, 1984), 66–81; quote from p. 70.
33. Dostoevsky, *Notes from Underground,* "Wet Snow," IV, pp. 54–55.
34. Ibid., VIII, p. 77.
35. Ibid., VI, p. 68.
36. Ibid., VII, p. 72.
37. Jackson, "Aristotelian Movement and Design," 72.
38. Dostoevsky, *Notes from Underground,* "Wet Snow," IX, p. 85.
39. Ibid., pp. 86–87.
40. G. Pattison, "Freedom's Dangerous Dialogue: Reading Dostoevsky and Kierkegaard Together," in *Dostoevsky and the Christian Tradition* (ed. G. Pattison and D. O. Thompson; Cambridge: Cambridge University Press, 2001), 237–56; quote from pp. 240–41.
41. Pattison, "Reading Dostoevsky and Kierkegaard," 240.
42. Jackson, "Aristotelian Movement and Design," 74.
43. The idea that Liza lives out the narrator's own ideas was first suggested to me by Kelsey Moore, a student at Iona College.
44. For a good and accessible discussion of the Oedipal dynamics of the novel, see M. Holquist, "How Sons Become Fathers," in *Fyodor Dostoevsky's* The Brothers Karamazov (New York: Chelsea House, 1988), 39–51.
45. It is on Alyosha that Dostoevsky apparently intended to focus the sequel. On Alyosha and the proposed sequel, see V. A. Vetlovskaya, "Alyosha Karamazov and the Hagiographic Hero," in *Dostoevsky: New Perspectives* (ed. R. L. Jackson; Englewood Cliffs, N.J.: Prentice-Hall, 1984) 206–26. Cf. R. P. Blackmur, "*The Brothers Karamazov:* The Grand Inquisitor and the Wine of Gladness," in *Critical Essays on Dostoevsky* (ed. R. F. Miller; Boston: G. K. Hall, 1986), 205–15, esp. 205. Blackmur hypothesizes that Dostoevsky intended a trilogy of novels.
46. F. Dostoevsky, *The Brothers Karamazov* (trans. C. Garnett; New York: Penguin Books, 1958) bk. 2, chap. 2, p. 53.

47. Dostoevsky, *Brothers Karamazov*, bk. 1, chap. 2, p. 22.

48. See the excellent discussions of memory and forgetting by R. L. Belknap, "Memory in *The Brothers Karamazov*," in *Dostoevsky: New Perspectives* (ed. R. L. Jackson; Englewood Cliffs, N.J.: Prentice-Hall, 1984), 227–42; and P. George, "Remembering the Dead: Kierkegaard and Dostoevsky," *Modern Believing* 35 (1994): 24–31.

49. The title of bk. 2, chap. 2 is "The Old Buffoon."

50. See the first paragraph of the novel: Dostoevsky, *Brothers Karamazov*, bk. 1, chap. 1, p. 19.

51. Dostoevsky, *Brothers Karamazov*, bk. 1, chap. 5, p. 36.

52. F. F. Seeley, "Ivan Karamazov," in *New Essays on Dostoevsky* (ed. M. V. Jones and G. M. Terry; Cambridge: Cambridge University Press, 1983), 115–36; quote from p. 122.

53. V. Kantor, "Pavel Smerdyakov and Ivan Karamazov: The Problem of Temptation," in *Dostoevsky and the Christian Tradition* (ed. G. Pattison and D. O. Thompson; Cambridge: Cambridge University Press, 2001), 189–225; quote from p. 199.

54. Dostoevsky, *Brothers Karamazov*, bk. 12, chap. 12, p. 698.

55. Cf. Seeley, "Ivan Karamazov," 115: "Thus Ivan Karamazov is the last of a line sometimes designated in Russian 'philosophizing doubles' because of their intellectual preoccupations and split personalities. His genealogy can be traced back through such 'heresiarchs' as Kirillov and Raskolnikov to the Underground Man." Seeley then offers an interesting psychological portrait of Ivan, showing the family resemblances among the Karamazovs.

56. S. Hackel, "The Religious Dimension: Vision or Evasion? Zosima's Discourse in *The Brothers Karamazov*," in *New Essays on Dostoevsky* (ed. M. V. Jones and G. M. Terry; Cambridge: Cambridge University Press, 1983), 139–68; quote from p. 165.

57. Webb, "Christian Agnosticism," 39.

58. Quoted by R. Pevear, "The Mystery of Man in Dostoevsky," *Sourozh* 66 (1996): 31–35; quote from p. 32.

59. J. Pelikan, *Fools for Christ: Essays on the True, the Good, and the Beautiful* (Philadelphia: Fortress Press, 1955) 80. Cf. Florovsky, "Quest for Religion," 53: "He used to claim that before him nobody, even in the West, had been able to present the atheistic case with the same fullness and with the same power as he had presented it. And he did so deliberately and conscientiously in order to demonstrate its fallacy."

60. Blackmur, "Wine of Gladness," 207.

61. Dostoevsky, *Brothers Karamazov*, bk. 5, chap. 4, p. 238.

62. Ibid. (emphasis in this translation)

63. Ibid., p. 239.

64. Ibid., bk. 5, chap. 5, pp. 247, 250.

65. J. Catteau, "The Paradox of the Legend of the Grand Inquisitor in *The Brothers Karamazov*," in *Dostoevsky: New Perspectives* (ed. R. L. Jackson; Englewood Cliffs, N.J.: Prentice-Hall, 1984), 243–54; quote from p. 249.

66. Dostoevsky, *Brothers Karamazov*, bk. 5, chap. 5, p. 252.

67. Pelikan, *Fools for Christ*, 74.

68. Florovsky, "Quest for Religion," 54.

69. Pelikan, *Fools for Christ*, 83.

70. Catteau, "Paradox of the Legend," 252–53.

71. Dostoevsky, *Brothers Karamazov*, bk. 5, chap. 5, p. 248.

72. Catteau, "Paradox of the Legend," 252.

73. Cf. Pelikan, *Fools for Christ*, 78: "Freedom may have been necessary for faith, but it was not necessary for conformity to the moral law. That could come by compulsion, and

according to the Grand Inquisitor, it was only through compulsion that the common people could be made to obey."

74. V. Terras, "The Art of Fiction as a Theme in *The Brothers Karamazov*," in *Dostoevsky: New Perspectives* (ed. R. L. Jackson; Englewood Cliffs, N.J.: Prentice-Hall, 1984), 193–205; quote from p. 198.

75. Cf. Gibson, *Religion of Dostoevsky*, 183–84: "And one thing at least is clear: the 'Legend' is written with a double mind by a man facing both ways. Intellectually, the author is with the Grand Inquisitor; affectively, he is moved by the Christ.... The contrast in the 'Legend' is between the freedom of Christ and compulsion (however high-minded) of a spiritual autocracy. Freedom and compulsion seem to have changed places, meanings, and values."

76. Cf. S. R. Sutherland, "The Philosophical Dimension: Self and Freedom," in *New Essays on Dostoevsky* (ed. M. V. Jones and G. M. Terry; Cambridge: Cambridge University Press, 1983), 169–85, esp. 183: "What is most significant about this for an account of Dostoevsky's views of freedom is its explicit rejection of the adequacy of individualistic accounts of freedom.... [T]he notion of human action which is based on an 'objective' view of human beings, and which ignores the web of social and reactive attitudes to which we belong, verges on incoherence."

77. Florovsky, "Quest for Religion," 51.

78. Kantor, "Problem of Temptation," 217.

79. Cf. Florovsky, "Quest for Religion," 54: "Dostoevsky's own option is obvious, even if he is speaking on behalf of Ivan. Actually, the alternative is false." Also cf. Pevear, "Mystery of Man," 34–35, who points to the experience of Dmitri as Dostoevsky's "answer" to Ivan and the Grand Inquisitor.

80. Dostoevsky, *Brothers Karamazov*, bk. 6, chap. 1, pp. 278–79.

81. M. Ziolkowski, "Dostoevsky and the Kenotic Tradition," in *Dostoevsky and the Christian Tradition* (ed. G. Pattison and D. O. Thompson; Cambridge: Cambridge University Press, 2001), 31–40; quote from p. 33. The article gives the literary and historical antecedents on which Dostoevsky drew for the character of Zossima, as does Hackel, "Zosima's Discourse," 139–68.

82. Dostoevsky, *Brothers Karamazov*, bk. 6, chap. 2, p. 310.

83. Pevear, "Mystery of Man," 33.

84. Gibson, *Religion of Dostoevsky*, 191–92.

85. Ibid., 202.

86. Kantor, "Problem of Temptation," 218 (emphasis in original).

87. Ibid., 218–19.

88. J. D. Frodsham, "Conflicting Theodicies—Some Modernist Literary Approaches to the Problem of Evil," *Religious Traditions* 5 (1982): 24–43; quote from p. 25.

89. Gibson, *Religion of Dostoevsky*, 201.

90. Dostoevsky, *Brothers Karamazov*, bk. 2, chap. 3, p. 58.

91. The contrast suggested by R. L. Jackson, "The Wound and the Lamentation: Ivan's Rebellion," in *Fyodor Dostoevsky's The Brothers Karamazov* (ed. H. Bloom; New York: Chelsea House, 1988), 119–35, esp. 120–24.

92. Dostoevsky, *Brothers Karamazov*, bk. 2, chap. 3, p. 60.

93. Hackel, "Zosima's Discourse," 152–53. On Zossima's concern for all "Creation," see also B. K. Ward, "Christianity and the Modern Eclipse of Nature: Two Perspectives," *Journal of the American Academy of Religion* 63 (1995): 823–43.

94. Gibson, *Religion of Dostoevsky*, 190.

95. Cf. Blackmur, "Wine of Gladness," 209, who calls the story of Zossima's life "the noble lie."

96. G. Rosenshield, "Mystery and Commandment in *The Brothers Karamazov*," *Journal of the American Academy of Religion* 62 (1994): 483–508; quote from p. 502.

97. M. J. Kurrick, "The Self's Negativity," in *Fyodor Dostoevsky's* The Brothers Karamazov (ed. H. Bloom; New York: Chelsea House, 1988), 97–118; quote from p. 108.

98. Florovsky, "Quest for Religion," 53.

99. Gibson, *Religion of Dostoevsky*, 194.

100. Dostoevsky, *Brothers Karamazov*, bk. 6, chap. 2, p. 303.

2. "The Eternal Feminine Draws Us Upward":
Feminine Wisdom in the Old Testament, Augustine, and Goethe's *Faust*

Introduction

From the ancient Israelite sages to present-day philosophers, men have struggled to understand the feminine side of God and themselves, a side that defies their categories because it is alien at the same time that it is attractive, indescribable at the same time that it evokes praise and wonder. The surprise is not that they most often preferred to refer to God in the images familiar to their own masculine lives (father, warrior, king) but that they dared to picture God as Mother and Lover at all. And while we may fault them for not consulting more with their own mothers, sisters, wives, and daughters about the "mysteries" of the feminine, I do not think their male perspective necessarily diminishes the truthfulness or relevance of the insights that they did attain from the outside. Women clearly understand or experience the feminine more directly than men do, but they don't necessarily love it more: The love of a son for his mother is as noble and humane, and as relevant to understanding her, as her daughter's love for her, or as her love for her children.

In this chapter we will examine the depiction of divine and human wisdom as feminine in Proverbs, Sirach, and the book of Wisdom. We will then look at Augustine's writings to see how he finally learned wisdom from his mother, Monica, and also at the character Faust in Goethe's play to see how he is saved from his own folly by the wisdom of Gretchen and Mary. In all of these works, the male authors rightly intuited the greater power and truth to be gained through humility and compassion rather than by the destructive pride of reason and objectivity.

Divine Wisdom in Proverbs, Sirach, and the Book of Wisdom

Several times in the book of Proverbs, a personified Wisdom addresses the audience, and this personification is female. This feminine portrayal of wisdom can be explained by the fact that the Hebrew word for "wisdom" is feminine (*hokmah;* it is also feminine in many other languages—*sophia* in Greek, *sapientia* in Latin, *sagesse* in French), but this is only a very partial explanation.[1] The gender of nouns does not dictate how they are described; the French word for "battle" *(bataille)* is feminine, but we would not usually use feminine images to describe a battle, and if we did, some comment or explanation would be required. Wisdom is presented to us as Lady Wisdom, an agent or aspect of the Lord, his special way of communicating with and through creation. Given the strict monotheism of the Israelites, she cannot be a separate goddess; in some way she is a feminine communication or manifestation of God, an idea that is expressed by these books in several ways.[2]

When Lady Wisdom first addresses her children, it is to entreat them, almost plead with them: "Wisdom cries out in the street; in the squares she raises her voice. . . . 'Give heed to my reproof; I will pour out my thoughts to you; I will make my words known to you'" (Prov 1:20, 23). When she speaks, it is with the honesty and care of a mother (see Prov 1:8; 6:20; 10:1; 31:2). Her words are truthful (Prov 8:6–9) and of infinite worth: "Take my instruction instead of silver, and knowledge rather than choice gold; for wisdom is better than jewels, and all that you may desire cannot compare with her" (Prov 8:10–11). This worth is partly a delayed gratification, for she promises her followers that she will give them wealth and power (Prov 8:15–16, 18, 21). But she also promises them another reward—"I love those who love me" (Prov 8:17)—and we know that in the biblical tradition as expressed in the Song of Songs (a book closely related to the Wisdom books), love (even in its merely human expression between a woman and man) is more valuable and powerful than anything else: "For love is strong as death, passion fierce as the grave. Its flashes are flashes of fire, a raging flame. Many waters cannot quench love, neither can floods drown it. If one offered for love all the wealth of his house, it would be utterly scorned" (Song 8:6–7). Finally, Lady Wisdom describes how, like a good mother or hostess, she spreads a lavish table of food and wine, both to entice people away from folly (also personified as female, Prov 9:13–18) and to reward them for coming to her (Prov 9:2–5).

But besides describing her relation to humans, Lady Wisdom gives an astonishing description of her relation to the Lord. She was the first being he created: "The LORD created me at the beginning of his work, the first of his acts of long ago. Ages ago I was set up, at the first, before the beginning of the earth" (Prov 8:22–23). She even seems to have helped God with the rest of his creation: "When he marked out the foundations of the earth, then I was beside him, like a master worker" (Prov 8:29–30).[3] And besides being God's helper, she was his playmate and the playful admirer of their handiwork: "I was daily his delight, rejoicing before him always, rejoicing in his inhabited world and delighting in the human race" (Prov. 8:30–31); or "I was delight day by day, playing before him all the time, playing on the surface of his earth, and my delight (was) with humankind."[4] Lady Wisdom brings joy to God at the same time that she finds joy in what they have made together. While God pronounces everything he makes "good" (Gen 1:1–31), Wisdom finds everything she makes with God joyful or delightful; while God commands, Wisdom plays. For all of human history, people in their moments of despair have accused God of "toying" with them, but this description of Wisdom playing with humanity is a statement of mutual joy, for she is glad to play with her children and to make them happy with her play.

Sirach gives similar but slightly different and more specific associations for Lady Wisdom.[5] As in Proverbs, Wisdom is described in Sirach as the first created thing: "Before all things else wisdom was created" (Sir 1:4). Similar to Proverbs, she comes down to all the earth: "From the mouth of the Most High I came forth, and mistlike covered the earth" (Sir 24:3). Sirach seems to take the generous table that Wisdom laid in Proverbs 9 and go one step behind the hostess to identify Wisdom with the delightful fruits given to people: "Like cinnamon, or fragrant cane, or precious myrrh, I give forth perfume. . . . I bud forth delights like the vine, my blossoms yield to fruits fair and rich. Come to me, you that yearn for me, and be filled with my fruits" (Sir 24:15, 17, 19). Sirach's new contribution to the wisdom tradition is to make particular Wisdom's presence among the Israelites (Sir 24:8–12) and to specify this presence further by identifying her with the Law (Torah—Sir 24:23). While this is a somewhat nationalistic and conservative move, one thing it does preserve beautifully is the experience of Wisdom bringing joy in everyday matters, for the Israelites as well as modern Jews have always associated joy and Torah, a tradition preserved liturgically in their celebration of Simchat Torah ("joy of/over Torah"), which follows Sukkot (Booths or Tabernacles). While the Torah was only given to Israel, Sirach ends his praise of Wisdom by connecting her to all of time and creation: "The first human never knew wisdom fully, nor will the last succeed in fathoming her. . . . Again I will send my teachings forth shining like the dawn, to spread their brightness afar off; again will I pour out instruction like prophecy, and bequeath it to generations to come" (Sir 24:28, 32–33).

The book of Wisdom (ca. 50 B.C.E.)[6] also describes Wisdom as present at creation (Wis 9:9) and even as the Creator herself: "If riches are a desirable possession in life, what is richer than wisdom, the active cause all things? And if understanding is effective, who more than she is fashioner of what exists?" (Wis 8:5–6). And while Wisdom was a special creation of the Lord in Proverbs and Sirach, the book of Wisdom makes her connection with God even more intimate, sacred, and awe inspiring: "For she is a breath of the power of God, and a pure emanation of the glory of the Almighty; therefore nothing defiled gains entrance into her. For she is a reflection of eternal light, a spotless mirror of the working of God, and an image of his goodness" (Wis 7:25–26). Here it is clear that Wisdom is not God's consort or offspring but his glory, purity, light, and image. She is an aspect or manifestation of him: "Wisdom is somehow identified with the Lord. The call of Lady Wisdom is the voice of the Lord; she is the revelation of God."[7] And the book of Wisdom also makes the image of Lady Wisdom as a lover more explicitly erotic, beautiful, and alluring: "I loved her and sought her from my youth; I desired to take her for my bride, and became enamored of her beauty. She glorifies her noble birth by living with God, and the Lord of all loves her" (Wis 8:2–3).[9] Wisdom is the way the Lord entices people to love him, and her presence in someone is a sign (and enticement?) of God's love: "In every generation she passes into holy souls and makes them friends of God, and prophets; for God loves nothing so much as the person who lives with wisdom." (Wis 7:27–28)

The reason wisdom is personified as feminine in these Old Testament books has long baffled commentators, who sometimes simply observe it and despair of an explanation: "Various reasons have been put forward to explain why Wisdom is personified as female. There are no satisfactory answers."[9] While this may be true from a linguistic or historical perspective,[10] I think that when one examines the feminine qualities that we have found in the Wisdom books associated with divine wisdom, it is clearer from a theological or psychological perspective why they had to depict her as female, and how her qualities complement the male qualities more often associated with God in the Old Testament.

First, Wisdom is associated with creation, helping God to create, and in particular, enjoying the creation, at the same time that she brings joy to the Creator. Although there are many masculine roles of creativity—father, author, artisan—and they often involve some loving relation and attachment to the thing created, none can have the level of intimacy and immediacy of motherhood,[11] of the created thing being a literal, physical part of the creator. And this special attachment necessarily entails greater feeling and compassion—literally, "suffering with"—than other creative acts. This is most obvious at the moment of birth, during which mother and child are in profound agony together, while the most the father can do is offer his support while looking on. And for a mother to entreat her children is quite different from a father commanding them. Lady Wisdom's call has an element of empathy or identification ("How could you do such a thing [to me]?"), rather than being rational, distancing, objectifying ("How many times did I tell you not to do that?"). Lady Wisdom does not try to put us in our place so much as ask us to put ourselves in her place, to come to her table and not spurn her advice and love. Female Wisdom is much closer to her offspring; she is "the primary link between God and humankind."[12] This feminine portrayal of wisdom imagines a divine presence that is much more vulnerable and accessible than the masculine images of father, judge, warrior, and king more usually applied to God in the Bible, and it is an enormous and valuable addition to the biblical concept of God.

Closely related to this depiction of Wisdom as feeling and rejoicing is the depiction of her as a lover. Although God the Father may be said to love his creation, he is not usually depicted as a lover, an important and powerful role that Wisdom fills: "One can perhaps better comprehend the power of Wisdom the lover, who can defeat death with life for those who love her. The image of the lover has the capacity to draw together the experiences of daily life and the experiences of faith."[13] If Wisdom's feeling and compassion emphasize the vulnerability and accessibility of God or Wisdom, then love and longing—of Wisdom for her human devotees and of them for her—make Wisdom accessible in a different way, while at the same time making her extremely powerful and vital to humans. As a lover, Wisdom is as demanding and rewarding as any we can imagine.

A mother is necessarily female, and her children's experience of her is necessarily and importantly different from that of a father, as well as complementary of his role. A lover is not necessarily female, but since the biblical books were almost certainly written by men, it is a given that they would depict a lover as female. Although such images necessarily went beyond their own experiences as men, they nonetheless answered to vital and primal experiences that almost all people have—the love of a child for his or her mother, the love between a woman and man—and they therefore make the image and the experience of God in the Bible that much more passionate and realistic. So as surprising as the female images for Wisdom may seem in the Bible, they ultimately make perfect sense for answering the spiritual needs of both ancient Israelites and modern Christians. Indeed, the power of these images in part explains the survival and appeal of Judaism and Christianity.

Feminine Wisdom for Augustine

Saint Augustine was born in 354 C.E. in Thagaste in North Africa.[14] At first a teacher of rhetoric, he lived in Rome and Milan before returning to North

Africa, where he became bishop of Hippo in 395. These were the waning days of the Roman Empire in the West. Rome was sacked by the Visigoths in 410, and Augustine himself died during the Vandal siege of Hippo in 430. The quantity and variety of Augustine's surviving writings give us a detailed and revealing look at his long career and development. They include dialogues, letters, and sermons, as well as doctrinal, polemical, and exegetical works. His vast intellect thoroughly analyzed every matter put before it, and at the same time, his deep emotion and passion come across clearly in how he wrestled with his own spiritual problems and how he compassionately counseled his parishioners. His most famous work, of course, is his *Confessions* (397). In this work he relates his own intellectual and spiritual journey. Intellectually, he explored Platonism, Manichaeiansm (a Gnostic-Christian group), and skepticism before being baptized Catholic in 387. Personally, he tells us of his relationships with his parents, colleagues, friends, son and the woman with whom he lived for thirteen years and who bore his son. His report is extremely revealing of his personality, and we know Augustine the man better than any of the other early church writers, better than many writers and philosophers since.

Augustine seems always to have had a problem with the masculine and feminine sides of his life. This struggle is contained in a concentrated form in his relationship with his parents. His mother, Monica, was an extremely devout and pious Christian. She was also a little obsessed with her one son (though Augustine had siblings, they are barely mentioned in his book), literally following him around the Mediterranean (even when he tried to escape). Her love for him seems to have been a bit overpowering, "relentless . . . all-absorbing . . . devouring,"[15] a "carnal affection."[16] And although every reader has noticed the touching and sincere love that Augustine expresses for her, he seems to have idealized her and worried about whether he could ever live up to her expectations, while at the same time he ran away from her and defied her expectations. As for his father, Patricius, there is hardly a word in the *Confessions* about him. He died when Augustine was seventeen, a fact Augustine mentions only in passing and without registering any emotion.[17] Though he apparently did not beat Augustine's mother, he was unfaithful to her, hot-tempered, and a pagan until almost the end of his life.[18] The one similarity his parents seem to have had is one that they passed on to Augustine in undiluted, concentrated form: "Both parents, however, had one quality in common: determination. . . . Augustine was able to make this quality his own. It is no mean achievement to have done so. We can see the result, above all, in the manner in which he hounded his ecclesiastical opponents, and stuck firmly to his own ideas."[19] For most of his life before writing the *Confessions*, Augustine idealized his mother's piety and disdained his father's worldliness and carnality; he felt intimidated and smothered by the former, and disgusted by the latter. This is surely not a very healthy mixture, and it is only when he gets beyond his conflicted and hostile attitudes toward his parents that he begins to lead a happy and meaningful life, as we shall see.

Augustine's struggles with the masculine and feminine disturb his professional life as well. Augustine recounts how he would sometimes leave the male-dominated world of rhetoric to indulge in the partly feminized pseudoscience of astrology. Augustine turns from the hustle and bustle and respectability of the exclusively male classroom and court to the silent darkness of the stars and the slightly embarrassing, furtive consultation of astrologers. It is significant how Augustine is turned away from astrology:

> There was at that time a certain man, wise, most highly skilled in the art of medicine.... When he learned from my conversation that I was given to the study of the books of the nativity calculators, he advised me in a kind and fatherly manner to throw them away.... "You," he said, "have the profession of rhetoric by which to maintain yourself in the world of men, and yet you pursue this delusion, not out of any need at home but of your own accord."[20]

A father figure turns him away from the mysteries of mother night and calls him back to the respectable "world of men." In the long run, however, astrology is much less spiritually dangerous to Augustine than the "world of men," with all its vain ambition and deadly pride. Astrology at least makes one feel weak and vulnerable before a supposedly higher power, while Augustine's worldly career only makes him feel falsely superior, invulnerable, and self-sufficient.

Augustine also struggles with the image of the masculine, patriarchal Christian God. He is lured away from Christianity because some people mock its supposedly anthropomorphic view of God: "Is God confined within a corporeal form? Does he have hair and nails?"[21] The idea that God might inhabit a human, male body is both ridiculous and disgusting to Augustine, and he therefore embraces Manichaeanism. The Manichees were a dualistic sect that Augustine followed for nine or ten years of his adult life.[22] Like most dualists, though they did not worship a goddess, they had a much larger and more prominent place for the feminine in their cosmology, a "lush, partly erotic mythology,"[23] at the same time that they ultimately disparaged either gender. Their worship is known to have been much more aesthetically pleasing than Catholic ritual of the time.[24] They believed that all living things consist of the masculine principles of heat, light, and dryness being trapped by the feminine principles of cold, dark, and wet. We are light, airy souls trapped in gross, wet bodies. So on the one hand, the Manichees could offer to Augustine a wonderfully antiseptic, genderless God without all the messy maleness of the biblical God: "Above all, as a serious and sensitive young man, Augustine could abandon the terrible father-figure of the Old Testament."[25] He describes his concept of God under Manichaean influence as a "pure, sexless mind"[26] or an "immense, shining body."[27] While this image of God was less objectionable to Augustine than that of an old man sitting on a throne somewhere, it was still limiting and impersonal. And on the other hand, Manichaean anthropology also allowed Augustine to disavow sin completely as an alien force that he carried around with his body but that was not essentially himself. He could ignore it and eventually jettison it, freeing himself from it without bearing any of its guilt or tarnish: "It gave joy to my pride to be above all guilt.... I loved to excuse myself, and to accuse I know not what other being that was present with me but yet was not I."[28] And he could arrogantly free himself *by himself.* As long as Augustine remained a Manichee, there was no need to acknowledge either a feminine side to himself or a masculine (or feminine) side to God, for both were gross impediments to understanding the true nature of people or God. Nor did he need to acknowledge guilt or seek help in conquering sin, for these too were misconceptions. Given his strong, independent personality, this avoidance of responsibility was probably an enormous attraction to him, but it was also exactly the reason it could not satisfy him completely or permanently, as inevitably he would see its shortcomings and its lack of integrity.[29]

Through all of these personal, professional, and religious struggles, Augustine has one passionate goal in mind—wisdom: "I was stirred up and enkindled and set aflame to love, and pursue, and attain and catch hold of, and strongly embrace not this or that sect, but wisdom itself."[30] But as long as he pursues it alone, it frustrates him. It is when he finally allows God to help and when he dedicates himself to helping others that real wisdom begins to come to him. He quits his job as a teacher of rhetoric, the "chair of lies"[31] he had occupied and on which he had put so many false hopes. Rather than lying to others, he withdraws from the world with his mother, son, and friends to seek wisdom together with them.[32] In one of his earliest extant works, a dialogue between himself and a personified Reason, Augustine describes the quest for a relationship with a personified Wisdom that is very feminine, even erotic:

> Reason: Now let us ask about what sort of lover of wisdom you are: you long to see and to hold her, with a most pure gaze and in an embrace that has no veil in between, naked as it were, in a way that she allows to only a few and most select of her lovers. Now if you burned with love for some

beautiful woman, wouldn't she be right not to give herself to you, if she found that you loved something besides her? So how can the purest beauty of wisdom show herself to you, unless you are ablaze for her alone?

Augustine: Why am I held back by this unhappiness and delayed by this miserable torment? Surely I have shown that I love nothing else, for anything which is not loved for its own sake is not really loved. I love only wisdom for her own sake, and only for her sake do I want to have, and fear losing, other things, such as life, peace, friends. How can my love of that beauty have a limit? Not only do I not begrudge her to others, but I even seek many more who will pursue her with me, long for her with me, grasp her with me, and enjoy her with me, and they will be my friends even more, the more the love of her is shared among us.

Reason: That is just how lovers of wisdom ought to be. She seeks such lovers, whose union with her is completely pure and without any defilement.[33]

As in the biblical tradition, Augustine personifies Wisdom as a lover to emphasize the challenge of the pursuit of her but the sweetness and desirability of the rewards. Augustine later criticizes these early works of his, saying that they "still breathed forth the school of pride."[34] Although these early writings may still contain an unhealthy amount of "pride," Augustine's selfishness and false sense of self-sufficiency seem to have diminished remarkably. He no longer seeks wisdom alone, nor does he stand before a class as an authoritative dispenser of it, but he seeks it humbly and passionately with his friends in a community of mutual love, trust, and dependence.

Shortly after his baptism, though, his mother dies, and this personal crisis causes a further reevaluation and rethinking of his life and relationships.[35] Augustine can finally stop idealizing his mother and accept what she has known all her life, that she is "an ordinary human being, an object of concern, a sinner like himself, equally in need of mercy."[36] And once he accepts Monica's humble evaluation of herself, he can express his own grief in the same way his emotional mother had long wept for him: "I took comfort in weeping in your sight over her and for her, over myself and for myself. I gave way to the tears that I had held back, so that they poured forth as much as they wished. I spread them beneath my heart, and it rested upon them, for at my heart were placed your ears, not the ears of a mere man."[37] Augustine has achieved the place where his heart can rest, the place he has longed for since the very beginning of the *Confessions*,[38] by learning from his mother how to affirm and accept an earthly love, with all its imperfections and finitude: "Augustine's description of his mourning achieves a paradoxical affirmation of *eros*—of the love of that which cannot last—within a context of *agape*."[39] Augustine even imitates Monica's wisdom and patience by finally accepting his imperfect earthly father, just as she had for so long: "[R]emember Monica, your handmaid, together with Patricius, sometime her husband, by whose flesh you brought me into this life ... my parents in this passing light, my brethren under you our Father in our Catholic Mother, and my fellow citizens in that eternal Jerusalem."[40] Monica's example of humility and love has redeemed her family and guided her brilliant but wayward son back through all his wanderings.

The ultimate problem with, as well as part of the attraction of, all the philosophies that Augustine had tried was not their (partial) truthfulness but their lack of humility, their "puffed up ... unnatural pride."[41] Augustine begins to overcome that pride as he humbly but very passionately seeks a female Wisdom with his friends. He also learns from his uneducated, emotional mother that real wisdom is not acquiring knowledge but acting on the knowledge of our fallen and limited state; this kind of knowledge naturally and automatically precludes pride and can result only in humility, love, and service. It is a lesson that helps him make peace with his past and then drives him forward to his new life as a bishop, humbly serving and loving others for the rest of his life.

Goethe's *Faust:* Gretchen and Mary Save Faust from Himself

Johann Wolfgang von Goethe's (1749–1832) writing captures much of the intellectual power and depth of the Enlightenment and Romantic periods in which he lived, ages that he came to epitomize even more than such brilliant and influential contemporaries as Immanuel Kant (1724–1804). Goethe is known for his brilliance and honesty but not necessarily for his orthodoxy. He did not think of himself as an atheist, however, but as holding a variety of theisms appropriate to his different intellectual endeavors: "When we do natural science, we are pantheists; when we do poetry, we are polytheists; when we moralize, we are monotheists."[42]

Goethe's greatest work is unquestionably *Faust*, an enormous drama based on the legendary life of a charlatan who lived in the first half of the sixteenth century.[43] The original Doctor Faust was thought to have practiced impressive magic, as well as university teaching and pederasty. After his death in 1540, legends quickly grew that he had acquired his magical powers through a pact with the devil, who had then whisked him off to eternal, hellish punishments.[44] Told this way, the tale is a straightforward one of godless rebellion leading to eternal damnation, and it remained popular in Goethe's time, during which he probably first encountered his future hero in the form of a comical puppet show of Faust's life and death. But Goethe's genius brooded over the diabolical doctor for more than sixty years and transformed his story from a straightforward, orthodox tale of damnation for lust and greed into a much more obscure, unorthodox, and, most of all, interesting tale of salvation and love. Like his creator, Faust is no atheist, but rather he seeks God in passionate and unusual ways.[45]

Goethe begins his version of Faust's story with a prologue in heaven based on the beginning of the book of Job.[46] The devil, here called Mephistopheles or Mephisto, speaks to the Lord, mocking him for giving his supposedly favorite creature a unique but partial gift that does more harm than good:

> I see alone mankind's self-torturing pains.
> The little world-god still the self-same stamp retains,
> And is as wondrous now as on the primal day.
> Better he might have fared, poor wight,
> Hadst thou not given him a gleam of heavenly light;
> Reason, he names it, and doth so
> Use it, than brutes more brutish still to grow.
> —*Prologue, lines 38–44*[47]

As in Job, the Lord proposes one servant who disproves the devil's accusation. But since Mephisto's accusation was about reason and not faith, the Lord proposes not a paradigm of faith like Job but rather a man of science and intense intellectual vigor and curiosity, Doctor Faust, a man who is anything but comfortable in his relation to the Lord or the world.

In Goethe's version, Faust is a scientist, philosopher, and medical doctor, but all his great learning only brings him misery, because, unlike those less intelligent, he can see how meager and useless is the knowledge he possesses:

> That we in truth can nothing know!
> That in my heart like fire doth burn.
> 'Tis true I've more cunning than all your dull tribe,
> Magister and doctor, priest, parson, and scribe;
> Scruple or doubt comes not to enthrall me,
> Neither can devil nor hell now appal me—
> Hence also my heart must all pleasure forego!
> I may not pretend, aught rightly to know,
> I may not pretend, through teaching, to find
> A means to improve or convert mankind.
> Then I have neither goods nor treasure,
> No worldly honour, rank, or pleasure;
> No dog in such fashion would longer live!
> —*Part 1, lines 11–23*

Especially painful to him is the praise and admiration he receives from the ignorant villagers, for he knows that his impotent, senseless medicine does more harm than good to them. Indeed, what career could be more likely to frustrate and madden a sensible and sensitive man than that of a medieval doctor, who could only diagnose, but possessed almost no methods to cure or alleviate suffering? Faust wants knowledge of life and life-giving knowledge,[48] and his attempts thus far have failed miserably and only brought greater suffering to others and miserable frustration to himself. Exactly as Augustine had turned away in frustration from the masculine pursuits of rhetoric and the courts to the pseudoscience of astrology, Faust turns away from science and medicine taught to him by his father to alchemy and conjuring, and his conjurations are increasingly feminine.[49] Even before the androgynous and rakish Mephisto offers his services to Faust, we see the doctor in his laboratory, summoning an earth spirit, a spirit who weaves on the loom of God (lines 163–64) and who rebuffs Faust like an angry lover, refusing his longing for "breasts" (line 104)—whether maternal or sexual—and mocking his pathetic and futile attempts at "sucking at my sphere" (line 136).[50] Neither masculine science nor feminine pseudoscience can give Faust the knowledge he craves; neither can soothe the turmoil in his own "breast"; (or "heart,"—which the poem uses both to refer to Faust's innermost self), and so he is on the brink of suicide. When he is momentarily soothed by religion and nature, it is by turning to the life-giving sun, also a feminine symbol.[51] What little, partial success Faust has had in his quest for knowledge has come when he has pursued a feminine, creative principle and not a masculine, controlling one.

Mephisto now appears to the desperate and vulnerable doctor and makes the famous pact. The devil will serve Faust in any way he asks, giving him every experience and pleasure that can be had, while Faust wagers his soul that none of this will ever fully satisfy him. It is not Faust's faith that will protect him from the devil's temptations but his restlessness, his inability to be satisfied with easy answers or diversions: "He knows that he must push forward into the uncharted future or die. Salvation cannot come by finding rest in anything. To be at rest is to be cursed."[52] Mephisto first takes Faust further into the feminine world of magic, taking him to a witch's kitchen for a potion (after showing him the ridiculousness of men drinking in a tavern, which utterly bores Faust). Under Mephisto's influence, Faust has given up his laboratory and retort for a kitchen and a bubbling cauldron.[53] But even this diabolical kind of feminine influence, a world of deception and control, gives Faust a glimpse of a higher kind of female figure when he sees a beautiful woman in a mirror there: "The image of the woman yet again embodies the goal of Faust's striving."[54] The vision captivates him with love and longing, but not lust. Mephisto senses that the mirror's influence is against his own devilish goals, and so he hurries Faust away from it.[55] This incident then leads directly to a far different encounter with a real woman when Faust falls in love with Gretchen, also called Margaret in the poem. At first Mephisto is all in favor of Faust's infatuation, for he thinks that it will lead him further under the influence of lust and sinfulness. But Mephisto soon realizes that Faust loves Gretchen precisely for her "simplicity and holy innocence, . . . meekness and humility" (lines 2839–41), and she herself is completely impervious to his devilish temptations.

But it is not just Gretchen's innocence or naivete that appeal to Faust or us. It is her wisdom, her experiential knowledge and loving acceptance of all the messiness and wonder of life (including sexual attraction), that captivate Faust. Her vivid description of prolonged suffering offers us a glimpse of her attractiveness:

> As soldier is my brother gone;
> My little sister's dead; the babe to rear
> Occasioned me some care and fond annoy;
> But I would go through all again with joy,
> The darling was to me so dear. . . .
> I reared it up, and it grew fond of me.
> After my father's death it saw the day;
> We gave my mother up for lost, she lay
> In such a wretched plight, and then at length
> So very slowly she regain'd her strength.
> Weak as she was, 'twas vain for her to try
> Herself to suckle the poor babe, so I
> Reared it on milk and water all alone;
> And thus the child became as 'twere my own;
> Within my arms it stretched itself and grew,
> And smiling, nestled in my bosom too. . . .
> At night its little cradle stood
> Close to my bed; so was I wide awake
> If it but stirred;
> Or while I was obliged to give it food,
> Or to my arms the darling take;
> From bed full oft must rise, whene'er its cry I heard,
> And, dancing it, must pace the chamber to and fro;
> Stand at the wash-tub early; forthwith go
> To market, and then mind the cooking too—
> To-morrow like to-day, the whole year through.
> —*Lines 2857–61, 2863–72, 2876–85*

Gretchen's life includes clear echoes of the life of Mary, the mother of Jesus: She is quite literally a virgin mother ("And thus the child became as 'twere my own") who buries her own child. In the world of folklore, Gretchen appeals to Faust or to us in the same way that Cinderella does—as a woman with strength, patience, endurance, courage, and engagement with the world and its problems—and not just as a damsel in distress.[56] While he has been studying life, she has been living it; while he has been feeling sorry for himself, she has been feeling for and helping others. Faust feels disordered, empty, suicidally depressed, and trapped, while in her he sees "order . . . plenteousness in poverty, and bliss in the 'prison' of her narrow surroundings."[57] Gretchen is no weak woman for Faust to win or possess, and this is exactly why she can derail Mephistopheles' plans, for that is the only image of her that his lewd mind can form. She is instead a paradigm of strength for him to wonder at and emulate: "He completely loses himself . . . in her world," and only with her does he speak "not with the self-assertion that we expect of him, but rather in self-surrender."[58] He loves her and needs her much more than he seduces her, even if some of the latter is still retained from traditional folk tales: "Faust is . . . released from his adverse role as seducer of Gretchen to indulge his affinity, his kinship, with her . . . his instinctive or deeper relation to her is not the one dramatically assigned to him but rather that of a worshipper in a not quite compatible sense."[59] This is love, not lust, and it teaches Faust to give, not take.

But Mephisto is able to win a temporary victory over Faust by tricking Gretchen into accidentally killing her mother, and by letting the physical aspects of Faust's love overwhelm his higher yearnings. Gretchen bears Faust's illegitimate child and all the humiliation that comes with giving birth to a child out of wedlock. She is driven insane by the ordeal, kills the child, and is executed for her crimes, refusing Faust's offer of escape. Unlike him, she may be insane, but she is not under the influence of the devil. While Faust is flitting with Mephisto from one orgy to the next, Gretchen is praying to Mary, with whose sufferings she identifies and on whose merciful, compassionate intercession she completely relies. By the end of part 1, Gretchen is saved by God because she takes responsibility for what she has done, begs God for forgiveness, and does penance, while Faust comes dangerously close to falling completely under Mephisto's power, fleeing responsibility or punishment as he pursues empty pleasures.

But Faust is saved in the end, much to the dismay of Mephisto and many orthodox readers, who see him as richly deserving hell after what he has done to the innocent Gretchen. The only thing that saves him in the end is his surrender of himself to Gretchen, who is now in heaven alongside Mary: "It is this same penitential dimension . . . so simple yet so profound, that saves her—and that finally, through her, saves Faust himself."[60] Directly opposite to the narrator of *Notes from Underground*, Faust can surrender and make himself completely vulnerable to the woman he used, humiliated, and destroyed. And when Faust surrenders to the Divine at the end, it is not to the foolish, boasting God the Father, the almost comical "ancient one" (line 110) of the prologue, but to the completely loving and accepting "Goddess" Mary (line 12103). The "Eternal Feminine" (line 12110) has drawn Faust's love up through all its manifestations, completing and perfecting all his loves "from Gretchen . . . through Sophia [Wisdom], which brings with it the best of our inner life, higher to Mary, who alone, as the supreme center of humanity, lifts the upward look into the miracle of the mystery."[61] In a brilliant and multilayered reversal, Mary here becomes both the example of obedience for men to follow and the object of their quest. She is therefore both the ultimate example of female submission to the masculine God and the ultimate object of male submission to a feminine goddess.

Just like Augustine, Faust ultimately finds his masculine, worldly, rational life and ambitions to be empty, meaningless, dead, and deadening. From Gretchen (and, in spite of himself, from the androgynous, lewd, but, most of all, playful, Mephisto)[62] he learns what we saw in the last chapter—that it is our loving relationships that bring us real happiness and fulfillment; it is not by acquiring money, pleasure, fame, or even knowledge that we are fulfilled, but by giving away ourselves. Losing ourselves in others, we find a higher and permanent existence: "To weave oneself into that super-individual sphere of existence, to put *my* creative stamp upon it and thus to survive in it—that and only that can bring man the highest happiness for which he strives."[63] It is only when Faust imitates the wisdom and humility of Gretchen that he can let go of his need to know and control, opening himself up to a whole world and life he has never known before, a "world of freedom and of authentic humanity, of morality and ultimately of monotheism."[64] It is the freedom and authenticity of love, the wisest act of all, as foolish as it makes us act sometimes, because it allows God into our lives, and allows us into his kingdom: "Love, not egoism, is both the principal instrument of Grace and the highest value."[65]

Conclusion: Feminine Wisdom

We have now seen a variety of depictions of Wisdom as feminine from widely varying cultures and time periods—ancient Israel, Roman North Africa, and Germany during the Enlightenment. As these authors have considered the feminine side of God and themselves, they have given us creative, compassionate, playful female images of God and humanity, but they have not suggested that these aspects are weaker than their male counterparts. To put it in the real world of our experience, do you necessarily obey or love your father more than your mother? Does she have less influence and control over your life than he does? Stereotypically masculine qualities are often quite ineffective and imprudent; sometimes the fragile bamboo bends and survives while the mighty oak topples over in the violent storm, and often the person who stands alone and refuses to cooperate or compromise with others ends up failing and falling alone. Flexibility and empathy are sometimes infinitely more powerful than rigidity and objectivity. This idea is deeply embedded in the Taoist description of the universe, its creation, and its maintenance:

> There was a beginning of the universe
> Which may be called the Mother of the universe.
> He who has found the mother (Tao)
> And thereby understands her sons (things),
> And having understood the sons,
> Still keeps to its mother,
> Will be free from danger throughout his lifetime.[66]

But while the Taoist tradition stresses the feminine side(s) of the universe and of its creative force, the Bible constantly stresses the masculine side(s) of God and the masculine experiences of its writers and (half of) their audience. Tao is described as mother, flowing water, hollow reed, the emptiness inside a vase—things that are powerful because of their giving, adaptable nature; God in the Bible is usually described as father, warrior, judge, and king—men who are powerful because of their ability to take things and make others conform to their will. Although certainly not as balanced and equal as the familiar concept of yin and yang (complementary opposites symbolized in the interlocking, overlapping black and white halves of a circle), the wisdom tradition is one part of Judaism and Christianity that does offer some balancing view of the feminine side of the universe and its Creator. The biblical wisdom tradition, as well as later literature adopting the image of a female divine Wisdom creating and loving her creation as she calls it back to herself, together provide a very important and potent minority opinion on God within the biblical tradition and subsequent Christianity. God the Father more usually commands and teaches, and our experience of him is therefore most often one of knowledge and obedience (or ignorance and disobedience). But Lady Wisdom creates, plays, and nurtures, and she is therefore experienced by us as a loving presence that is much harder to ignore. Together these images of both masculine and feminine form a much fuller picture of God and a much more satisfying experience of him/her.

Likewise, the depiction of the wise woman, as opposed to the more usual image of the male sage or philosopher, also weaves through these works. Just as divine Wisdom fills up and balances the image of God, feminine, human wisdom gives a fuller and more accurate picture of our humanity. Both Augustine and Faust finally find happiness when they are no longer satisfied with semi-feminized lives or religions but instead find real female figures and qualities that can lead them to a God beyond stifling gender roles. Monica and Gretchen help them find a God who no longer tests, threatens, or makes demands of them (like a bad father); nor smothers, stifles, or emasculates them (like a bad mother); but forgives and perfects them (like a good parent, lover, or Savior). Augustine and Faust painfully learn that there are limits to reason, independence, and ambition, typically masculine qualities that need to be offset and balanced by the qualities of intuition, cooperation, and humility. Perhaps no person in Christian tradition exhibits these qualities more fully than Mary, who in the Bible exclaims in utter humility and submission, "Here am I, the servant of the Lord; let it be with me according to your word" (Luke 1:38), an impoverished young woman (scholars tell us she was probably twelve or thirteen)[67] eagerly taking upon herself the further shame and degradation of bearing an illegitimate child just because God's angel has told her to do so. And later she takes the humbling mysteries of God and keeps them "in her heart" (Luke 2:19, 51), holding on to God through intuition and feeling, rather than reason or logic. Goethe takes this to an even more mysterious and marvelous level by showing how Mary embodies human and divine wisdom: "The Eternal Feminine / draws us upward" (lines 12,110–11). Mary or Sophia (Wisdom) is truly a female Savior, a Salvatrix, and by emulating her wisdom, we learn to be like her at the same time that we begin to let her save us.

Notes

1. Cf. R. E. Murphy, *The Tree of Life: An Exploration of Biblical Wisdom Literature* (2d ed.; Grand Rapids: Eerdmans, 1990), 146: "It is simply not adequate to say that the Hebrew noun *hokmah* is feminine gender."

2. Cf. Murphy, *Tree of Life*, 133: "In the biblical context the figure of Wisdom cannot be conceived as hypostasis or person because of the strict monotheism of the postexilic period. Whatever association Wisdom may have had in an earlier era, she is best understood in her biblical expression as a communication of God." On the possible prebiblical goddess that may lie behind the figure, see his discussion of Lang in *Tree of Life*, 137–38, 147–48.

3. The meaning of the verse is mysterious; see Murphy, *Tree of Life*, 136.

4. Translation by Murphy, *Tree of Life*, 136.

5. Sirach models his description on Proverbs 8; see P. W. Skehan and A. A. Di Lella, *The Wisdom of Ben Sira: A New Translation with Notes* (New York: Doubleday, 1987), 331–38; Murphy, *Tree of Life*, 139–40.

6. On the date, see Murphy, *Tree of Life*, 83.

7. Murphy, *Tree of Life*, 138.

8. Cf. J. L. Crenshaw, *Old Testament Wisdom: An Introduction* (Atlanta: John Knox Press, 1981), 178: "Since the book we are discussing purports to come from Solomon's hand, it elevates the *erotic relationship* with Wisdom" (emphasis in original).

9. Murphy, *Tree of Life*, 146.

10. Though C. V. Camp, *Wisdom and the Feminine in the Book of Proverbs* (Sheffield, U.K.: Almond Press, 1985), presents a persuasive case for the historical situation in which this depiction could have formed.

11. Cf. Camp, *Wisdom and the Feminine*, 79–84, who discounts maternal images for Wisdom.

12. Ibid., 272.

13. Ibid., 111.

14. For excellent biographies of Augustine, see P. Brown, *Augustine of Hippo: A Biography* (Berkeley: University of California Press, 1967); H. Chadwick, *Augustine* (Oxford: Oxford University Press, 1986). For an analysis of Augustine's works with some biography, see J. J. O'Donnell, *Augustine* (Boston: Twayne Publishers, 1985).

15. Brown, *Augustine of Hippo*, 30.

16. *Confessions* 5.8.15. All quotations from Augustine's *Confessions* are from the translation by J. K. Ryan, *The Confessions of St. Augustine* (New York: Doubleday, 1960).

17. *Confessions* 3.4.7. See the discussion in Brown, *Augustine of Hippo*, 30–31.

18. *Confessions* 9.9.19.

19. Brown, *Augustine of Hippo*, 31.

20. *Confessions* 4.5.5. Augustine does not completely abandon astrology until later; see *Confessions* 7.6.8–10.

21. *Confessions* 3.7.12. See also K. Paffenroth, "Paulsen on Augustine: An Incorporeal or Nonanthropomorphic God?" *Harvard Theological Review* 86 (1993): 233–35.

22. On the Manichees, see Brown, *Augustine of Hippo*, 46–60; O'Donnell, *Augustine*, 3–4; Chadwick, *Augustine*, 11–17.

23. Chadwick, *Augustine*, 13.

24. Cf. ibid.: "Church people could be specially impressed by the fine parchment and calligraphy of Manichee sacred books and by the special solemnity of their music."

25. Brown, *Augustine of Hippo*, 49.

26. *Confessions* 4.15.24.

27. Ibid., 4.16.31.

28. Ibid., 5.10.18. Cf. Brown, *Augustine of Hippo*, 51: "For Augustine, the need to save an untarnished oasis of perfection within himself formed, perhaps, the deepest strain of his adherence to the Manichees"; Chadwick, *Augustine*, 11: "One would not expect such a religion to have attractions for a young man to whom sex was important (unless it were that one could attribute all one's lower impulses to the powers of darkness and disown personal responsibility)."

29. Cf. Brown, *Augustine of Hippo*, 53: "More than anything, perhaps, it had enabled the young Augustine to disown, for a time, and at a heavy cost, disquieting qualities that he would only later come to accept, both in his God and, one may suspect, in himself. These were the hard, 'paternal' qualities associated with the omnipotent Father of Catholic belief: a Father capable of righteous anger, of inflicting punishment, His unique goodness separated by an unbridgeable gulf from the intimate guilt of His sons."

30. *Confessions* 3.4.8.

31. Ibid., 9.2.4.

32. Ibid., 9.4.7–12.

33. Augustine, *Soliloquies* (trans. K. Paffenroth; Hyde Park: New City Press, 2000), 13.22–23. Cf. the similarly erotic imagery in *On the Free Choice of the Will* 2.37. Thanks to Phillip Cary for pointing out this latter passage to me.

34. *Confessions* 9.4.7.

35. The following discussion is based on my "Book Nine: The Emotional Heart of the *Confessions*," in *A Reader's Guide to Augustine's Confessions* (ed. Kim Paffenroth and Robert P. Kennedy; Louisville: Westminster/John Knox Press, 2003).

36. Brown, *Augustine of Hippo*, 164.

37. *Confessions* 9.12.33.

38. Ibid., 1.1.1: "You arouse him to take joy in praising you, for you have made us for yourself, and our heart is restless until it rests in you."

39. A. H. Hawkins, "St. Augustine: Archetypes of Family," in *The Hunger of the Heart: Reflections on the* Confessions *of Augustine* (ed. Donald Capps and James E. Dittes; Society for the Scientific Study of Religion Monograph Series 8; West Lafayette, Ind.: Society for the Scientific Study of Religion, 1990), 237–54; quote from p. 249.

40. *Confessions* 9.13.37.

41. Ibid., 7.9.13.

42. An aphorism attributed to Goethe, quoted by J. Pelikan, *Faust the Theologian* (New Haven: Yale University Press, 1995), 19.

43. Though it was apparently not meant for presentation on the stage; see W. P. Andrews, *Goethe's Key to Faust: A Scientific Basis for Religion and Morality and for a Solution of the Enigma of Evil* (Port Washington, N.Y.: Kennikat Press, 1913), 9.

44. On the Faust legend, see the introduction to *Goethe's Faust* (ed. and trans. W. Kaufman; New York: Doubleday, 1961), 12–18; see also Andrews, *Goethe's Key to Faust*, 33–35.

45. Cf. Pelikan, *Faust the Theologian*, 20.

46. On the comparisons with Job, see the breathtaking essay by C. Zhitlowsky, "Job and Faust" (trans. P. Matenko; in *Two Studies in Yiddish Culture*; Leiden: E. J. Brill, 1968), 71–162. See also J. K. Brown, *Goethe's Faust: The German Tragedy* (Ithaca, N.Y.: Cornell University Press, 1986), 44–46.

47. J. W. von Goethe, *Faust. Part 1* (trans. Anna Swanwick; New York: P. F. Collier, 1909–14). All quotations from pt. 1 are from this translation.

48. Cf. Brown, *Goethe's Faust*, 50: "Faust seeks direct perception of the cosmos without the mediation of words: both in its immediacy and in its object, this is a form of gnosis on the typical Neoplatonic model."

49. Cf. the observations of K. Adam, *Saint Augustine: The Odyssey of His Soul* (trans. D. J. McCann; New York: Macmillan, 1932), 17–18: "Augustine at this point of his life is a Faust-like figure. Between him and Goethe's Faust, as has been justly observed, there are many points of contact. In both there is the same passionate struggle for truth and for happiness of soul. In both an important part is played by astrology and demonism, by woman's love and worldliness. In both there is a despair of truth and a longing for death. And—to pass quickly to the end—in both is the same salvation through the 'revelation of love that unfolds into blessedness.'"

50. On the contrast between the earth spirit and the immediately preceding vision of the macrocosm, see Brown, *Goethe's Faust*, 52–56.

51. See Andrews, *Goethe's Key to Faust*, 12–13.

52. W. Sundberg, "The Demonic in Christian Thought," *Lutheran Quarterly* 1 (1987): 413–37; quote from p. 420. Sundberg significantly ties this restlessness to that described in Pascal, whom we will examine in the fourth chapter.

53. The movement obviously parallels that of Macbeth from war and politics into the feminine and diabolical world of witches; see Brown, *Goethe's Faust*, 95–96.

54. Brown, *Goethe's Faust*, 87; cf. B. Fairley, *Goethe's Faust: Six Essays* (Oxford: Clarendon Press, 1953), 97–98.

55. Cf. Brown, *Goethe's Faust*, 88: "Our earlier insight about the role of Mephistopheles and of magic necessarily precludes, I think, any possibility that this image is demonic or false."

56. Though I was familiar with the identification of Cordelia and Cinderella, I'd never thought of Gretchen this way until Ms. Matilda Siconolfi of Iona College pointed this out in class. Compare Gretchen to Snow White or Rapunzel, who seem to be much more purely victims, and who are locked away in a tower or hidden in the woods, away from the world and its dangers; and in higher literature, Gretchen is clearly modeled on Shakespeare's Ophelia, but is much more active and strong.

57. R. Anchor, "Method and Family in Goethe's *Faust:* Gretchen's Mother and Gretchen Tragedy," *Historical Reflections* 23 (1997): 29–48, 37.

58. Fairley, *Goethe's Faust*, 54.

59. Ibid., 48–49.

60. Pelikan, *Faust the Theologian*, 113.

61. Ibid., 125, quoting Balthasar.

62. Cf. Brown, *Goethe's Faust*, 101: "Thus the two [Gretchen and Mephisto] do not, like good and bad angels, pull Faust in opposite directions, but both work together to keep Faust striving. Paradoxically, Gretchen and Mephisto serve identical functions."

63. Zhitlowsky, "Job and Faust," 130 (emphasis in original).

64. Pelikan, *Faust the Theologian*, 108.

65. Ibid., 118, quoting Dye.

66. Lao Tzu, *The Way of Lao Tzu (Tao-te ching)* (trans. W. T. Chan; New York: Macmillan, 1963) chap. 52; cf. chaps. 1, 25, and 28.

67. See J. B. Green, *The Gospel of Luke* (Grand Rapids: Eerdmans, 1997), 86.

3. "Reason in Madness":
The Wisdom of Folly in the New Testament and *King Lear*

Wisdom and Folly in the New Testament

Throughout the New Testament, the words for "wisdom," "wise," "wisely," or "make wise" are most often used in the same positive ways as their Hebrew equivalents were used in the Old Testament. They are applied to Jesus, to God, and to his faithful followers.[1] Most of the New Testament applies the Old Testament idea of divine and human wisdom directly to the present situation as a positive attribute to be admired in God and pursued in our own lives. In the case of God, wisdom is a divine attribute that shows God's vast superiority as Creator; in the case of humans, wisdom is a God-given gift of insight and discernment that renders people enlightened and better able to serve God.

But alongside this positive portrayal of wisdom are dissenting or qualifying voices, writings that adapt the Old Testament concept of wisdom rather than apply it directly. Sometimes these are criticisms of someone or something that seems "wise" but is not so in reality—there is apparent wisdom, and there is real wisdom.[2] Sometimes this contrast is made more pointed, as when there is not just the mistake of judging something as wise that isn't, but rather a real conflict between two different kinds of wisdom, an earthly one and a heavenly one: "Such wisdom does not come down from above, but is earthly, unspiritual, devilish. For where there is envy and selfish ambition, there will also be disorder and wickedness of every kind. But the wisdom from above is first pure, then peaceable, gentle, willing to yield, full of mercy and good fruits, without a trace of partiality or hypocrisy" (Jas 3:15–17). And more surprisingly, in what is regarded by many as the earliest gospel tradition about Jesus, the sayings common to Matthew and Luke (the so-called Q source),[3] a tradition that several times depicts Jesus as a teacher of wisdom,[4] there is a saying that makes the contrast not between two competing kinds of wisdom, but between wisdom on the one hand and simplicity or childishness on the other: "I thank you, Father, Lord of heaven and earth, because you have hidden these things from the wise and the intelligent and have revealed them to infants" (Matt 11:25 // Luke 10:21). Alongside the conventional idea of wisdom, some New Testament writings formulated an implacable conflict between differing kinds of wisdom, and the superior kind was identified with people who are normally thought of as the opposite of "wise"—people who are simple, unsophisticated, weak, and vulnerable.

Although Paul can speak of wisdom in the same positive way as other New Testament writers, it is this contrast between conflicting kinds of wisdom that his theological creativity really elaborated in his Corinthian correspondence. Faced with a cosmopolitan, worldly congregation steeped in Greek culture, philosophy, and religion, Paul's language and the issues he addresses are markedly different from those in his other epistles.[5] Though less explicitly theological than Romans or Galatians, the Corinthian letters are just as fundamental to Paul's message of Christianity, as they constantly return to the radical reconfiguration in human life and relationships that has been brought about by the life, death, and resurrection of Jesus. As Paul is trying to impress upon his Corinthian audience the unexpected demands and outlook of their new life in Christ, he launches into an impassioned paragraph that goes to the heart of his Gospel, putting it in terms of a paradoxical new wisdom and folly that defy expectations:

> For the message about the cross is foolishness to those who are perishing, but to us who are being saved it is the power of God. For it is written, "I will destroy the wisdom of the wise, and the discernment of the discerning I will thwart." Where is the one who is wise? Where is the scribe? Where is the debater of this age? Has not God made foolish the wisdom of the world? For since, in the wisdom of God, the world did not know God through wisdom, God decided, through the foolishness of our proclamation, to save those who believe. For Jews demand signs and Greeks desire wisdom, but we proclaim Christ crucified, a stumbling block to Jews and foolishness to Gentiles, but to those who are called, both Jews and Greeks, Christ the power of God and the wisdom of God. For God's foolishness is wiser than human wisdom, and God's weakness is stronger than human strength. (1 Cor 1:18–25)

Wisdom in either the Old Testament or the Greek world implies and promises a life of success and respect, not a miserable, shameful death on a cross.

If the Corinthians are to follow a crucified Christ, they must cast off their old ideas of wisdom and accept a divine wisdom that is foolishness by worldly standards, for it is a wisdom that came down to us in the one who served, suffered, and died for others in weakness and humility.

Perhaps even harder to accept are the implications that this divine wisdom has for its devotees, implications to which Paul turns in the following verses. Just as God did not choose a conventional king or sage as his Son, so too the followers of this foolishness are not those who are normally valued or respected in their world: "Consider your own call, brothers and sisters: not many of you were wise by human standards, not many were powerful, not many were of noble birth. But God chose what is foolish in the world to shame the wise.... God chose what is low and despised in the world, things that are not, to reduce to nothing things that are" (1 Cor 1:26–28). To follow a God who is so foolish as to die for his creation, or to follow the penniless, illegitimate son of a Jewish peasant girl, is to bring upon oneself a similar life of service, weakness, and ridicule, as Paul demonstrates in his own life: "And I came to you in weakness and in fear and in much trembling. My speech and my proclamation were not with plausible words of wisdom" (1 Cor 2:3–4). About a year later, Paul finally explodes in anger against the Corinthians' intransigence or relapse into their old ways, and he gives a "fool's speech" in which he sarcastically defends himself by boasting of the same respectable but worthless and ungodly qualities that his opponents claim. He then turns to boast of the really important, legitimating parts of his ministry, his humiliating sufferings, concluding with a statement of what really qualifies him as an apostle, or what would qualify his readers as Christians, if they could allow such folly to rule their own lives: "If I must boast, I will boast of the things that show my weakness" (2 Cor 11:30). We are all weak before God and others; Paul only teaches his followers the wisdom of admitting, accepting, and building on this weakness, for such wisdom is the only real way to overcome our weakness and limitations.

Whereas older Wisdom literature offered a lifestyle that would minimize or avoid suffering, and some Wisdom books such as Job tried to provide some kind of answer or context for it, Paul offered the Corinthians a divine wisdom that embraced suffering and demanded it of her followers. This must have been as hard a demand for them as it is for us, but the alternatives are ultimately less attractive, for they only deny and postpone the inevitable, clinging to empty, fleeting dreams as if they were eternal: "Yet among the mature we do speak wisdom, though it is not a wisdom of this age or of the rulers of this age, who are doomed to perish" (1 Cor 2:6). In a world in which six of the Seven Wonders of the World exist only in our imagination, the Eternal City of Rome was sacked and burned sixteen centuries ago, and the Thousand Year Reich lasted twelve years, who would deny that the foolishness of God might well be a good deal more powerful and wise than anything we have to offer to ourselves? (Indeed, let us hope that it is, as the longevity of our supposedly eternal accomplishments seems to be shrinking steadily.) But the temptations to cling to earthly things and to avoid the inevitability of suffering are powerful indeed (they are usually called "wise"), as we will see in *King Lear*.

Overview of *King Lear*

Shakespeare's (1564–1616) *King Lear* is amazingly simple in its outline: an old king unwisely divides his kingdom between his two evil daughters while disowning his good daughter, and the two evil daughters destroy him, their sister, and each other. Its complexities and profundities do not lie in its plot or even in its characterizations, the two places modern audiences would usually look for understanding. In its setup, plot, and characterizations, everything about the play is archetypal, like a fairy tale; its two wicked daughters and one good daughter have always suggested to audiences and critics the Cinderella story.[6] I think the play's genius is in two other qualities it has in abundance. First is its placing of such archetypal characters into scenes of shattering dramatic power and violence, cataclysms that are apocalyptic in their scope and overtones—the first explosive scene of Lear's tantrum, the world-shattering storm, the mock trial presided over by fools and madmen, the sadistic eye gouging, the heartrending death scene: Even on the page these leave an indelible impression. And second are the poetic speeches given by almost every character as they share with us their deepest feelings and thoughts about the unfolding apocalypse. No one can read or hear these lines without pausing to consider them long and hard.

The play opens with Lear, the king of Britain, at the height of his power—and the depth of his folly. He comes forward in a very public spectacle before the wedding of his youngest daughter, Cordelia, and announces that he will divide his kingdom between his three daughters. Even more shocking, he proposes to base the division of the kingdom upon their public protestations of their love for him. His two eldest daughters, Goneril and Regan, give empty, hyperbolic speeches and receive their rewards immediately, before Cordelia speaks, demonstrating that the scene is only for show and that it is not really a contest at all: It didn't matter what Goneril and Regan said, because the prizes were awarded before all the "contestants" participated. When Lear turns to Cordelia, however, she first refuses to answer and then gives a sincere answer, but one that has struck generations of readers as a very cold and detached statement of her love: "I love your Majesty / According to my bond, no more nor less" (1.1.92–93). Lear explodes, dividing her part of the kingdom between the other two and giving her to the king of France without a dowry. When Lear's faithful servant Kent tries to defend Cordelia, Lear banishes him from the kingdom.

Lear proposes to live alternately in the castles of Goneril and Regan, keeping a retinue of one hundred knights at his disposal. While at Goneril's castle, he is rejoined by a disguised Kent, whom he takes on as a follower. We also meet there his Fool, a character who can tell Lear things much more unpleasant than Cordelia and Kent tried to say in the first scene but in such a way that he can get away with it and, more importantly, in a way that renders Lear capable of listening:

> LEAR: Dost thou call me fool, boy?
> FOOL: All thy other titles thou hast given away; that thou wast born with . . .
> Now thou art an O without a figure. I am better than thou art now: I am a fool, thou art nothing.
> —*1.4.141–43, 183–85*

Just a few lines earlier, Lear was incapable of tolerating Kent and Cordelia when they respectfully referred to him as "Father," "King," and "Majesty," while the Fool's role allows him to call Lear a "fool" and "nothing," as well as numerous other names, most all of which seem to imply a playful disrespect: "nuncle" (1.4.111, 125, 148, 163, and *passim*), "shealed peascod" (1.4.190), "hedge-sparrow" (1.4.206), "Jug" (1.4.215), and "Lear's shadow" (1.4.221). Goneril's assessment of the Fool as "all-licensed" (1.4.191) is quite accurate.

But while at Goneril's, we find that there is nothing at all playful in the disrespect she shows to her father. She objects that his retinue is "disordered . . . deboshed and bold" (1.4.232) and dismisses half of them without Lear's knowledge. Lear flies into another rage and leaves for Regan's castle. Regan, however, is warned of his approach by Goneril, and leaves her castle with her husband, the Duke of Cornwall, so that they're not home when Lear arrives. Lear's company, Regan, Cornwall, and Goneril all meet at the castle of the Earl of Gloucester, where the two daughters subject Lear to the final humiliation: They tell him that they will not let him into either of their homes with even one follower of his own. He must live the end of his life alone, friendless, with not one vestige of his former life left to him, with not even the smallest, cheering illusion about who is now in charge. Lear prefers the elements to their hospitality, and he leaves with Kent and the Fool, going out into a storm more savage than any Kent can remember (3.2.45–49), while Goneril and Regan tell Gloucester to lock the doors to keep them out. They wander around, Lear raging against what has happened to him, until Kent finds them a hovel for shelter, in which they find a partly naked madman.

Meanwhile, Shakespeare has constructed a parallel plot about Gloucester and his children. Gloucester has a legitimate son, Edgar, and an illegitimate son, Edmund. Edmund conceives a plan to trick his father into thinking that Edgar is going to try to kill Gloucester, hoping thereby to inherit his title and lands though totally willing to improvise as the situation unfolds. Gloucester falls for the deception, while Edmund simultaneously tricks his half brother into fleeing, thereby making the accusations seem all the more likely.[7] Edgar is alone in the wilderness and assumes the disguise of a madman to protect himself; he is the one whom Lear, the Fool, and Kent find in the hovel, and for the rest of the play their plots are intertwined. Gloucester finds them, gives them shelter, and sends Lear to Dover to meet up with a French army led by Cordelia, while Edgar again wanders off into the wilderness, still in disguise. Edmund gives this information to Cornwall, who rewards him by giving him all of Gloucester's lands. Cornwall then gouges out both of Gloucester's eyes before being killed by a servant who objects to the torture. Gloucester is left to wander helplessly outside, where Edgar sees him and helps him. Gloucester intends suicide, so Edgar tells him he has led him to the top of a cliff; in reality they are on a plain, so when Gloucester throws himself forward, he is unhurt. Edgar then pretends to be a bystander at the bottom of the supposed cliff and tells Gloucester that he saw him float down like a feather. Gloucester's "miraculous" salvation convinces him not to attempt suicide again.

As they are speaking, Lear enters, having gone mad because of what Goneril and Regan did to him, but more so because of what he did to Cordelia: "A sovereign shame so elbows him; . . . / . . . these things sting / His mind so venomously that burning shame / Detains him from Cordelia" (4.3.42, 45–47). Lear is eventually reunited with Cordelia, while Edgar defends his father from Goneril's evil servant Oswald, killing him. The forces of good appear to be winning, and the forces of evil under Goneril, Regan, and Edmund are rapidly unraveling, as both women lust after Edmund and are in deadly competition over him. However, they have managed to raise an army to repulse the French force, and in the ensuing battle between the French and British forces, Lear and Cordelia are taken prisoner by Edmund, who orders them executed.[8] In a duel Edgar mortally wounds Edmund, who, before he dies, sends a messenger to save Lear and Cordelia from execution. At the same time, Goneril poisons Regan, then kills herself. Again the tide seems to have turned in favor of the good characters. But Edgar relates how his father's weak heart finally gave out when Edgar finally revealed himself to him, and then Lear enters, carrying the body of Cordelia. It is an image of desecration and destruction so complete and irrevocable that it overwhelms the three surviving characters:

KENT:	Is this the promised end?
EDGAR:	Or image of that horror?
ALBANY:	Fall and cease.

—5.3.264–65

Kent is hopeless, Edgar is resigned, Albany is overcome, and none of them can console Lear or one another. Lear tells us that he killed the evil servant who had killed Cordelia, then the king himself dies a few lines later. Kent expresses his intention to die soon (suicide?), Albany abdicates his power, and Edgar is left to carry on, providing his own commentary on the situation that relates it back to the first scene (at which he was not present): "The weight of this sad time we must obey, / Speak what we feel, not what we ought to say" (5.3.324–25).[7] We have watched in horror as two families and a kingdom have been destroyed as they struggled to learn the value of this statement.

It is the play's overwhelmingly apocalyptic and bleak imagery, action, and especially ending that lead many to deny its Christianity entirely. Harold Bloom scoffs at "Christianizers of this pagan play" and their "irrelevant transcendental moralizings"[8] and finally dismisses all such claptrap: "That pretty much makes Christianity as irrelevant to *Macbeth* as it is to *King Lear*, and indeed to all the Shakespearean tragedies."[9] This is true only if one believes that a play to which Christianity is relevant must necessarily have a happy ending, as though Christians cannot be anguished or cannot give a Christian response and meaning to anguish on the stage. Such a caricature may well be true for the plays on which Shakespeare based his play. I completely agree that "nowhere in Shakespeare's play is there the sentimentalized Christianity so characteristic of its predecessor,"[10] Shakespeare having abandoned sentimentality for "complexity, ambiguity, and dubiety."[11] But unless these latter qualities are considered un-Christian, I see nothing to diminish the relevance of Christianity to the play, and some Christians of not inconsiderable faith and influence have been capable of a good deal of doubt: "One notes that Pascal and Kierkegaard thought of themselves as Christians."[12] Never mind the more obvious case of the book of Job, the Scriptures and subsequent Christian literature include numerous examples of unanswered prayers and shameful deaths and disappointments: "In the Psalms, and even in the Epistles, our deliverance is often an object of faith and hope but sometimes emphatically not of experience. You may repent and confess and obtain forgiveness and learn patience and reassume your proper place in the world, and still things may not turn out well. Cordelia may die."[13] Such tragedy is not antithetical or even peripheral to Christianity; it is at its very heart: "Like Job, *King Lear* is part of this Wisdom Literature tradition. . . . Tragedy is Wisdom Literature dramatized."[14]

Put another way, it seems very odd to suggest that the play's apocalyptic tone renders it un-Christian, when Christianity began as an apocalyptic sect and maintains at least the vestiges of its origins. The Gospel of Mark, regarded by most as the earliest Gospel, probably did not originally contain an account of the resurrection and therefore ends as bleakly as anything in Shakespeare, its hero betrayed, denied, abandoned, and shamefully killed, crying out to a God who does not answer.[15] But perhaps the intervening centuries have rendered "sentimentalized Christianity" so commonplace and apocalyptic Christianity so weird and primitive that a play more closely identified with the latter is no longer recognizable to us as Christian. Christianity, or any apocalyptic worldview, believes in redemption but denies that final redemption is possible or even compatible with the way the world is *now:* "On this side of eternity, there are at best fleeting though magnificent moments of glad grace, such as the one we witness between Lear and Cordelia.... [S]uch moments ... are finally unworldly, in the world but not of it."[16] The play is inescapably nightmarish, but it is an undeniably Christian nightmare: "Shakespeare, like Jung, seem[s] to feel that the New Testament Apocalypse, having already produced 'a universal religious nightmare,' is an encounter with essential human experience—is as much the province of poets and dramatists as of theologians and historians."[17]

Not surprisingly, the play is from Shakespeare's dramatic maturity and the height of his genius, probably first performed in 1605, the year after *Othello* and the year before *Macbeth*. But comparison with those two plays and with the slightly earlier *Hamlet* (1601) shows the different challenges presented to us by *King Lear*. The heroes in the other tragedies are enormously appealing—ambitious, successful, decisive (in the case of Othello and Macbeth), or deeply thoughtful (in the case of Hamlet). They are paradigms of Aristotelian tragic heroes—great men with just one fatal flaw, one that throughout the play we are eager to forgive or overlook, or which we desperately hope they will fix before it is too late. But it is very hard indeed to call Lear appealing, as Shakespeare seems to go out of his way in the first two acts to make him as unappealing as possible: In the first scene alone he shows such loathsome qualities as "wicked pride, self-will, self-love, vanity, choler, egoism, senile puerility, a crass materialism which views love as a commodity to be bartered and traded, tyranny, sloth, and want of courage"[18]—a potent, shocking litany of shortcomings indeed; and when he is later laid low, he turns into a miserable, bitter, complaining, spiteful, self-pitying old man. While the observation that Lear is deeply loved by all the good characters in the play certainly needs to be taken into consideration,[19] it cannot check our distaste for him, though it may put it in some larger context; their steadfast love for him seems to put the characters who love such a miserable old man in a better light, but not him.

Further, while it is abundantly clear what is wrong with Lear, where is his greatness? He is too old to have Hamlet's vitality and potential, but he could have at least the memory of the kind of martial virtue of Macbeth or Othello. Did he win battles, vanquish foes, build great palaces or castles, govern wisely and make the people happy? He certainly may have, but there is absolutely nothing in the play to indicate this, and his anguish in Act 3, the beginning of his descent into madness and revelation, hints at serious problems in his reign and in his life:

> Poor naked wretches, wheresoe'er you are,
> That bide the pelting of this pitiless storm,
> How shall your houseless heads and unfed sides,
> Your looped and windowed raggedness, defend you
> From seasons such as these? O, I have ta'en
> Too little care of this! Take physic, pomp;
> Expose thyself to feel what wretches feel,
> That thou mayst shake the superflux to them
> And show the heavens more just.
> —3.4.28–36

Apparently Lear's reign left something to be desired. And, more importantly for him as a person, we have before us on stage an eighty-year-old man who seems to be thinking of the misfortunes of others for the first time in his life: There is the real tragedy. This is why modern retellings of the story sometimes portray the king as more bloodthirsty and successful to make him more appealing—and to make his downfall seem more just, as punishment for past violence, rather than the unraveling of a faulty, misguided life. Director Akira Kurosawa embellishes the story this way brilliantly in his film *Ran*, in which the Lear character seems to be combined with Macbeth. He is a savage and successful warrior-king who tries ineffectually to stop the violence now that he is on top, but is dogged by the demons of his bloody past. All this is fine as new art, but it is not the image or meaning of Shakespeare's *King Lear*, which works in a different way than other tragedies. It works by having a hero who is so ordinary and unexceptional—not in rank and wealth, to be sure, but in the more important qualities of his personal and emotional state.[20] Lear is weak and frail in a way that Hamlet, Othello, and Macbeth are not, nor are Oedipus and Orestes. In this respect, at least, Arthur Miller's *Death of a Salesman* may have made the same point as *King Lear* more than other plays have. It is crucial for this tragedy that we see someone like us realize and be destroyed by the mistakes of his life, mistakes that are not enormous crimes like those of other tragic heroes (parricide, matricide, regicide, wife murdering, incest, cannibalism), but rather the fairly mundane act of insensitivity to others, especially those dearest to him.[21] *King Lear* seems all too familiar, in a way that Bloom quite rightly describes as making us feel "uncomfortably at home."[22] This is exactly why *King Lear* is more difficult and uncomfortable to experience than the other tragedies but also exactly why it has greater power and relevance to us.

Worldly Wisdom in *King Lear*

Let us now consider the depiction of wisdom and folly in what many consider Shakespeare's greatest play. In terms and images very reminiscent of the New Testament, the characters who behave foolishly according to the world's standards, especially the Fool, Cordelia, Kent, and Edgar, turn out to have real, life-giving, divine wisdom; on the other hand, the characters obsessed with being wise by worldly standards, typified by Goneril, participate in a fatal folly, a blinding self-absorption that makes them not only cruel and rapacious but ultimately miserable and self-destructive. Especially interesting in this analysis is the insight it offers us into Lear himself, for it sees his transformation not as redemption in the fullest, or more optimistic, sense but as the absolutely necessary and painfully beautiful preparation for redemption, the enlightenment and transformation of a man from normalcy to truth, from appearance to reality, from bondage to freedom—as difficult and fatal, and therefore tragic, as the movement there has been.

If the selfless Fool, Edgar, Kent, and Cordelia lead Lear to real, divine wisdom, then it is probably not surprising that the chief spokesperson for the falsifying and deadly wisdom of the world is Goneril, a Shakespearean villain devoid of even the minimal humanity of a Iago or Richard III, who often fascinate us, while she can only horrify and repulse. She is a truly apocalyptic character who deserves every one of the horrific, animal labels applied to her in the play, one who easily could have spoken the inhuman line of the Flannery O'Connor character the Misfit, that there is in life "no pleasure but meanness."[23] Without the sincere and eloquent, if cruel, soliloquies of Edmund, and without his sense of shame and self-defensiveness,[24] all of Goneril's strikes are preemptive, the height, or depth, of an earthly wisdom of self-interest, always seeking to stay one step ahead of her opposition, and always assuming that everyone is really or potentially her enemy. Edmund's evil is reactive and partly understandable, given the first lines of the play, in which he is publicly humiliated in what seems like a routine way by his unthinking, lecherous father; Goneril's is proactive, motiveless, gratuitous, beyond understanding. And unlike Edmund or the Misfit, a further problem with Goneril is how well she fits into polite society, thereby giving free and murderous reign to her evil wisdom. Her penultimate line in the play was a hairbreadth away from becoming completely and irrevocably true:

"[T]he laws are mine" (5.3.159). Only the second time we see her, she is already referring to her father as an "Old fool" (1.3.19), and immediately following this, she tells him to "make use of your good wisdom" (1.4.210) and "be wise" (1.4.230), while behind his back she ridicules his "dotage" (1.4.284). She finds nothing unusual or inappropriate in bolting the doors on her eighty-year-old father in the midst of a hellish storm: she says it is the fault of "his folly" (2.4.286), and her sister too calls their gratuitous cruelty "wisdom" (2.4.302). No characters could better illustrate James' description of earthly wisdom: "Such wisdom does not come down from above, but is earthly, unspiritual, devilish. For where there is envy and selfish ambition, there will also be disorder and wickedness of every kind" (Jas 3:15–16).

In the characters of Goneril and Regan, Shakespeare has exaggerated and perverted the worldly wisdom of self-preservation and shrewd calculation that we see in the biblical tradition and elsewhere into hideous creatures that have practiced rapacity and cruelty so thoroughly that they have now become "natural" urges followed for their own sake (cf. Lear's many appeals to "nature," and his anguished cry that Goneril is "unnatural"—2.4.273), rather than temporary concessions to practicality. It is this exaggeration that in fact makes Goneril and Regan's self-interested acts self-destructive, for the sisters lack all sense of balance, order, and restraint, never mind goodness or virtue. In Goneril, this deficiency is expressed especially in her pursuing Edmund with her husband still alive, an action that is not "merely" sinful but impractical and that leads to all the deaths at the end; in Regan, it is expressed in her insistence that Gloucester's eye-gouging be pursued beyond the normal or "acceptable" bounds of torture at the time (the servants do not protest the first eye-gouging, only the second), leading directly to Cornwall's death, to the hostility of the common people against them, and again indirectly to all their deaths.[25]

Goneril and Regan's lust is a good focus for understanding their kind of wisdom. What finally is the difference between love and lust? One needn't think theologically or ethically, just in a straightforward description. What is lust but love minus all concerns for other people, a desire to get with no desire to give? Or, a little more cynically, what is love but lust with a lot of concern for the other person added? I do not mean to minimize the importance of this addition; indeed, Shakespeare maximizes it in *King Lear*. As 1 Corinthians indicates and as Kent, Cordelia, the Fool, and Edgar practice, love is a very daunting and "foolish" exercise, totally focused on the needs of another person, who may not appreciate or benefit from it, while ignoring one's own needs and safety. As Bloom emphasizes in his nihilistic analysis, it ruins or kills all its devotees in the play: "Its value . . . is less than negative: it may be stronger than death, but it leads only to death."[26] On the other hand, lust initially looks much wiser and more practical than love: it seeks something pleasurable that you want, it ignores inconvenient consequences, it seeks to maximize gain while minimizing cost, and it may result in you passing on more of your genes to the next generation than your more conservative and repressed neighbors. So what's not to like?

While love is an arduous and sometimes fatal trial, subtracting its concern for the other and reducing it to lust as Goneril and Regan do only make it an enslaving addiction or affliction,[27] and still just as fatal. Indeed, Edmund's greater power and appeal in the play are because he maintains an icy, almost inhuman control over his urges, apparently feeling none of the lust of the women who pursue him. Even his power grab and his distaste for his father and half-brother seem matter-of-fact and unemotional: his plans for exterminating them are as cold and methodical as what one would use against large, bipedal vermin. The good characters suffer and are killed because they courageously and foolishly overcome the natural urge of self-preservation—they literally lack the sense to come in out of the rain—while Goneril and Regan are destroyed by foolishly succumbing to their appetites, both natural and unnatural. Our possession of natural urges or appetites is neither wise nor foolish; it is simply a fact. But the control or (dis)use of such urges can be wise or foolish. Goneril and Regan have refused the natural urge of filial love until it has atrophied into nonexistence (quite possibly in reaction to Lear's own bad parenting),[28] while they have replaced it by overindulging the unnatural urge of cruelty and the natural appetite of sexual desire, making these into psychological monstrosities or addictions that destroy them. On the other hand, Edgar and the Fool, the characters antithetical to Goneril and Regan, pose riddles that "insist on the alien aspect of Nature and on all that detracts from man's sense of his own dignity—corns, chilblains, lice, and the mere pricking of sexual desire."[29] The Fool neither denies the presence or necessity of such "prickings" nor advocates for them in the bawdy humor typical of Shakespeare's comic characters;[30] he only makes fun of such urges, and of the people who give in to them or who deny their reality. The only advocates for unrestrained appetite are Goneril and Regan (and Lear in his madness as he speculates with bitterest irony about the source of their evil), and they are anything but humorous or wise.

Also extremely revealing of Goneril's "wisdom" is its contrast with Albany's new "folly" in Act 4, what has been called his (belated and ineffectual) "detonation.... a timed explosion, a retarded awakening to human evil and a transformation from confused disinterest to engaged commitment."[31] This is the first time someone other than Lear has stood up to Goneril and her "wisdom," and she reacts to her husband exactly as she did to her father, calling him a "fool" and his words "foolish" five times in the heated exchange (4.2.28, 37, 54, 58, 61). She had earlier chastised her husband in similar, though much less offensive, terms: "You are much more atasked for want of wisdom / Than praised for harmful mildness" (1.4.334–35). Goneril twists positive, Christian images into ugliness and insult; for her, pity for the weak is not the milk of human kindness but "cowish" (4.2.12) and "milk-livered" (4.2.50; cf. the earlier "milky kindness" at 1.4.332), and Christ's admonition to turn the other cheek is spat out of her mouth as an accusation of cowardice and impotence (4.2.51). Goneril is unspeakably evil, but her analysis of others is quite accurate. She has rightly understood Albany's "folly" as Christlike "folly" and her reaction to it is what we would expect from worldly "wisdom"—derision and disgust. But unlike the case in Act 1, something must have changed in Albany's anatomy or psyche, such that he is now as assertive as Goneril, and he rightly diagnoses her "wisdom" as anything but: "Wisdom and goodness to the vile seem vile; / Filths savor but themselves" (4.2.38–39). To follow an earthly "wisdom" that mocks compassion and praises cruelty is to descend into a cannibalistic, self-destructive hell, breaking all the "natural" ties that make life livable or worth living: "Humanity must perforce prey on itself, / Like monsters of the deep" (4.2.49–50).

But if Goneril is the most consistent and horrifying spokesperson for her kind of worldly wisdom, it is more important for the meaning of the play that at the beginning the hero himself is dangerously close to his evil daughters' point of view, as there is a family resemblance in general: "Lear and all three daughters suffer from a plethora of prides."[32] Although nowhere in the play could we say that Lear behaves with his evil daughters' cruelty, or their "predatory self-seeking,"[33] it is not unfair to observe that the dominant male lion of the pride need not be predatory; his females bring him what he needs without him behaving in a ruthless or violent manner.[34] Likewise, the aged Lear can be calm and generous so long as all the other people play the roles that he has imperiously and without consultation assigned to them. But the fragility of his calm and the hollowness of his generosity are obvious as soon as Cordelia refuses to speak her assigned lines. And the way Lear rewards mere flattery as soon as Cordelia shows herself unwilling to express her real affection satisfactorily is as ugly as the flattery itself, and much more catastrophic. Lear tries to use his authority and the kingly "patina of symbolic paternalism"[35] to get what he wants, just as Goneril and Regan use the outer shows of filial or sororal affection and loyalty to get what they want; in the beginning he is as addicted to and manipulative of appearances as they are. To be sure, his appetites are quite different and more humane and elevated than theirs: he has acquired in his undescribed past the political power for which they lust, and in which he apparently has little interest, as he divests himself of it with far too little thought. Lear's needs are purely emotional, but because his desires are much less mundane and much more personal than theirs, his selfish and manipulative pursuit of them is perhaps even uglier.

While sharing his evil daughters' taste for appearances, showmanship, and the opinions of others, Lear also shares their taste for violent retaliation, another quality that has a patina of justice or common sense upon it. Lear's need for revenge is clear in the first scene, but in its sequel in Act 1, Scene 4, it seems even more obscene, as it now lacks the spontaneous, explosive quality of a man losing his temper, as in the first scene, and instead has become both pettier and more venomous. And for a man who can't take even the mildest of criticism, Lear certainly can dish it out in a most disgusting manner. After a long scene of bickering, and before he even knows that Goneril has dismissed half his retinue, Lear prays in front of her in the most ungodly way imaginable:

> Hear, Nature, hear; dear goddess, hear:
> Suspend thy purpose if thou didst intend
> To make this creature fruitful.
> Into her womb convey sterility,
> Dry up in her the organs of increase,
> And from her derogate body never spring
> A babe to honor her. If she must teem,
> Create her child of spleen, that it may live
> And be a thwart disnatured torment to her.
> —1.4.266–74

There is clearly something profoundly wrong—morally, spiritually, psychologically—with a man who directs such obscene curses against his daughter, no matter how badly she has behaved. Exactly like his evil daughters, for the first two acts of the play, Lear selfishly and deceitfully manipulates people to get what he wants, and when he is slighted, he viciously—if ineffectually at that point—retaliates with no consideration for the other person. Though not as diseased as they are, clearly years of playing the role of king, of being what other people expect and having people do and say what he expects, have made Lear into a man who has little respect for the truth, who automatically believes in the justice of his own cause, and who tends to react with revenge and savagery, not forgiveness, compassion, or even understanding.

The worldly wisdom that uses and manipulates appearances and that values the superficial distinctions and gradations of the social hierarchy is repeatedly illustrated by the play's fascination with clothing. In the play clothes are never used for protection from the elements, as Lear rightly diagnoses in his explosion against Goneril and Regan's cruel "reason":

> O reason not the need! Our basest beggars
> Are in the poorest thing superfluous.

> Allow not nature more than nature needs,
> Man's life is cheap as beast's. Thou art a lady:
> If only to go warm were gorgeous,
> Why, nature needs not what thou gorgeous wear'st,
> Which scarcely keeps thee warm.
> —2.4.259–65

Lear and his daughters know perfectly well what they are doing. All their "reasons" for stripping him of his retinue are legitimate but deliberately ignore the deeper reality, that clothes really do make the man: "In 2.4 the sisters are scrupulously, icily polite, even solicitous, as they ignore what is staring them in the face, that they are stripping Lear of his self."[36] The ladies wear clothes that not only *show* their social status as princesses but also *create* that status. Throughout the play, language (whether in verbal, symbolic, meteorological, or fashion statements) is part of reality, not merely a reflection of reality (and on this crucial point, both Cordelia and Lear are profoundly wrong in their disagreement over the [in]ability to speak about love). Goneril and Regan seek to take away any remaining trappings of kingship from Lear not for reasons of mere practicality but because they want to rob him of all status and make it clear to him and everyone else that he is under their control, not vice versa. As Lear notes, they want to reduce him to a merely animal or biological existence; like a pathetic stray animal they have found, they will feed and shelter him but nothing more. They will show him none of the respect due a king or father, and they will allow him to show none of the authority of those roles either; they will not even leave him the minimal dignity of a man.

But Lear still values clothes and what they represent at this point, and part of his horribly painful education is that he must learn not to value them. He learns that clothes are not only part of what makes us human, as opposed to animal, but are also mechanical, contrived, and artificial, thereby threatening our humanity in a different way. There is something intrinsically disingenuous, stilted, and stifling about clothes: They not only create our social roles but also trap us in them and falsify our nature, for they are part of "the whole structure of values and practices that govern, protect, and *disguise* men in society."[37] And as wrong and sadistic as Goneril and Regan are for "stripping" their father, there is something profoundly inhuman or subhuman about someone who overvalues clothes and the social hierarchy they represent. Such false values are illustrated by the character most removed in status and personality from Lear, the craven toady Oswald. The honest Kent twice says that this vile creature was made by a tailor (2.2.50, 53), an insult that I had previously passed over (Kent has a long and colorful litany of them directed at Oswald, "base football player" [1.4.82] being perhaps the most memorable), until Phyllis Rackin offered the insight that this places Oswald irrevocably in the inhuman realm that overvalues clothes and social hierarchy: "Since he is nothing but clothes, he is inhuman. . . . If the poor, bare, forked animal needs clothes to distinguish him from the beasts, the thing made by a tailor lacks even the natural affections that distinguish the beasts from inanimate things."[38] Oswald cannot "distinguish value from rank,"[39] and for the first two acts of the play, Lear cannot either, just as he cannot distinguish any inner value from its outward appearance. It is only when Lear painfully overcomes the distinctions on which his life (and to a large extent ours) has been based that he can begin to see and enter a higher reality: "When the divisions are erased and the individual has been exposed as the 'poor thing' Lear discovers him to be—that is the portal of the Kingdom of God."[40] Lear literally and symbolically shows his rejection of the deadly, falsifying nature of clothes and rank when he begins to disrobe in act 3 (3.4.103), and again in his scene of madness in Act 4 (4.6.170, see below). In this scene he insists upon his kingship (4.6.196), even saying that he is "every inch a king" (4.6.106). Apparently Lear has achieved a new kind of dignity and worth not founded on appearances and convention, and he reiterates the disrobing gesture and its meaning with his dying breath (5.3.310). As painful and fatal as this movement has been, it has improved Lear and elevated him above the false life and values he shared with his evil daughters and Oswald at the beginning of the play.

Even more painful—because it is both a more elevated and a more basic human urge—is the lesson Lear has to learn about justice in this world. When he has cast himself out into the storm to flee the worse buffetings of his daughters' cruelties, Lear cries out against the injustices done to him and expresses his pious hope that the gods will speedily reassert their justice:

> Let the great gods
> That keep this dreadful pudder o'er our heads
> Find out their enemies now. Tremble, thou wretch,
> That hast within thee undivulgèd crimes
> Unwhipped of justice. Hide thee, thou bloody hand,
> Thou perjured, and thou simular of virtue
> That art incestuous. Caitiff, to pieces shake,
> That under covert and convenient seeming
> Has practiced on man's life. Close pent-up guilts,
> Rive your concealing continents and cry
> These dreadful summoners grace. I am a man
> More sinned against than sinning.
> —3.2.49–60

The power of the storm scenes lies in the outrage we feel along with Lear against what is happening to him, and the exhilaration we feel at his Job-like defiance: His "passionate protest against injustice and humiliation affirms human dignity despite the most relentless pressure of cruelty, cynicism, and degradation."[41] Just as his ordinariness renders him more accessible to us, so does his all too human protest: "Lear appeals primordially to the universal outrage of all those acutely conscious of their own mortality."[42]

But as much as we sympathize with Lear and thrill at his defiance, he—and much more importantly *we*—must learn two very painful truths.[45] Without lapsing into shrill, nagging "Bildadism"[43] and foolishly thinking that his suffering is somehow commensurate with what he has done, it is nonetheless crucial for Lear's enlightenment that he recognize that he is responsible for this situation. Secondly, he must accept that there will be no divine retribution meted out against those who have wronged him. It is clear from the beginning and end of Lear's speech quoted above that the erroneous but comforting beliefs in divine justice and in his own (relative) innocence go hand in hand in his mind, and most often in ours: "Let the great gods / . . . Find out their enemies now . . . / . . . I am a man / More sinned against than sinning" (3.2.49, 51, 59–60). (Gloucester expresses the same futile and blinding wish for justice in 4.1.64–71.) As long as Lear tries to defend himself and wait for the gods to vindicate him, he will be crushed by his daughters' cruelty while remaining blind to his own sins.

The first of these lessons comes to Lear relatively easily, even if he postpones the full ramifications of his guilt for much longer. As early as Act 1, Scene 4, he can admit his error—"O Lear, Lear, Lear! / Beat at this gate that let thy folly in" (1.4.261–62)—and a little later, even his guilt—"I did her wrong" (1.5.21). The second lesson—that in this life there is no justice, whether human or divine; that the gods or God will not lift one divine finger to end or even mitigate human suffering—understandably takes Lear much longer to accept, for it is a vision too horrible to contemplate, too shattering of everything he holds valuable and meaningful.[44] But as long as he holds on to this comforting but false vision of divine justice, it will crush and blind him, for it is a "fiendish burden of justice . . . a delusional vision."[45] The mad Lear finally and fully comes to this realization in Act 4 while speaking to the blind Gloucester:

LEAR: Thou hast seen a farmer's dog bark at a beggar?
GLOUCESTER: Ay, sir.
LEAR: And the creature run from the cur. There thou mightst behold the great image of authority—a dog's obeyed in office.
Thou rascal beadle, hold thy bloody hand!
Why dost thou lash that whore? Strip thy own back.

> Thou hotly lusts to use her in that kind
> For which thou whip'st her. The usurer hangs the cozener.
> Through tattered clothes small vices do appear;
> Robes and furred gowns hide all. Plate sin with gold,
> And the strong lance of justice hurtless breaks;
> Arm it in rags, a pygmy's straw does pierce it.
> None does offend, none—I say none! I'll able 'em.
> Take that of me, my friend, who have the power
> To seal th' accusers lips. Get thee glass eyes
> And, like a scurvy politician, seem
> To see the things thou dost not. Now, now, now, now!
> Pull of my boots. Harder, harder! So.
>
> —*4.6.152–70*

It is a shocking and horrible conclusion for a king to have to reach: A life of authoritative commands is equated to the barking of a dog, and a life of dispensing "justice" is recognized as nothing but hypocrisy, injustice, and violence. But Edgar rightly evaluates the truth of Lear's speech in the next line: "Reason in madness" (4.6.172). Lear's realization is as necessary and redemptive as it is shattering, for it is only when Lear can let go of his false political and theological worlds that a new world and outlook can dawn on him, "the remarkably Christian conclusion that in this world there is no continuing city and that we are 'strangers and sojourners' (see Lev. 25:23) without expectation of the cessation of intrigue or warfare in the here and now."[46] As depressing as it is for Lear (and for us) to renounce the possibility of justice in this life and accept God's silence at his suffering, it lets him see a higher realm, as "he awakens to an ultimate reality . . . which foretells his final unutterable epiphany."[47] This surrender is exactly like Job's, who finally understands the utter poverty of his former life and values and comes to accept God in all his frightening mystery: "I had heard of you by the hearing of the ear, but now my eye sees you; therefore I despise myself, and repent in dust and ashes" (Job 42:5–6).

In the end, Lear is rescued from himself, cured of his madness and his addiction to the worldly wisdom that has defined and ruined his life. Although Bloom asserts that there is no positive side to Lear's story, he clearly agrees with this assessment of the negative, of what Lear has learned to reject and despise: "Lear's prophecy fuses reason, nature, and society into one great negative image, the inauthentic authority of this great stage of fools."[48] Bloom can reasonably reject any positive meaning, because the price of Lear's realization is so staggering, even by the standards of tragedy, and its outcome offers no clear compensation. Unlike the book of Job to which it bears so much resemblance, the ending of *King Lear* gives no recompense to the destroyed hero for all his suffering, but only the respite of death: "The parallels with the Book of Job serve to mark the ending of *King Lear* not as an adaptation but a bitter Beckett-like parody."[49] Anyone who can read the last seventy lines of the play or see them acted on stage with dry eyes must be a "stone," as Lear himself accuses (5.3.258). As we look at the horror on stage, even though we might long for a different ending, we know not only that a different ending *cannot* be but that it positively *should not* be: "The theatrical point of the play's ending, then, seems to be that the theatre's capacity to show us what we want is firmly denied. We are not going to get what we want; we are going to have to watch the tragedy that has been building in the play from the start."[50] Any alternative ending that we could come up with would be a "remedy [that] would give more discomfort than the disease,"[51] a cruel kindness, as Kent also describes similar attempts to "help" Lear: "He hates him / That would upon the rack of this tough world / Stretch him out any longer" (5.3.314–16). This is not (only) because Shakespeare is smarter or wiser than we are but because in life, as in the play, suffering not only is inevitable but can also have infinite value, with the corollary that enlightenment not only is eminently avoidable but is also very painful: "The spiritual meaning of suffering has nowhere been more fully communicated than in *King Lear*."[52] The transformation from spiritual death to life gains us immortality at the expense of the mortal, as Paul also wrote, "What you sow does not come to life unless it dies. . . . What is sown is perishable, what is raised is imperishable. It is sown in dishonor, it is raised in glory. It is sown in weakness, it is raised in power" (1 Cor 15:36, 42–43). Lear and Cordelia would have died eventually, but without this ending, they may not have known how much they loved each other, they may not have faced how much they had hurt each other, and that would have been a much worse tragedy.

Having considered the negative side of Lear's education or redemption—what it is he must unlearn, what it is he must be redeemed from—let us now consider the positive side—what he learns, or the state into which he is redeemed. If Goneril's worldly wisdom shows Lear the painful meaninglessness and worthlessness of his former life, the foolish love and trust of Cordelia, Kent, the Fool, and Edgar show him what has real worth.[53]

"And My Poor Fool Is Hanged": The Foolish Wisdom of *King Lear*

That something wonderful and awful happens to Lear in his final moments is acknowledged by all, but exactly what that is has been interpreted in quite different ways, and ways that, like the alternative happy endings proposed by some, trivialize or overlook the deeper reality that Lear has achieved. Some think Lear is imagining that Cordelia is still alive, and therefore he dies in joy, receiving some recompense or escape from all the horror[54]—a happy ending, but a pathetic one, I think, if our hero can die only in a happy delusion that has replaced the vicious delusion that his former life has been. Redemption is a change of state: For Lear to go from a deluded, unhappy state to a deluded, happy state is clearly a kind of change, but not the right one, leaving his life and death still in untruth. On the other hand, some have suggested that Lear at the end sees the truth that Cordelia is alive in heaven.[55] This to me is too naively optimistic, and, more important, disconnects the last scene from the rest of the play, for what does Lear's suffering—the constant, overwhelming theme of the play—have to do with Cordelia being in heaven? A deceased loved one being in heaven is a pleasant enough thought that anyone could arrive at without the personal and national cataclysm we have seen unfold. If one is to feel uplifted by the ending of the play, if Lear's suffering is to have meaning for himself and us, it would have to be because his spurning of the deadly, worldly wisdom described above has also led him to embrace something new and vivifying: "Those who have felt the play to be about redemption have had trustworthy feelings, but those who have tried to make it doctrinally Christian, or who have seen Cordelia as a Christ figure, have missed the play's powerful expression of spiritual transformation."[56] Lear has been transformed because he has been led to the terrible and fatal, but true and liberating realization that his life has been a lie, at the same time that Cordelia, Kent, Edgar, and the Fool have shown him the goodness and truth that have always been right in front of him. Cordelia is not a Christ figure, for her death is not redemptive, but her life and the lives of these other Christlike characters *are* redemptive, for they lead Lear to truth, compassion, and love.

The Fool and Cordelia embody truth more than do Edgar and Kent, who are in disguise and therefore participate in well-intentioned deception. The Fool and Cordelia always speak the truth to Lear, regardless of the consequences or whether he wants to hear it. As foolish as this is by earthly, self-seeking wisdom, it is wise by the standards of heavenly wisdom: "But the wisdom from above is first pure . . . willing to yield . . . without a trace of partiality or hypocrisy" (Jas 3:17). Truth is also a fundamental part of love, which "rejoices in the truth" (1 Cor 13:6), and there is no questioning the depth and sincerity of the love that the Fool and Cordelia have for Lear. Their roles as loving truth tellers to Lear are so identical that Lear finally confuses them in his last speech, "And my poor fool is hanged" (5.3.306), a conflation that has been called a "divine confusion";[57] we may call it at least a wise and loving one. Truth is also something that has been sorely and devastatingly lacking in Lear's life. An essential part of the truth is that it is usually uncomfortable and unacceptable to us, as Cordelia's speech is unacceptable to her foolish father in the first scene and as the Fool's speeches are to the worldly-wise Goneril. This unacceptable, confrontational side of truth telling fits in with the biblical depiction of prophets as fools or madmen, including Paul's description of himself (2 Cor 11:23), "prophecy having historic associations with madness and being the medium in which, historically, the paradoxes of reason and madness, folly and wisdom are unfolded.... [T]he Fool's prophecy is essential to *King Lear*—a quintessential manifestation of its cosmos."[58] Through their foolish devotion and self-sacrifice to the truth, Cordelia and the Fool teach Lear its infinite value at the same time that he is learning of the deadly worthlessness of lies and appearances.

But there are deep limitations even in this foolish but noble devotion to the truth. As wise as these characters are compared to the evil Goneril or the self-deluded Lear, no one possesses the whole truth. Their perspective is therefore "slant and incomplete . . . merely part of the truth."[59] The role of incomplete, humanly held truth is therefore mostly negative. It can and should correct people who erroneously believe that they possess the whole truth, the primary role of the Fool toward his master, Lear: "After all, the Fool's function is to tell subversive truths to a court society foolish enough to think its own truths are *the* truth."[60] And even partial truth can expose those who tell lies as if they were the truth, the role of the Fool and Cordelia toward her evil sisters: "He [the Fool] can formulate the tenets of worldly wisdom with a clarity that worldly wisdom often prefers to blur. He defines the predatory self-seeking of Goneril and Regan."[61] Partial truth can point out the inadequacy of other partial truths and the evil of falsehood, but it cannot offer a completely satisfying alternative, since it is itself only partial truth.

A further complication or imperfection in one's devotion to truth is in its motives, which are quite susceptible of slipping into selfishness and self-righteousness. Indeed, one could hazard that no virtuous inclination is more susceptible to this corruption than the supposed devotion to truth: Who among us has not hurt someone else, and then justified it by saying that we were just being honest, or that it was for their own good, when really it was because we like being right and putting others in their place? Such a selfishness hidden in her supposed selflessness often has been detected in Cordelia's actions in the first scene, succinctly and famously summed up as her "faulty admixture of pride and sullenness."[62] She has plenty of her father's stubbornness, "the old man's willfulness,"[63] and at least a little of her sisters' devotion to propriety and rationality at the expense of emotion: "Cordelia is justified in all that she says, but not loveable."[64] Cordelia seems to value truth over love: "Cordelia is more concerned with the spiritual pride of her integrity, at the beginning, and the righteousness of her position vis à vis her sisters, at the end, than with love. Her self-image interferes with her ability to love."[65] Furthermore, her ideas about love are not at all true (at least as expressed in the awkward, disastrous first scene): "Her ideas are only a variation on Lear's; she too thinks of affection as a quantitative, portionable medium of exchange of goods and services (1.1.95–104)."[66] Cordelia loves the truth, but she does not know the truth about love; it is not something she can teach her father but something they must learn together.[67] The Fool, on the other hand, becomes irrelevant to Lear because he *is* capable of teaching Lear the truth: "When Lear has absorbed the Fool's truths and begins to utter them himself, the Fool becomes redundant."[68] Either way, it is clear that while truth is a necessary (and often painful) part of love, love abides longer and dwells deeper within us than the truth; it is eventually "what Lear now needs more than the truth."[69] Built on a foundation of truth, love takes us much higher than truth alone could: "Love never ends" (1 Cor 13:8).

The other two good characters who help Lear overcome his evil daughters and himself are Kent and Edgar, and they embody compassion much more than do Cordelia and the Fool. After the first scene, they do not practice the kind of "tough love" that Cordelia and the Fool force upon Lear; rather, they practice the literal meaning of compassion (or sympathy) by "suffering with" Lear throughout his ordeal.[70] Like the truth, compassionate suffering is a part of both New Testament love and wisdom: Love "bears all things . . . endures all things" (1 Cor 13:7); "But the wisdom from above is . . . full of mercy and good fruits, without a trace of partiality or hypocrisy" (Jas 3:17). The goodness and purity of Kent and Edgar's motives and feelings are even less in question than Cordelia's, as she herself acknowledges, "O thou good Kent, how shall I live and work / To match thy goodness?" (4.7.1–2). They are much more present to Lear and his suffering than the physically absent Cordelia or the mentally distant Fool. Cordelia in the first scene and the Fool throughout mock Lear's pain (in a therapeutic but still painful way), while Kent and Edgar suffer it with him, experiencing pity and empathy for him that are almost unbearable. Edgar bears the pains of his blinded father as stoically as he can, but his emotions overcome him— "[aside] I cannot daub it further. / . . . Bless thy sweet eyes, they bleed" (4.1.52, 54)—as they did earlier when he met the wronged Lear—"My tears begin to take his part so much / They mar my counterfeiting" (3.6.59–60). Edgar later gives a rather pious and unemotional diagnosis of his father's eye gouging—"The gods are just, and of our pleasant vices / Make instruments to plague us. / The dark and vicious place where thee he got / Cost him his eyes" (5.3.171–74)[71]—but cannot help exclaiming when he sees the ruined king, "O thou side-piercing sight!" (4.6.85).[72] And Kent expresses the ultimate empathy and sacrifice for his king in his final lines: "Break, heart, I prithee break![73] . . . / I have a journey, sir, shortly to go. / My master calls me;

I must not say no" (5.3.313, 322–23). Goneril and Regan cling to inhuman reason and hypertrophied lust, Edmund lacks all emotions, and even Cordelia is a bit too self-composed and self-assured, but Kent and Edgar are pure, unerring, and healing passion and feeling, Lear's "physician[s]" as Kent labels himself (1.1.163).[74]

But exactly as Cordelia and the Fool's devotion to truth has its shortcomings, so too does human compassion, as noble and beautiful as it is. Kent throughout seems more concerned with Lear's physical safety—that he be clothed, sheltered, kept dry and warm—than with his spiritual well-being. This concern with the merely physical even seems to overtake the Fool, replacing his concerns for Lear's more substantive, inner improvement.[75] Edgar too seems mostly concerned with keeping his father alive. This is a common shortcoming of compassion: How many of us are eager to alleviate the more obvious physical ailments of other people, especially our children, while we deny or overlook deeper and potentially more harmful emotional needs because we just don't know how to deal with them? Feeding, clothing, or sheltering someone can be costly, but it is totally straightforward compared to the nebulous and open-ended goal of making someone happy. Ultimately, no one can do that for another person; they can only lead and love by example, and at this Kent and Edgar are powerful and purposeful: "It is part of the play's developing purpose to transform us . . . from devils of rational intellect, into Gods of known and feeling sorrow."[76] If Cordelia and the Fool show Lear how to live (and die) for the truth, Kent and Edgar show him what it is to live (and die) for another person. They pity Lear so that he can learn to stop pitying himself and begin to pity others, they suffer with him so that he can learn how to overlook his own suffering and begin to suffer with others, and they alleviate his suffering so that he can learn how to help and love others: "Love is patient; love is kind" (1 Cor 13:4).

While Shakespeare has used Edgar, Kent, Cordelia, and the Fool to emphasize and point to some of the shortcomings of parts of human love, it is clear that together they embody unconditional love in the most pure and noble way imaginable. Lear has given each of them every reason not to love but despise him, and they have steadfastly refused, though the world dissolves around them. The line spoken of Cordelia, "Thou hast one daughter / Who redeems Nature from the general curse" (4.6.201–02), could just as easily apply to all of them. Cordelia and Edgar together, through truth and compassion, redeem the nature of children from deceit and cruelty, just as the Fool and Kent do so for the nature of servants. And their unconditional love finally leads Lear to love unconditionally as father and king, and redeems his own nature, as we will see.

How much has Lear learned to appreciate and live according to this kind of foolish wisdom before he dies? There are glimpses of his education or improvement in act 3 when Lear shows concern and compassion for the Fool (3.4.23–27) and for the disguised Edgar (3.4.61–73). Later, in his reunions with Cordelia and finally with Kent, Lear shows how much he has learned from them. While the whole tragedy of the play was set in motion by Lear's foolish, childish, tyrannical demand that others speak of their love for him (1.1.54, 86, 90), he enters the stage for the last time saying that he will now speak (5.3.258–60)—speak of his dead daughter and his love for her. While part of Lear's madness is brought on by his repeated, inhuman refusal to weep (1.4.287–88; 2.4.278–81), he can learn from Cordelia (4.7.71; 5.3.23) how to bring himself even to this show of weakness (3.7.62; 5.3.283). Whereas he cursed and punished Cordelia in the first scene, he puts himself completely at her disposal in the end, ready to accept punishment from her—"If you have poison for me, I will drink it" (4.7.72)—and eager to beg for her forgiveness—"Pray you now, forget and forgive" (4.7.85). He tearfully thanks Kent when his servant reveals the faithful service he has given "his enemy king" (5.3.221). And while Gloucester couldn't stand being in the presence of the loved one he had wronged (dying as soon as Edgar reveals himself), Lear only wants to be with his beloved, serving and loving her as they both serve "God" (the only singular use of "God" in the play):

> Come, let's away to prison.
> We two alone will sing like birds i' th' cage.
> When thou dost ask me blessing, I'll kneel down
> And ask of thee forgiveness. So we'll live,
> And pray, and sing, and tell old tales, and laugh
> At gilded butterflies, and hear poor rogues
> Talk of court news; and we'll talk with them too—
> Who loses and who wins; who's in, who's out—
> And take upon 's the mystery of things
> As if we were God's spies; and we'll wear out,
> In a walled prison, packs and sects of great ones
> That ebb and flow by th' moon.
> —5.3.8–19

Lear has learned that he is "a very foolish fond old man" (4.7.60), but this is a totally different "folly" than Kent diagnosed in the first scene (1.1.149); it is the folly that knows enough to admit its weakness and its dependence on other people and on God, rather than rashly and foolishly asserting its independence or dominance over them. Lear has now achieved the folly that sees and values things as they really are, the folly that makes weakness into a value: "When we come crying hither, we bring with us the badge of all our misery; but it is also the badge of the vulnerabilities that give us access to whatever grandeur we achieve."[77] This, of course, is no longer folly at all, but real sight and knowledge, the highest wisdom one can achieve—a loving humility, a humble love.

Lear's newfound "folly" is radically, steadfastly opposed to Goneril's worldly, self-seeking "wisdom" and to Lear's own tyrannically egoistical behavior in the first scene: "In a world of lust, cruelty and greed, with extremes of wealth and poverty, man reduced to his essentials needs not wealth, nor power, nor even physical freedom, but rather patience, stoical fortitude, and love; needs, perhaps, above all, mutual forgiveness, the exchange of charity."[78] Lear has learned that love "does not insist on its own way" (1 Cor 13:5); in his final scenes he is completely focused on others and the loving service and gratitude he can offer them. Nothing could be more childish than his behavior in the first scene, yet by the end he has finally given up his "childish ways" (1 Cor 13:11), and he spends what is left of his life practicing a mature, giving, caring, properly parental love. No longer a child, he can enter his final scene carrying his dead child in his arms, an image meant to evoke a pietà, the image of Mary holding the dead body of her son Jesus.[79] (As we saw in Chapter 2, there are few images of a love that is higher, more patient, or more perfect than that of Mary.) This development in Lear is as heroic and miraculous as any imaginable, a monumental and truly life-giving transformation, even (or especially) if he happens to stop breathing shortly thereafter:[80] "Lear dies . . . with his whole being launched toward another. . . . [T]he image is deeply tragic; yet it is also, in the play's terms, a kind of victory."[81] Indeed, to learn to love truly is about the only thing that could possibly be worth all the pain he has endured.

Conclusion: Folly as a Higher Wisdom

Consider the "fool's speech" I gave above in praise of lust (and one could easily transform the speech to relate it to any self-centered, acquisitive behavior), about how it garners so many tangible, immediate rewards with minimal effort or risk. Now suppose that we could simply discount what happens to Goneril and Regan as fanciful poetic justice with little relevance to our own lives; we can easily imagine a lust-filled life without all that bloodshed and violence. If you are afraid of disease, you can trust modern science and practice "protected sex." If divine rather than biological punishment has got you down, go ahead and discount the seemingly unlikely possibility of retribution in an afterlife. Even so, could any mature person look at such a pragmatic description of selfishness and say, "Yes, that is exactly what I would like to have; thank you for laying it out in such clear and unambiguous terms. I would most definitely like to devote all my life and energy to pursuing just that goal. I think I'll get started right away"? Call me hopelessly optimistic, but I would find that very hard to believe. The rewards of lust, while tangible and immediate, are so utterly paltry that no real man or woman would knowingly choose them, or if they did, no one of even average depth and sophistication could remain satisfied with them for an entire lifetime. Or consider it in terms of what human beings "naturally" praise and value. Every culture that has ever prospered has built statues and monuments and written songs, poems, and plays to honor people who dedicated or sacrificed their lives out of love for their country, or for God, art, or knowledge. Who would raise one stone or one syllable to someone who dedicated his or her whole life to greed or lust, even if they didn't overtly hurt people along the way? Henry Ford has improved my life much more directly and noticeably than any artist or composer, but I certainly don't admire him, and I would rather poke myself in the eye than sing a hymn to him. I might envy Bill Gates for his money, or Hugh Hefner for his young girlfriends, but I don't envy either of those men their lives. It would never occur to me to call them "wise," certainly not "blessed," not necessarily even "happy," nor would I expend one minute trying to be like them or to get some of what they have. And if anyone thinks that is only because I am a "fool," just consider the other extreme. No one is so far gone in greed and selfishness that they would not call Mother Theresa, Jesus, or Buddha both very "wise" and very "happy"—all people who died penniless and celibate but who valued other things that really matter, things that can make human life "blessed."

And finally, for a minute let's forget about great villains or heroes, whether dramatic or religious—just consider the events of your own life. When you consider all the things you have done to get money, power, or sex or to fulfill some other selfish desire, are you really proud of *all* those actions? Are those the moments for which you would like to be remembered? Aren't there more than a few moments of selfishness that you would like to take back, or at least that you hope no one else finds out about or remembers? Most of us are content if we haven't done anything *too* shameful in pursuit of our selfish goals. Now consider the things you have done for someone or something you love, the things you have done with no thought of how they would benefit you but only out of devotion to another person or to an idea. Whatever those actions are in your individual case—whether they relate to family, friends, God, knowledge, art, or even sports—and even (or especially) if some of those actions may strike you later as embarrassing or ludicrous, I'm willing to wager that in your most honest and private moments you wouldn't give up any one of them for any other "gain," because there is no other "gain" with which they are comparable or commensurate. They are of a wholly other order—"transcendent" in theological language—because you transcend yourself and your limitations through them, rather than remaining trapped and limited in your individuality. I am the same pathetic person even if I win the lottery, for nothing essential has changed about me, but I become a little less pathetic when I love someone or something outside of myself and begin to live a new life for other people and ideals and not only for myself. From a worldly perspective, nothing could be more foolish than giving without thought of recompense, but nothing could recompense us more fully and unexpectedly, for this kind of giving rewards us with a new wisdom that values the things that are true, beautiful, and eternal.

Notes

1. As applied to Jesus, see Matt 11:19; 13:54; Mark 6:2; Luke 2:40, 52; 7:35; Col 2:3; Rev 5:12. As applied to God, see Luke 11:49; Rom 11:33; 16:27; Eph 3:10; Rev 7:12. As applied to his faithful followers, see Matt 7:24; 10:16; 12:42; 23:34; 24:45; 25:2, 4, 8, 9; Luke 1:17; 11:31; 12:42; 16:8; 21:15; Acts 6:3, 10; 7:10, 22; Rom 16:19; 1 Cor 3:10; 6:5; 12:8; Eph 1:8, 17; 5:15; Col 1:9, 28; 3:16; 4:5; 2 Tim 3:15; Jas 1:5; 3:13, 17; 2 Pet 3:15; Rev 13:18; 17:9.

2. Rom 1:14 (ambiguous), 22; 11:25; 12:16; Col 2:23; 2 Pet 1:16.

3. On Q, see J. S. Kloppenborg, *The Formation of Q: Trajectories in Ancient Wisdom Collections* (Harrisburg, Pa.: Trinity Press International, 2000).

4. Matt 11:19 // Luke 7:35; Matt 12:42 // Luke 11:31; also in the temptation scene: See K. Paffenroth, "The Testing of the Sage: 1 Kings 10:1–13 and Q 4:1–13," *The Expository Times* 107 (1996): 142–43.

5. On the situation in Corinth, see the introduction in F. F. Bruce, *1 and 2 Corinthians* (New Century Bible Commentary; Grand Rapids: Eerdmans, 1971), 18–25.

6. See, e.g., T. McFarland, "The Image of the Family in *King Lear*," in *On King Lear* (ed. L. Danson; Princeton: Princeton University Press, 1981), 91–118, esp. 98; S. Booth, "On the Greatness of *King Lear*," in *William Shakespeare's King Lear* (ed. H. Bloom; New York: Chelsea House, 1987), 57–70, esp. 67–68.

7. Malcolm and Donalbain similarly bring suspicion on themselves by fleeing in *Macbeth*.

8. 5.3.254 makes it sound as though only Cordelia was to be executed, while in 5.1.67–68 it sounds as though both were to be killed.

9. The lines are assigned to Albany in the Quarto; see the discussion by M. J. Warren, "Quarto and Folio *King Lear* and the Interpretation of Albany and Edgar," in *William Shakespeare's King Lear* (ed. H. Bloom; New York: Chelsea House, 1987), 45–56.

10. H. Bloom, *Shakespeare: The Invention of the Human* (New York: Riverhead Books, 1998), 484, 486.

11. Ibid., 521.

12. J. Wittreich, "'Image of that Horror': The Apocalypse in *King Lear*," in *The Apocalypse in English Renaissance Thought and Literature* (ed. C. A. Patrides and J. Wittreich; Ithaca, N.Y.: Cornell University Press, 1984), 175–206; quote from p. 179.

13. W. R. Elton, *King Lear and the Gods* (San Marino, Calif.: Huntington Library, 1968), 71.

14. J. L. Murphy, *Darkness and Devils: Exorcism and King Lear* (Athens: Ohio University Press, 1984), 213.

15. L. Basney, "Is a Christian Perspective on Shakespeare Productive and/or Necessary?" in *Shakespeare and the Christian Tradition* (ed. E. B. Batson; Lewiston, N.Y.: Edwin Mellen Press, 1994), 19–35; quote from p. 35.

16. S. Marx, *Shakespeare and the Bible* (New York: Oxford University Press, 2000), 62.

17. On the ending of the Gospel of Mark, see R. T. France, *The Gospel of Mark: A Commentary on the Greek Text* (Grand Rapids: Eerdmans, 2002), 685–88.

18. M. Schwehn, "*King Lear* beyond Reason," *First Things* 36 (1993): 25–33; quote from p. 32. Cf. C. L. Barber, "On Christianity and the Family: Tragedy of the Sacred," in *Twentieth Century Interpretations of King Lear: A Collection of Critical Essays* (ed. J. Adelman; Englewood Cliffs, N.J.: Prentice-Hall, 1978), 117–19, esp. 119: "In their dramatized lives they are in time, and in the human condition where Lear's demand and Cordelia's sacrifice to it lead to total, tragic loss. . . . But the realization of them in the theatre takes them out of time, so that there is a kind of epiphany as we finally see them, a showing forth not of the divine but of the human, sublime and terrible as it reaches towards the divine and towards destruction."

19. Wittreich, "'Image of that Horror,'" 188.

20. R. Nevo, "On Lear and Job," in *Twentieth Century Interpretations of King Lear: A Collection of Critical Essays* (ed. J. Adelman; Englewood Cliffs, N.J.: Prentice-Hall, 1978), 120–22; quote from pp. 120–21.

21. Bloom, *Invention of the Human*, 479.

22. Cf. Bloom, *Invention of the Human*, 493: "Lear, beyond us in grandeur and in essential authority, is still a startlingly intimate figure, since he is an emblem of fatherhood itself."

23. This point is made well by McFarland, "Image of the Family," 95, through comparison with *Hamlet:* "The situation in *Hamlet*, by contrast, is almost flamboyant; it has the specialness of things that happen only once, in the realm of the hypothetical, and to others than ourselves. . . . A shipwreck happens to others, not to us; and Oedipus, Orestes, and Hamlet find themselves in unthinkable situations that accentuate our own security as spectators. . . . The situation in *King Lear* involves a different model of experience, an image of family life that is neither flamboyant nor unique. On the contrary, it is in significant respects almost commonplace."

24. Bloom, *Invention of the Human*, 476.

25. F. O'Connor, "A Good Man Is Hard to Find," in *Flannery O'Connor: The Complete Stories* (New York: Farrar, Straus and Giroux, 1972), 132.

26. Cf. S. L. Goldberg, "On Edgar's Character," in *Twentieth Century Interpretations of King Lear* (ed. J. Adelman; Englewood Cliffs, N.J.: Prentice-Hall, 1978), 115: "Edgar . . . is a true member of the Gloucester family, all of whom in one way or another seem insecure and anxious about themselves, and whose characteristic psychic style is defensive beside the bolder, more challenging, self-confidently active style characteristic of the Lear family."

27. Cf. J. C. Rice, "The Empathic Edgar: Creativity as Redemption in *King Lear*," *Studia Mystica* 7 (1984): 53: "The belief in rational structures of experience also accounts for the absurd brutality of the villains' acts. It is as unrealistic to expect to insure the future through violent brutality as through praying to a virtue rewarding God."

28. Bloom, *Invention of the Human*, 486.

29. Cf. ibid., 484: "The gods in *King Lear* do not kill men and women for their sport; instead they afflict Lear and Edgar with an excess of love, and Goneril and Regan with the torments of lust and jealousy."

30. On Lear's similarity to Goneril and Regan and his complicity in their evil, cf. McFarland, "Image of the Family," 104: "Thus Lear's action, not in becoming angry with

Cordelia, who has herself acted with some of the old man's willfulness, but in disclaiming paternal care, propinquity, and property of blood, is, if we like the rhetoric of good and evil, the beginning of the evil in the play's progression of events; it is an action of the same order as those of Goneril and Regan"; and Bloom, *Invention of the Human*, 509: "The foregrounding of this play would involve a long career of outbursts, which presumably helped convert Regan and Goneril into mincing hypocrites."

31. L. C. Knights, "On the Fool," in *Twentieth Century Interpretations of King Lear: A Collection of Critical Essays* (ed. J. Adelman; Englewood Cliffs, N.J.: Prentice-Hall, 1978), 122–23; quote from p. 123.

32. Cf. Elton, *King Lear and the Gods*, 317: "In contrast to his traditionally ithyphallic comic role and to the concerns for the flesh shared by Touchstone, Feste, Pompey, and Lavache, *Lear*'s 'all-licens'd' Fool seems paradoxically repressive and antiprogenitive. 'Down, wantons, down!' is his theme."

33. Ibid., 298, 300.

34. Bloom, *Invention of the Human*, 508.

35. Knights, "On the Fool," 122.

36. Cf. the animal imagery used by Alfred Harbage in his introduction to the Pelican edition of *King Lear* (New York: Penguin, 1970), 19: "Cornwall is less repellent than Goneril and Regan only as the mad bull is less repellent than the hyena, they less repellent than Oswald only as the hyena is less repellent than the jackal."

37. McFarland, "Image of the Family," 100.

38. Basney, "Christian Perspective on Shakespeare," 32.

39. P. Rackin, "On Edgar: Delusion as Resolution," in *Twentieth Century Interpretations of King Lear: A Collection of Critical Essays* (ed. J. Adelman; Englewood Cliffs, N.J.: Prentice-Hall, 1978), 123–25; quote from p. 124 (emphasis added).

40. Rackin, "On Edgar," 124–25.

41. Ibid., 125.

42. Rice, "Empathic Edgar," 59.

43. Nevo, "Lear and Job," 122.

44. Bloom, *Invention of the Human*, 510.

45. This is true dramatically as well as morally, as recognition is a crucial element in Aristotle's analysis of tragedy. See Marx, *Shakespeare and the Bible*, 64. "Recognition . . . denotes the character's shift of perception, perspective, and attitude that develops as the plot unfolds . . . recognition implies that the character discovers a deeper truth that somehow was already known but ignored."

46. Nevo, "Lear and Job," 121.

47. Cf. Schwehn, "*King Lear* beyond Reason," 31–32: "And we find what we would expect to find given our analysis of Lear and Edgar, namely, that both of them insist against all appearances that the gods are finally just. . . . Nowhere in any of these men's theologies is there a place for a deity who 'maketh his rain to fall upon the evil and upon the good.'"

48. Rice, "Empathic Edgar," 53.

49. C. Davidson, "History of *King Lear* and the Problem of Belief," *Christianity and Literature* 45 (1996): 285–301; quote from p. 296.

50. Marx, *Shakespeare and the Bible*, 65.

51. Bloom, *Invention of the Human*, 515.

52. Marx, *Shakespeare and the Bible*, 77.

53. Basney, "Christian Perspective on Shakespeare," 34.

54. Booth, "On the Greatness of *King Lear*," (1987), 69.

55. Rice, "Empathic Edgar," 58.

56. Knights, "On the Fool," 123: "It is through him [the Fool], therefore, that we come to see more clearly the sharp distinction between those whose wisdom is purely for themselves and those foolish ones—Kent, Gloucester, Cordelia, and the Fool himself—who recklessly take their stands on loyalties and sympathies that are quite outside the scope of any prudential calculus."

57. Thus Bloom, *Invention of the Human*, 486: "The joy that kills Lear is delusional: he apparently hallucinates, and beholds Cordelia either as not having died or as being resurrected."

58. The position of some cited by Marx, *Shakespeare and the Bible*, 77.

59. Rice, "Empathic Edgar," 58–59.

60. H. C. Goddard, "*King Lear*," in *William Shakespeare's King Lear* (ed. H. Bloom; New York: Chelsea House, 1987), 9–43; quote from p. 34. Cf. the discussions of the identification of the Fool and Cordelia by Elton, *King Lear and the Gods*, 324; S. Booth, "On the Greatness of *King Lear*," in *Twentieth Century Interpretations of King Lear: A Collection of Critical Essays* (ed. J. Adelman; Englewood Cliffs, N.J.: Prentice-Hall, 1978) 98–111, esp. 103–04; and J. L. Calderwood, "Creative Uncreation in *King Lear*," in *William Shakespeare's King Lear* (ed. H. Bloom; New York: Chelsea House, 1987), 121–37, esp. 126–27. Calderwood makes the common observation that the same actor may have played both parts.

61. J. Wittreich, "*Image of That Horror*": *History, Prophecy, and Apocalypse in King Lear* (San Marino, Calif.: Huntington Library, 1984), 49, with an excellent discussion of the Erasmian and biblical background to the idea of the Fool in the play following on pp. 50–53. Cf. the much less relevant discussion of other associations with "fool" in Bloom, *Invention of the Human*, 493.

62. Calderwood, "Creative Uncreation," 126.

63. Ibid. (emphasis in original).

64. Knights, "On the Fool," 122.

65. Samuel Taylor Coleridge, quoted by J. F. Danby, *Shakespeare's Doctrine of Nature: A Study of King Lear* (London: Faber & Faber, 1949) 115. Cf. Bloom, who repeatedly refers to her "recalcitrance" (e.g., *Invention of the Human*, 508).

66. McFarland, "Image of the Family," 104.

67. Booth, "On the Greatness of *King Lear*" (1987), 67.

68. Rice, "Empathic Edgar," 51.

69. Booth, "On the Greatness of *King Lear*" (1987), 67.

70. Cf. Schwehn, "*King Lear* beyond Reason," 31: "But over the course of a *lifetime*, a pilgrimage, the love between the best parents and the best children can be and often is 'equalized'. . . . Between parents and children, love is a matter of living in a loving manner *over time*" (emphasis in original).

71. Calderwood, "Creative Uncreation," 126.

72. Ibid., 127.

73. Cf. J. Adelman, introduction to *Twentieth Century Interpretations of King Lear: A Collection of Critical Essays* (ed. J. Adelman; Englewood Cliffs, N.J.: Prentice-Hall, 1978), who points to Edgar's "Christ-like compassion—literally *feeling with*" (p. 4, emphasis in original).

74. Rice, "Empathic Edgar," 57, suggests that Edgar does this "to alleviate the immediately experienced suffering of Edmund." This is a quite likely interpretation and further emphasizes Edgar's compassion and empathy.

75. Clearly a reference to Christ's suffering; see Basney, "Christian Perspective on Shakespeare," 32. Cf. Adelman, introduction, 4–5.

76. Line assigned to Lear as his final line in the Quarto.

77. The observation of Elton, *King Lear and the Gods*, 289.

78. Cf. Calderwood, "Creative Uncreation," 126: "Lacking employment, he grows more and more concerned with practical affairs—the coldness of the night and lack of shelter."

79. Rice, "Empathic Edgar," 52.

80. M. Mack, "The World of *King Lear*," in *Twentieth Century Interpretations of King Lear: A Collection of Critical Essays* (ed. J. Adelman; Englewood Cliffs, N.J.: Prentice-Hall, 1978), 56–69; quote from p. 69.

81. K. Muir, "On Christian Values," in *Twentieth Century Interpretations of King Lear: A Collection of Critical Essays* (ed. J. Adelman; Englewood Cliffs, N.J.: Prentice-Hall, 1978), 120.

82. The identification of Barber, "Tragedy of the Sacred," 119.

83. Cf. Bloom, *Invention of the Human*, 509, who sees no transformation: "Lear's enormous changes, his flashes of compassion and social insight, essentially are emanations of his wholeheartedness, rather than the transformations Bradley and most subsequent critics have judged them to be." Partly this must be some overly fine distinction, as "change" (especially one that is "enormous") and "transformation" are usually taken as synonyms. And partly this is just the observation that there is continuity as well as change in Lear: Clearly he is changed (for the better) at the end, and clearly there remains something of the old, explosively emotional Lear.

84. Mack, "The World of *King Lear*," 57.

4. The Inadequacy of Reason in Ecclesiastes and *Pensées*

Introduction

We have seen, then, how some of the unremarkable, commonsensical observations on life and success from Old Testament Wisdom literature were replaced in later literature by challenging, revealing reflections on the necessity of evil and folly for human life to be free, meaningful, or good. But we have also seen how within the biblical wisdom tradition itself, surprising formulations—such as feminine Wisdom—and reformulations—such as being a fool for Christ—had been developed; the tradition was no more conservative than most, and it was a good deal more adaptive and creative than some. Even within the Old Testament tradition itself, challenges had been raised against traditional wisdom formulations. Such challenges are epitomized in the books of Job and Ecclesiastes (Qoheleth): "Thus the authors of Job and Qoheleth are wise men in revolt against the unexamined assumptions of their colleagues."[1] These authors saw two related stumbling blocks for traditional wisdom: the inability of humans to understand the divinely instituted order of the universe, and the especially painful example of this lack of understanding in the experience of innocent, unexplainable suffering. These authors therefore are not merely an overturning or denial of wisdom so much as they are a reexamination of it to bring it into agreement with the phenomena; if one is to explain human life, one must first describe it accurately. But as we will see, such honesty comes at a great price of comfort, probably even of piety. All of us need to hear painful truths, but none of us likes to, nor do we particularly appreciate or honor those people who force us to hear such truths. And as uncomfortable and challenging as the biblical authors now made their reformulation of wisdom, the French mathematician, philosopher, and theologian Blaise Pascal would make it even more so, pushing the investigation further into reconsidering human reason and happiness.

Ecclesiastes

Within the Old Testament, the Wisdom books stand out as unusual, and within the Wisdom corpus, Ecclesiastes has struck readers for millennia as even more unconventional than the rest of wisdom.[2] The composition of Ecclesiastes (the Greek-Latin form of the Hebrew word *Qoheleth* in Eccl 1:1, 12; 7:27; 12:9–10, by which the book and its author are also known) is not much debated. For most of Christian history the book has been attributed to Solomon, but it is now commonly attributed to an author writing shortly after 300 B.C.E.[3] God's inscrutability is what so bothers the author of Ecclesiastes. Ecclesiastes questions God's goodness and justice because of his experience of pleasure and boredom: "I kept my heart from no pleasure. . . . Then I considered all that my hands had done and the toil I had spent in doing it, and again, all was vanity and a chasing after wind" (Eccl 2:10–11). But it is not just pleasure that is empty; *everything* is empty, even wisdom itself: "Then I saw that wisdom excels folly as light excels darkness. . . . Yet I perceived that the same fate befalls all of them" (Eccl 2:13–14). If anything, pleasure receives more praise in the book than wisdom (Eccl 2:24; 3:12–13, 22; 5:18–19; 8:15; 9:7–9; 11:7–10). It is not pain but the utter pointlessness of life that bothers Ecclesiastes so much, causing him even to hate life, for if life doesn't mean anything or result in anything, if it is the most ludicrous and protracted of dead ends, what could possibly be the reason for loving it? "So I hated life, because what is done under the sun was grievous to me; for all is vanity and a chasing after wind" (Eccl 2:17). And for this pointless life, Ecclesiastes blames God: "It is an unhappy business that God has given to human beings to be busy with" (Eccl 1:13).

But for all his bleakness, it is extremely significant that two options that would seem quite consistent with his outlook—suicide and atheism—are never entertained by Ecclesiastes: "Qoheleth refused to view suicide as a way of resolving the immense existential anxiety in which he moved and breathed"; "Qoheleth was no atheist, nor did he regard God as irrelevant to human affairs. He took for granted not only the existence but also the omnipotence of the one God."[4] This seeming inconsistency may provide us with a key to understanding Ecclesiastes. As he honestly and diligently examines life and God, he can find nothing in either of them worthy of love, but neither can he despise or reject either of them. He unconditionally accepts both and even has some enjoyment of them, even if this enjoyment is in an overall context of frustration or bewilderment: "He simply accepts God on

God's terms. That is his faith. These terms are mysterious, so extreme that Qoheleth can call life's venture a vanity or absurdity (intending this as an objective fact, not as an insult). I have called this faith."[5] While this may not be as full or satisfying as most people's idea of faith, it is certainly a foundation for faith, as one must know the truth about God before one can love or trust God. Ecclesiastes does not blame God, but expresses painful honesty that what God does and allows to happen cannot simply be called "good": "Qoheleth never utters a word of reproach or hostility towards [God]. . . . God, then, is responsible for the state of the world, and this includes the things which Qoheleth perceives as injustice and oppression. But God's *motives* are entirely incomprehensible."[6] Ecclesiastes' honesty also leads to the realization that the frustration and dissatisfaction one feels in life paradoxically come because of a divine gift: "He has made everything suitable for its time; moreover he has put a sense of past and future into their minds, yet they cannot find out what God has done from the beginning to the end" (Eccl 3:11). Human beings are different from animals (though Ecclesiastes then equates them—Eccl 3:18–22) in their tantalizingly incomplete knowledge of eternity and infinity, of things beyond themselves that they cannot fully comprehend or achieve. While it is fair to say that this is "a gift of dubious value,"[7] it is a gift that opens us up to higher mental and spiritual longings at the same time that it frustrates those longings. Ecclesiastes does finally believe we are made in God's image (Gen 1:27), but our reflection of divinity is neither perfect nor unproblematic: It may indeed be exactly what causes us pain and dissatisfaction, as we live in a world that falls far short of either divinity or our expectations. Ecclesiastes teaches the value and divine origin of such higher expectations, while at the same time he counsels his readers to have the patience and acceptance to endure their frustration.

Ecclesiastes ruminates on the meager meaninglessness of human life, and he comes to the conclusion that the human mind is inadequate to understand either God or the universe. But once we learn this painful truth of the inscrutability of God and the universe, we can still will to accept and even embrace God and God's creation. It also leads to a less meaningless experience of life, for life is now seen as pointing to an ultimate meaning and reality beyond itself. We have seen that remaining in the realm of the rational is to a large degree to remain in the world of self-interest and limitation, while this new attitude of wonder frees us to experience the limitless mystery of life and God.

Pascal

For the first part of his short life, Blaise Pascal (1623–62) achieved remarkable success and fame with his work in mathematics and physics. But in his final years Pascal turned to theology. When he died, he left the notes for what he intended to be a final, comprehensive "apology" for the Christian religion as he saw it. These notes are now published as the *Pensées*, or "thoughts." By reading through the *Pensées* as we now have them, one can see how many senses "apology" had for Pascal. Pascal intended to defend Christianity from its detractors. He also wanted to persuade both Christians and non-Christians of the reasonableness of Christianity, to show them that it was not merely superstition: To outsiders, Pascal's defense of Christianity may have been intended to promote missionary activity; to those who were already Christians, his apology would be reassurance. But as Pascal defends Christianity against charges of irrational superstition, he also insists that Christianity is not merely a series of reasonable propositions that will carry conviction to any rational person. In this respect, religion is definitely not like mathematics for Pascal. But like mathematics, religion needs not so much to be defended as to be defined properly: No one doubts the truthfulness or utility of *some kind* of mathematics or religion, but one may well doubt the truth of a particular mathematical equation or theological proposition. For Pascal, Christianity is attacked, ridiculed, and abandoned by so many because it has been ill-defined and misunderstood. So the most important sense of his "apology" is to offer a definition of Christianity that is both accurate and understandable to those who do not already believe in Christianity. Let us consider definitions of Christianity that fall short of these criteria, and why Pascal or we might desire a new definition. It is clearly accurate to say "Christians believe that a supreme being created the universe and now guides its progress." But as Pascal himself observes, by itself this is a definition of deism, not Christianity.[8] It is accurate but incomplete, for it focuses exclusively on an element of Christianity that is neither unique to nor definitive of it. At the other extreme, it is a very full and powerful definition of one's experience of Christianity if one says "I am a Christian because I have been born again and bathed in the blood of Christ." But since the person saying this is probably not dripping with any bodily fluids, his or her language is clearly metaphorical and highly personal and subjective; it would be meaningless to a non-Christian, and possibly confusing to a fellow Christian, who might use different metaphorical language to describe his or her experience or who might mean something quite different by the same metaphor. Pascal wants a definition of Christianity that will allow both Christians and non-Christians to discuss and compare their beliefs with one another, and one that will finally grasp what is essential and not accidental in the religion.

Like Ecclesiastes, Pascal's writing is characterized by melancholy, a quality of which Herman Melville says, "All noble things are touched with that."[9] Melville mentions Pascal as one of those "sick men," whom one must read and understand if one is to "break the green damp mould with unfathomably wondrous Solomon,"[10] that is, if one is to conquer human mortality and limitation by confronting and defying them.

Even more important, the ruminations of both Ecclesiastes and Pascal are profoundly anthropocentric and experiential. Pascal pointedly disparages the possibility or the utility of proving the existence of God[11] and instead focuses on proving what kind of human nature we possess that makes a certain kind of God necessary if we are to be saved: "That is why I will not try to prove here by reasons from nature either the existence of God, or the Trinity, or the immortality of the soul, or anything of that sort . . . because such knowledge, without Jesus Christ, is useless and sterile."[12]

So from the general similarities of melancholy and anthropocentrism, we will now consider more specific points of similarity between Pascal and the Old Testament wisdom tradition, especially in regard to human nature and the inadequacy and use of reason to understand God and life.

Human Nature in Pascal

It may be well to start out with Pascal's most succinct and categorical statement on human nature: "How empty, yet full of filth is the human heart!"[13] But what is really interesting is what leads Pascal to this sobering and dismal conclusion. Unlike many others, such as Dostoevsky, Pascal does not arrive at this idea of human depravity by accumulating examples of moral failings or atrocities. Indeed, when he does mention immoral actions, his objection to them is more often incredulity at the stupidity of such actions than outrage at their immorality. When describing enormous human violence and brutality, he merely thinks it should be carried out more sensibly and practically: "When it is a question of deciding whether one should go to war and kill so many people, or condemn so many Spaniards to death, it is one person who decides, and he is even an interested party: it should be an impartial third party."[14] Pascal is here very much in accord with the biblical wisdom tradition that sees evil and folly as synonymous.[15] Pascal shows this vividly in his repeated mention of "Cleopatra's nose," the supposed attractiveness of which senselessly caused thousands of deaths.[16] And although, as we will see later, Pascal elaborates on the physical and mental shortcomings that go along with this human wretchedness, they do not seem to be his primary evidence for it. Rather, what he points to repeatedly is an emotional or psychological problem at the center of every human being: the inability to be happy. It is this psychological focus that makes Pascal's work different and more compelling than other apologies: "The Apology on the whole conforms to the general pattern of traditional Christian apologetics. Only in his psychological approach does Pascal depart from the traditional procedure."[17]

For Pascal, our inability to be happy is shown most clearly (and ironically) in our constant attempts to make ourselves happy, for if we were capable of true happiness, all of this activity would be unnecessary, and would even lessen our happiness:

> If our condition were truly happy, we would not need to divert ourselves from thinking about it. . . . If humanity were happy, then they would be more so, the less they were diverted, like the saints and God. Yes: but isn't someone happy who enjoys diversion? No: because it comes from elsewhere, from outside, and therefore one is made dependent, and is always liable to be troubled by a thousand accidents, and such disturbances are inevitable.[18]

Incapable of true happiness, we therefore settle for distraction from our unhappiness.[19] But besides its dependence on outside influences, which make it a fragile and vulnerable kind of happiness, a further problem with distraction is that it must inevitably end. Eventually we will win whatever game or sport we are playing, or get a great job or promotion or book contract, or have sex with the person whom we have been pursuing, or capture the animal we have been hunting, and then we will realize that what we thought we wanted doesn't make us happy at all: "We do not long for an easy, peaceful state that would allow us to think about our unhappy condition . . . but rather for the turmoil that keeps us from thinking about it and diverts us. This is the reason we like the chase better than the capture."[20]

But more frightening even than the dissatisfying nature of distractions would be the possibility that they might succeed in distracting us forever:

> The only thing that consoles us for our miseries is diversion, but it is also the greatest of our miseries. It is the main thing that keeps us from contemplating ourselves, and it imperceptibly makes us lose ourselves. Without it we would be bored, and boredom would push us to look for a more secure way of escape. But diversion amuses us and imperceptibly takes us to our death.[21]

The fact that we constantly distract ourselves proves to Pascal our wretchedness, our inability to be happy. But we might be so successful at distracting ourselves that we remain unhappy (but distracted) forever: "Since our true good has been lost, everything appears equally good to us, even our own destruction, even though it is simultaneously so contrary to God, to reason, and to nature. . . . Thus we never live, but only hope to live; and since we are always preparing to be happy, it is inevitable that we should never be so."[22] Pascal here envisions a numbing oblivion of losing ourselves in our distractions, which we should not think of as limited to such obviously self-destructive activities as drug abuse or gambling. What makes distractions more dangerous and insidious is that they might be the most normal, even necessary or commonly admired parts of our lives: Our careers, relationships, and goals threaten us the most, for they may make us so busy at becoming something that we forget to be anything at all, until it is too late.[23] (On the other hand, entertainments may not destroy us so long as they are recognized and experienced as the occasional, temporary, and trivial things that they really are, rather than permanent distractions from who we really are.)[24]

So Pascal believes that humans are irredeemable wretches, incapable of goodness or happiness. Actually, it is not so simple as that at all. For just as our unhappiness is ironically shown by our constantly trying to make ourselves happy, so too a certain kind of nobility and greatness are shown precisely in our wretchedness:

> All of these miseries prove humanity's greatness. They are the miseries of a great lord, the miseries of a dispossessed king. . . . Humanity's greatness is so obvious that it can even be deduced from their misery. What is nature in animals, we label as misery in humans, because we recognize that, although human nature today is like that of the animals, it is because humans have fallen from a better nature which was once their own. . . . To summarize: if humanity had never been corrupted, they would innocently and with assurance enjoy both truth and happiness; but if humanity had always been only corrupt, they would have no idea either of truth or of blessedness.[25]

For Pascal, human wretchedness and greatness are inextricably related, and they immediately and unambiguously imply each other: "'Grandeur' and 'misery' are not, however, simply mixed . . . but mutually determine one another as well"; "Human greatness and misery .. continually point back and forth to each other through the structure of desire."[26] As we saw in Ecclesiastes, we would not be wretched if we did not have some concept of a higher purpose and meaning for our lives, a concept of which our present life falls miserably short. On the other hand, we would not be great if we were not conscious of our wretchedness, for then our present life would satisfy us and it would never occur to us to call it imperfect, unhappy, or fallen: "Thus it is miserable to know that one is miserable, but it is great to know that one is miserable."[27] Without consciousness of our wretchedness, we would accept and enjoy our mortal lives for what they are, just as (as far as we can tell) animals do. But our wretchedness instead points us beyond ourselves and beyond the physical world we inhabit, because it shows us that we are not fully "at home" here:

Human greatness is constituted in part by an awareness of an otherness: the very desire for something "other" that lies outside our present understanding implies that we are not totally enclosed within the codes we use to define our objects of desire. The otherness implied by desire creates misery because it makes us sense all that we are currently lacking. But it also points to our greatness because, unlike animals, we can be aware of our misery and imagine a better state.[28]

We constantly hope and strive for things we cannot achieve on our own, and fail to accomplish the things we should, for only humans are capable of being less than they ought, precisely because they long to be more than they are.

Pascal's Use of Ecclesiastes

Pascal uses Scripture continually, and for many different purposes. It is a frequent part of his attacks on Judaism and Islam,[29] and it is a large part of his discussion of the problematic nature of miracles, which serve both to save and condemn.[30] But what we are interested in here is an examination of which Scriptural passages and characters Pascal focuses on to illustrate and elaborate his idea of the dual nature of human beings as both great and wretched.

Pascal significantly pairs the two greatest figures of the biblical wisdom tradition—Job and Solomon—to illustrate the dichotomy he sees at the center of human nature: "Solomon and Job have known and spoken best about human misery: one was the happiest person, the other the unhappiest; one knew by experience the vanity of pleasures, and the other the reality of pain."[31] These two men typify for Pascal the extremes of human experience—extreme and lasting pleasure and pain—and they show how at either extreme, one comes to the same conclusion about human nature: It is wretched because of its greatness, and it is great because of its wretchedness.

Although he mentions only "misery" or "wretchedness" directly, it is clear from his other comments related to Job and Solomon that he thinks they show us both sides of human nature. Here Pascal has directly mentioned Solomon's realization of the vanity or emptiness of pleasure, but elsewhere he comments on the futility of great knowledge, the other quality for which David's son was known. Knowledge is vain because we pursue it only for our own pride, not to help or educate others, but only to show off in front of them: "Curiosity is only vanity. Usually one only wants to know something in order to talk about it."[32] Such curiosity is usually vain in its object as well, pursuing knowledge of creatures rather than Creator, but this is a misguided object that Solomon was able to overcome: "David [and] Solomon never said, 'There is no vacuum, therefore there is a God.'

They must have been cleverer than the cleverest of those who came after them, for all of those use such proofs."[33] Solomon realized the wretched inadequacy of human knowledge, but this is also proof of human greatness: Imperfect knowledge makes one unhappy only because one retains some idea of what perfect knowledge would be. Ignorance is not bliss: "Ecclesiastes shows that humanity without God is in total ignorance and inevitable unhappiness. For one is unhappy who wills, but cannot do. Now one wants to be happy and assured of some truth, but one can neither know, nor can one stop wanting to know."[34] But Pascal believes that finally even this ignorance can be useful:

> Knowledge has two extremes which meet. The first is the pure, natural ignorance in which all people are born. The other extreme is reached by great souls who, having run through everything that humans can know, find that they know nothing, and they return to that same ignorance from which they departed; but it is a wise ignorance which knows itself.[35]

This is no longer vain curiosity or knowledge that seeks to dominate others or believes that it can know everything, but rather a "wise ignorance," a humbled and self-reflective knowledge that knows and accepts the truths that it cannot change or ignore. It cannot finally fix the human soul, but it can take a large step in diagnosing its illness.

Pascal finds the cure in the Pauline pairing of Adam and Christ: "Adam the figure of the one that was to come."[36] Pascal will even present it as the totality of all Christian belief: "All of faith consists in Jesus Christ and Adam."[37] But what is interesting is that while we can intellectually accept this solution, we cannot understand it:

> It is, however, an astonishing thing that the mystery furthest from our understanding, that of the transmission of sin, is that thing without which we can have no knowledge of ourselves. . . . We can conceive neither Adam's state of glory, nor the nature of his sin, nor the manner of its transmission to us. These are things which happened in a state of nature completely different from our own, and which go beyond our present capacities. Knowing all this is useless to our escape; all that it is important for us to know is that we are miserable, corrupt, separated from God, but redeemed by Jesus Christ.[38]

Pascal uses the scriptural pairs Job/Solomon and Adam/Christ in a way similar to how he uses the contrast between our knowledge of our own nature on the one hand and our knowledge of and longing for God on the other. Pascal believes we can understand and describe our own nature, which will then point us to a knowledge of God and a longing to be with God that we will never fully understand or realize in this life. Likewise, we can understand Job and Solomon all too well, for their experiences and reflections on their experiences are all too familiar to us as humans, and their pain and inadequacy point us to the other pair of Adam and Christ as the cause of and solution to this human condition, but in a way that cannot be fully understood or appreciated by us in this life. For Pascal the human mind cannot object to Adam's sin or Christ's redemption as illogical or nonsensical, but it also cannot explain or understand these concepts. It is enough for him if the mind can reason inductively from particular experiences of human wretchedness and greatness—such as those of Job and Solomon—to the general "rule" that would explain those experiences as the result of Adam's sin, and a believer could then hope for a resolution of those experiences with Christ's redemption: "From the viewpoint of faith, the story of the Fall and Redemption thus seems to subsume and give meaning to the misery of humankind's inability to satisfy its desires, in particular its desire for a transcendent truth."[39]

The Inadequacy and Use of Reason in Pascal

Pascal has, to my mind, the most nuanced idea of the use of reason in human life and faith. But as often happens, nuanced ideas are more complex and harder to understand than simple ideas and are therefore less popular. The simpler role of reason as adequate for understanding everything, epitomized in Descartes and the main thrust of the Enlightenment, has influenced most of our thought for the last four hundred years with nary a nod toward the nay-saying Pascal. On the other hand, the simple denial of reason has had plenty of advocates, whether in popular culture or piety, or in the refined and beautiful thought of Kierkegaard. But Pascal complicates his thought by giving a role to reason, but a limited and not ultimate role: "But Pascal had the greater problem, since he accepted the role of reason in determining truth more readily than did Kierkegaard."[40] A rationalist would simply say that we can know everything by reason, and an irrationalist or antirationalist would say that nothing we can know by reason is of very much importance, but neither has a problem with reason. Pascal, on the other hand, has a lot of trouble explaining to us what exactly the right role of reason would be.

For a philosopher and mathematician, Pascal is surprisingly blunt in his ridicule of reason and his frankness of its limitations: "How ridiculous is reason, thrown about in every direction by any wind! . . . Anyone who chose to follow only reason would be rightly judged by others to be an idiot."[41] But Pascal cannot imagine religion without reason: "If one offends the principles of reason, our religion will be absurd and ridiculous."[42] This would be merely superstition or custom, neither of which cares a whit for reason (consider the absurdities of fashion), and both of which are also constantly changing. And as weak and limited as reason is, Pascal knows how integral and undeniable it is to humans: "One ought to know when one ought to doubt, when one ought to affirm, and when one ought to submit. One who doesn't do this doesn't understand the power of reason."[43] Reason is weak, but it is persistent and nagging, like some small breeds of dog or a cold that you can't quite shake. If it is set aside, it will keep coming back until it is satisfied or vanquished. If we affirm something without really being convinced of it, we will never be sure that we questioned and probed it enough; our belief in such an idea will never be solid or completely sincere but always weak, halfhearted, and coerced. To accept without conviction is to shrug at the idea, not embrace it; such acceptance cannot be the basis of any real relationship to the truth or to God.

Now comes the really innovative part of Pascal's thought. What if there are very important truths about God and ourselves that cannot be explained by or to reason? What should reason do? It cannot explain them, but it cannot simply affirm them, lest doubts persist and render the affirmation permanently weak and lifeless. But a wonderful thing about reason is that it can know and diagnose its own limitations: "The final step of reason is to recognize that there are an infinity of things that go beyond it; it is just deficient if it can't even go as far as knowing that."[44] Reason is not silenced or denied by something else, but it acknowledges itself that there are realms beyond it, about which some other part of the human being will have to decide. It is not defeated; rather, it graciously surrenders. Like most philosophers, Pascal is short on examples (though he gives more than many other philosophers), but I think these meaningful realms beyond reason are clear and numerous enough in our lives. Without even bringing God into it, it would seem that our relationships, our vocation (not career, mind you, but vocation, the feeling that we have been called to do something), and our experiences of goodness or beauty (or their opposites) go beyond reason, though reason would not object to them. It would simply stand aside during these experiences, the way the sense of smell is uninvolved when reading a book. Reason itself must make this acknowledgment of and submission to the super-rational (the way one would sniff a book if one wanted to be sure that the sense of smell is uninvolved with its appreciation), thereby making the submission itself reasonable, to prevent any later doubts: "It is thus right that it submit, when it judges that it ought to submit. . . . There is nothing so consistent with reason as this rejection of reason."[45] Reason therefore is inadequate but utterly necessary for faith or love: "But only rational thought is able to accept its own limitations by saluting its mysterious powers of self-transcendence. The submission of reason, far from being its abdication or annulment, is its last and best achievement."[46] Like a telescope that cannot take us to the stars but that lets us know the stars are there and fans the flames of our desire to get there, reason points us to what lies beyond itself. With blunt realism concerning the limitations of reason and a keen insight into the psychology of doubt and belief, Pascal has shown how reason is the basis for something that is not itself reasonable (or unreasonable). Unable by itself to determine ultimate meaning or value, reason nonetheless makes the quest for these possible.

Conclusion: Reason and the Heart in the Encounter with God

For Pascal, what constitutes a true, complete, and beneficial encounter with God? "It is the heart that perceives God, and not reason. That is what faith is: God perceived by the heart, not by reason."[47] So the heart is the only organ or faculty that can truly perceive and relate to God, but what exactly Pascal means by "heart" is not quite clear. While it is clear that it "feels" things, it is not just or primarily emotion or feeling, for it also "knows" and "understands." It usually seems roughly equivalent to "intuition" but could also mean "essence."[48] At least twice "heart" seems strangely to be equated with animal, mechanical "instinct."[49] Although it is usually contrasted with reason, it seems to be a part of the mind or intellect, and not mere feeling: "This power is not opposed to the intellect nor is it even different from intellect; it is its loftiest part."[50]

But while words may fail to grasp fully what he means by "heart," Pascal is much clearer about what it does, and what it does is impossible finally for either reason or feeling. Pascal says that people who understand through the heart are "wise" and see "with the eyes of the heart."[51] The heart does not think things or figure things out, both of which imply a profound gap between knower and knowledge in the detached, sterile, and dead relation of reason to object. But nor does the heart simply get swept away by ideas—this is the pure, almost passive experience of feelings and emotions. The heart grasps, accepts, seizes, makes things its own and folds them into itself: "Knowledge presupposes love. One will know the truth—really know it, in the most profound sense, with the passion of appropriation—to the extent that one is loving."[52] And in knowing and loving, the heart also gives itself to what is known: "Really to know something is to give oneself to it, follow its lead, let it shape and guide one's thought"; "The heart . . . discerns and it loves, and in it knowledge and feeling . . . are mutually helpful."[53] Imagine the difference between dissecting a cadaver and getting to know and have a relationship (good or bad) with a live human being: After either experience, one could surely be said to "know" more about human beings, and both may even be useful parts of one's education and maturing (I have never dissected a human body, but my dissections of animals have all left me with a deep awe at the mystery of life), but there really could be no question over which is finally more valuable and humanizing.

It is also the heart that determines the object(s) of love, and these decisions are neither reasonable nor unreasonable; they are simply of a different order or kind:

> The heart has its reasons, that reason cannot comprehend: one knows this from thousands of examples. I say that the heart naturally loves the universal being and itself, as it has accustomed itself to do so; but it can choose to harden itself against either one of these. You have rejected one and kept the other: is it according to reason that you love yourself?[54]

Self-love is therefore not unreasonable (or reasonable), but it can be unwise, for it can render one incapable of loving God or other people, and it turns one instead inward to the self, which is only partially and very provisionally worthy of love. Wisdom, on the other hand, would turn one from self-love and open one up to the proper set of valuations: "All bodies together with all minds and all their products are not worth the least impulse of charity, which is of an infinitely higher order."[55] So, having used reason to understand certain realities of human nature, Pascal believes that one should then use a different faculty of the heart to will oneself to love God and others rather than oneself. "Know thyself" is the function of reason and is the foundation or starting point for the more important commands "Love the Lord your God with all your heart . . . and your neighbor as yourself" (Luke 10:27);[56] these are acts of the heart. Knowing oneself is to understand one's finitude, while loving the Lord and people is to see one's goal in the infinite: "Man is what he is because of the infinite for which he is made. His self-surrender is, at the same time and by the same token, his self-surpassing."[57] Such love is also the beginning and goal of all wisdom, which perceives that connectedness to God and others is the path of true, ultimate self-fulfillment, as foolish and difficult as it may seem at first.[58]

Notes

1. R. B. Y. Scott, *The Way of Wisdom in the Old Testament* (New York: Macmillan, 1971), 140.
2. See the discussion in ibid., 136–40.
3. See the discussion of authorship and dating by R. N. Whybray, *Ecclesiastes* (New Century Bible Commentary; Grand Rapids: Eerdmans, 1989), 3–14.
4. Crenshaw, *Old Testament Wisdom*, 123; Whybray, *Ecclesiastes*, 27.
5. Murphy, *Tree of Life*, 58.
6. Whybray, *Ecclesiastes*, 27.

7. Crenshaw, *Old Testament Wisdom*, 134.

8. Pascal, *Pensées* (Garden City, N.Y.: Doubleday, 1961), fragment 556 (449). All quotations from Pascal are my translation. The first number refers to the fragment number (hereafter abbreviated "fr.") in the Brunschvicg edition, and the number in parentheses refers to the fragment number in the popular English translation by A. J. Krailsheimer (New York: Penguin, 1966), based on the edition of M. Lafuma. For a discussion of the various editions, see R. J. Nelson, *Pascal: Adversary and Advocate* (Cambridge: Harvard University Press, 1981), 229–34.

9. Melville, *Moby-Dick*, chap. 16, "The Ship," 68.

10. Ibid., chap. 96, "The Try-Works," 355.

11. Cf. L. Kolakowski, *God Owes Us Nothing* (Chicago: University of Chicago Press, 1995), 124, who finds that the most prominent proofs in the *Pensées* are those "we come across when we turn our attention, not to stars and plants, not even to prophecies and miracles, but to ourselves, to our spiritual constitution."

12. Pascal, *Pensées*, fr. 556 (449).

13. Pascal, *Pensées*, fr. 143 (139). Krailsheimer's rendering is less literal but wonderfully succinct: "How hollow and foul is the heart of man!" T. V. Morris, *Making Sense of It All: Pascal and the Meaning of Life* (Grand Rapids: Eerdmans, 1992), 32, puts it even more pithily: "We are . . . full of crap."

14. Pascal, *Pensées*, fr. 296 (59).

15. See Crenshaw, *Old Testament Wisdom*, 80–91.

16. Pascal, *Pensées*, fr. 162 (413), fr. 163 (46), fr. 163b (197).

17. Sr. M. L. Hubert, *Pascal's Unfinished Apology: A Study of His Plan* (New Haven: Yale University Press, 1952), 145.

18. Pascal, *Pensées*, fr. 165b (70), fr. 170 (132). For a comparison between Augustine and Pascal on this point, see J. Morgan, *The Psychological Teaching of St. Augustine* (London: Elliot Stock, 1932), 176.

19. Cf. Kolakowski, *God Owes Us Nothing*, 133: "The goal is not to show us that we tend to embellish our image for our own comfort as well as for the eyes of others, but to make us realize that, whatever we might think, we are really unhappy, and only pretend not to feel our pain. . . . [W]e come to see that we spend most of our time seeking an illusory escape from reality into all sorts of 'divertissements.'"

20. Pascal, *Pensées*, fr. 139 (136).

21. Ibid., fr. 171 (414).

22. Ibid., fr. 425 (148), fr. 172 (47).

23. Cf. Kolakowski, *God Owes Us Nothing*, 134–35: "Anything we do—useful or not, necessary or otherwise—is at the service of the devil if it is not done for God's sake; if it is not, in people's minds, an act of obedience to the divine commandments and of praising the Lord. Any other goal—not only pleasure or gain but the sheer necessity of sustaining one's own life—is illicit if it is the goal in itself."

24. Cf. Morris, *Making Sense of It All*, 34: "What is wrong is our *always* using such activities as diversions in such a way as to keep us from *ever* having to grapple with the big issues of life" (emphasis in original).

25. Pascal, *Pensées*, fr. 398 (116), fr. 409 (117), fr. 434 (131); on human greatness in Pascal, cf. R. H. Soltau, *Pascal: The Man and the Message* (Westport, Conn.: Greenwood Press, 1970; originally published 1927), 119–21.

26. R. Guardini, *Pascal for Our Time* (trans. B. Thompson; New York: Herder & Herder, 1966), 54; S. E. Melzer, *Discourses of the Fall: A Study of Pascal's* Pensées (Berkeley: University of California Press, 1986), 82.

27. Pascal, *Pensées*, fr. 397 (114).
28. Melzer, *Discourses of the Fall*, 82.
29. E.g., Pascal, *Pensées*, fr. 446 (278), fr. 592 (204), fr. 730 (324), fr. 774 (221). See also D. Wetsel, *Pascal and Disbelief: Catechesis and Conversion in the* Pensées (Washington, D.C.: Catholic University of America Press, 1994), 177–242.
30. E.g. Pascal, *Pensées*, fr. 564 (835), fr. 808 (846), fr. 839 (854), fr. 843 (840). Cf. Nelson, *Adversary and Advocate*, 186: "In Pascal's theology, miracles do not convince and they are far from converting. As Pascal will maintain in his projected *Apology for the Christian Religion*, miracles may even *confound* belief" (emphasis in original). This position opposes the more simplistic view that Pascal considers miracles unambiguous "proof"— e.g., D. Adamson, *Blaise Pascal: Mathematician, Physicist and Thinker about God* (New York: St. Martin's Press, 1995), 78–81, 183–85.
31. Pascal, *Pensées*, fr. 174 (403).
32. Ibid., fr. 152 (77).
33. Ibid., fr. 243 (463).
34. Ibid., fr. 389 (75). The relevance to Solomon is greater since Pascal would have accepted the attribution of Ecclesiastes to him.
35. Ibid., fr. 327 (83).
36. Ibid., fr. 656 (590), quoting Rom 5:14.
37. Ibid., fr. 523 (226).
38. Ibid., fr. 434 (131), fr. 560 (431).
39. Melzer, *Discourses of the Fall*, 87. Cf. H. M. Davidson, *The Origins of Certainty: Means and Meaning in Pascal's* Pensées (Chicago: University of Chicago Press, 1979), 47: "At the end of this process, in the fact of our incomprehensibility—for we are in the midst of a discussion of reason and what it can understand of our condition—we look for some principle of explanation. Pascal tells us that it is the mystery of original sin. That represents one degree of intelligibility, one step in the pacifying of the mind and the removal of obstacles."
40. R. Hazelton, *Blaise Pascal: The Genius of His Thought* (Philadelphia: Westminster Press, 1974), 191. Cf. Guardini, *Pascal for Our Time*, 117: "Pascal knows nothing about the absolute incommensurability which Kierkegaard erects between God's holiness and man who is not only a 'sinner,' but 'sin.'"
41. Pascal, *Pensées*, fr. 82 (44).
42. Ibid., fr. 273 (173).
43. Ibid., fr. 268 (170). I can't help thinking that Kenny Rogers' song "The Gambler" does a good job of conveying a similar sentiment, I assume unbeknownst to the author.
44. Ibid., fr. 267 (188).
45. Ibid., fr. 270 (174), 272 (182).
46. Hazelton, *Blaise Pascal*, 202.
47. Pascal, *Pensées*, fr. 278 (424).
48. The preferred identifications of Hazelton, *Blaise Pascal*, 99–104.
49. Pascal, *Pensées*, fr. 395 (406), 252 (821).
50. Hubert, *Pascal's Unfinished Apology*, 136, quoting J. Chevalier. Cf. Guardini, *Pascal for Our Time*, 129: "'Coeur' is itself mind: a manifestation of the mind."
51. Pascal, *Pensées*, fr. 793 (308).
52. Guardini, *Pascal for Our Time*, 133.
53. Hazelton, *Blaise Pascal*, 102; Hubert, *Pascal's Unfinished Apology*, 136, quoting Chevalier.
54. Pascal, *Pensées*, fr. 277 (423).

55. Ibid., fr. 793 (308). In the parallelism of this fragment, people are either carnal, intellectual, or wise, according to whether they value bodies, minds, or charity.

56. Cf. Matt 22:37–39; Mark 12:30–31; Lev 19:18; Deut 6:5.

57. Hazelton, *Blaise Pascal*, 202.

58. Cf. Morris, *Making Sense of It All*, 191: "The heart is the deepest point of contact for emotions, attitudes, and beliefs. It is also the deepest source for human actions. . . . It may involve connectedness that is mental (intellectual), attitudinal (emotional), and volitional (involved with will and action) and thus, in its completeness, spiritual."

5. The Meaning of Suffering in Job and *Moby-Dick*

Introduction

While Ecclesiastes focused on the seeming meaninglessness of life, the author of Job was most troubled by the undeniable presence of innocent suffering in this life. Older wisdom had relied on overlooking or minimizing this problem by treating it as an exception to certain observable rules: "This sense of an unseen structure of reality was correlated with the observation that good or bad behavior had appropriate consequences—if not always, at least often enough to establish this as a general rule."[1] But a theology and morality based on experience that also promises certain results from adhering to it must change if there are enough experiences that do *not* correspond to the vision of the world put forth. If the good perish and the wicked triumph often enough, then a theology that simply denies this observation cannot survive. Thousands of years later the novelist Herman Melville would join the author of Job in his unorthodox quest to redefine wisdom. In both of these authors, there is such a profound sense of duty to the truth— of saying what must be said, with little or no regard for the consequences or the reactions—that such voices of integrity demand a full and sympathetic hearing from us if we ourselves are to increase in our experience and understanding of the truth.

Job

We will possibly never know when and how the book of Job came to be in the form we now have. Clearly there seem to be compositional "seams" in the work between the prose and poetry, and possibly between different parts of the poetry, as well as sharp differences in outlook and tone, but when and in what order the parts became united is debated.[2] I will speak of the work as a whole, and not of its parts, for this is how it has been received in the tradition. The story as we have it is as simple, mysterious, and powerful as any from any culture or time. Once upon a time, in the land of Uz, there was a man named Job. He was blameless in every respect, sacrificing to God piously and frequently. This man was also fortunate in all his worldly affairs, being blessed with numerous children, possessions, and servants. But one day God pointed this faithful man out to one of the "sons of God," Satan, a heavenly being whose assignment seems to be to prowl around the earth and examine people's conduct and prosecute them (his name means "accuser" or "adversary") for their misdeeds if necessary. God was understandably proud of and impressed with his servant Job, but Satan was not. Satan thought that Job was so pious and faithful only because these qualities garnered him such enormous blessings and that if those blessings were removed, Job would immediately lose his faith and curse God. So God allows Satan to conduct this test of Job's faith. All of Job's children, possessions, and servants are destroyed in a series of cataclysms. But Job only says, "The LORD gave, and the LORD has taken away; blessed be the name of the LORD" (Job 1:21). So Satan continues his assault on Job, afflicting him with some horrible disease that covers his entire body with sores. But Job merely replies, "Shall we receive the good at the hand of God, and not receive the bad?" (Job 2:10). Because of his remarkable response to suffering, Job would be known throughout history for his patience or "endurance" (Jas 5:11).

But the story does not end there. Three friends of Job appear and speak with him. They speak for a very long time indeed—and then a fourth man appears to speak. This enormous middle of the book is very repetitive, as Job over and over protests his innocence and the unfairness of what has happened to him, and his friends flatly assert that he must have done something to deserve all of this suffering: "Think now, who that was innocent ever perished? . . . Know then that God exacts of you less than your guilt deserves" (Job 4:7; 11:6). But along the way, Job desires more. He wants to lodge a complaint with God himself: "But I would speak to the Almighty, and I desire to argue my case with God" (Job 13:3). And this request is answered, for God appears and speaks to Job. God's speech is, however, in many ways the most irrelevant in all of literature: "The divine speeches seem completely irrelevant failing as they do to provide any answers to the problem of innocent suffering and divine justice."[3] While Job has been asking for thirty-five chapters why he is suffering this way, God offers insights that seem less than helpful; for instance, he points out that he made the sea and the stars as well as much less impressive creatures such as the donkey and the ostrich.

Somehow, Job at least finds this answer satisfactory, and the source of a new knowledge and a new relationship with God: "I had heard of you by the hearing of the ear, but now my eye sees you; therefore I despise myself, and repent in dust and ashes" (Job 42:6). God then gives back to Job everything he had before (and more), and Job lives happily ever after.

Again, the story is deceptively easy to retell, but what it finally means has never been decided, and some would even despair of ever finding its meaning: "Is it possible to understand the Book of Job?"[4] But human beings would not return to the story over and over throughout millennia of Jewish and Christian history if it did not mean something; the meaning may be elusive or paradoxical, but it is not empty.

If we would even come close to understanding Job, we would have to understand the last five chapters and three confusing things that happen there: God's enigmatic speeches, Job's ambiguous replies, and God's unexpected rebuke of Job's friends and affirmation of Job. In what possible sense are God's speeches here an answer to Job's questions? Although they start out as such, they cannot finally be a bald assertion of power, the divine equivalent of the ineffective parental reply to a recalcitrant child, "Because I say so!" This is because the things in creation to which God points include not only the powerful and awesome but also the merely weird; they do not make you cower so much as they make you shake your head. God's point is not that he is powerful and in total control of the world but that the world is mysterious, irrational, unexplainable by or to any human, possibly even a little unexpected to God himself: "The maker of all things is astonished at the things He has Himself made."[5] As with the old riddle "Can God make a rock so big that God can't lift it?" the answer here is that God has made a universe so strange that even God can't explain or justify it, at least not to any other being, if even to himself. So although the author does not connect all the dots for us, the first answer to Job's question of why he is suffering would seem to be that his suffering is as mysterious and unexplainable as the rest of God's creation. Although this response does not finally answer Job's question or explain his experience, it does put it in perspective—a very large, weird perspective, one that humbles the mind, not consoles it.

God continues his reply in a way that relates it more closely to Job's experience and concedes much to Job's previous attack on God's justice: "The first speech extols the mysteries of nature, while the second indirectly acknowledges the force of Job's attack upon God. . . . The second divine speech addresses Job's complaint somewhat more directly and comes very close to an admission that God found the task of ruling the world a difficult one."[6] God challenges Job now not with the mystery of creation but with the mystery of evil: "Look on all who are proud, and bring them low; tread down the wicked where they stand. Hide them all in the dust together; bind their faces in the world below. Then I will also acknowledge to you that your own right hand can give you victory" (Job 40:12–14). In answer to Job's question of whether God is just, God can only reply that he is not just in any way that would be recognizable by human standards, for human justice is based on punishing the wicked, while God's justice is somehow based on allowing evil to exist and even to thrive. Again, this reply does not explain evil so much as it places it in context and spells out its implications: "[God] speaks as the one who bears the burden of the moral government of mankind. . . . Is [Job] really prepared to say that he knows what justice must mean in its total context?"[7] Evil is again the precondition for human freedom and meaning, for these cannot exist unless God allows humans the freedom to disobey him and destroy themselves and each other (and once in history, even to kill him): "Yet with all this omnipotence, there is one thing the Almighty cannot do. . . . God cannot coerce the love and service of mortals."[8] As strange and painful as human life is, God can only assert that it must be this way if people are to have real relationships with him.

All of this pain and wonder first cause Job simply to fall silent (Job 40:4–5): "His answer is not defiant, but it is vague enough to be either humble or evasive; it is not an admission of any wrong."[9] But Job then does something that has been variously translated and interpreted in Job 42:6: "Therefore I despise myself and repent in dust and ashes." The ambiguity of the response begins at the verbal level: There is no direct object for the first verb, the relation between the second verb and the "dust and ashes" is unclear, and the range of possible translations for both verbs is wide. The verse is often taken to mean that Job now thinks it was wrong to question God, or that what he said about God was wrong; as we will see, in light of Job 42:7–8, this cannot be the right interpretation. Job does not regret what he said, he does not reject or repudiate it, but rather he decides to act and think differently in the future: "It would be mistaken to see here repentance for all that he has said, or even merely for certain statements that he made. The repentance should be interpreted as a change of mind."[10] This is a change in attitude, not just a change in thought, and it is directed toward the future, not the past.

But what has Job changed his mind about? Again, it cannot be his evaluation of God's (in)justice, for God himself finally defends Job's position when he says to Eliphaz, "My wrath is kindled against you and against your two friends; for you have not spoken of me what is right, as my servant Job has. . . . [M]y servant Job shall pray for you, for I will accept his prayer not to deal with you according to your folly; for you have not spoken of me what is right, as my servant Job has done" (Job 42:7–8). Any interpretation must deal with these verses, which, unlike everything else in the last five chapters of the book of Job, are utterly unambiguous; Job was right and his friends were wrong. So I take it that what Job changes his mind about, what he vows not to do in the future, is seeing the world the way his friends did. He rejects their worldview, a worldview that he more or less shared: "The warrants for Job's argument do not differ appreciably from those employed by his friends to refute him."[11] Although they spent most of the book disagreeing as to Job's innocence, Job and his friends shared a fundamental and misguided assumption: that God was explainable and understandable in human terms, that God was a small, domestic God, like a guardian angel, who could be predicted, appeased, cajoled, tamed. (Indeed, there may even be a hint of this domestication and trivialization of God at the beginning of the book, in the way that Job routinely sacrifices to God just in case someone in his family had sinned; perhaps significantly, when Job gets everything back at the end of the book, the text does not say that he continues to sacrifice to God.) Everything in God's speeches in Job blows this image away as a very small, self-centered piety; the God of Leviathan (or, one could add, the God of cancer, or the Holocaust, or AIDS, or September 11) is a great deal more, and less, than that. If one can stare down this vision of what God is, as Job does, one can have a new and fuller relation with God: "I had heard of you by the hearing of the ear, but now my eye sees you" (Job 42:5).

What might this new relation with God be like? If my interpretation of the last five chapters of Job is correct, then I would say that it will be a relationship that includes both confrontation and surrender, questioning and acceptance, doubt and trust—and all of these from both partners in the relationship. Indeed, elsewhere in the wisdom tradition, it is the soft, comfortable relationships that are harmful and dangerous, while the confrontational ones are really loving and beneficial: "Well meant are the wounds a friend inflicts, but profuse are the kisses of an enemy. . . . Iron sharpens iron, and one person sharpens the wits of another" (Prov 27:6, 17). To remove half of the relation—to excise confrontation, questioning, and doubt—is not piety but folly, as God labels it in Job 42:8. On the sinister side, it is the kind of folly also shown powerfully in Elie Wiesel's modern version of Job, *The Trial of God*,[12] in which the only character who will defend God, who counsels all the other characters around him only to surrender to God's will with complete trust and without question, is finally revealed to be none other than Satan, the enemy of God and the prince of lies. He beguiled the other characters to stop questioning or accusing God, but their questioning was the basis of their relation with God after the horrors they had witnessed, and they are left with nothing. Accepting evil is part of the fuller relation with God to which Job comes, and to which the book invites us, but calling evil good is not. If we are to have a relationship with a God who is finally incomprehensible to us, then I would think God would have to accept our agonized questioning at the same time that we would have to accept God's agonized inscrutability, for it must pain both us and God that he cannot make himself understandable to us.

Job's acceptance of the inscrutability of God and of evil leads to a deeper relationship with God, a relationship that makes much less sense than loving a God who rewards us, for we instead trust a God from whom we can ultimately have no guarantees. But as frightening as this relationship might be, how different is it from loving another person, the power and mystery of which we have seen in earlier chapters? Life is known in truth for its contingency and vulnerability, and this new attitude of acceptance and trust frees us to experience God and ourselves anew, humbled but wiser.

Herman Melville

Familiar to most English speakers is the American novelist Herman Melville (1819–91). He was raised Calvinist and married to a Unitarian, though he came up with his own brand of skeptical, confrontational theism, and he lived his adult life sailing all over the world while fathering four children.[13]

Most readers remember Melville as the author of some vivid if overwrought tales of adventure on the high seas. Indeed, during his life and for decades after it, his reputation was not even that high, and he died in bitterness, disappointment, and obscurity.[14] But from the 1920s on, critics have come to a deeper appreciation of his work, and especially of his masterpiece, *Moby-Dick* (1851): "Had there been no *Moby-Dick*, Herman Melville surely would have belonged to literary history, not to literature, and as a minor curiosity at that."[15] Like any truly great work of literature, the book works on many levels that are still being studied and debated. As an adventure story it has worked very effectively on generations of readers: A Nantucket whaling captain, Ahab, has become obsessed with the sperm whale that crippled him by biting off one of his legs, so he enlists a crew of men from around the globe to go hunt the monster, which turns on them and kills them all, except for our narrator, Ishmael. Told this way, the story works fine as a movie or a children's story, much like *Treasure Island*, with plenty of suspense and action.[16] The story is also a deep psychological drama of obsession and a descent into self-destructive madness very similar to many of Dostoevsky's works. Moreover, the book has deep but elusive political overtones. Melville never fails to remind the reader of the peculiarly American nature of the whaling industry and of Ahab's ship, the *Pequod*, and his crew, but Melville's tone varies wildly between patriotic praise of the whalers' ingenuity and bravery, and disgust at their careless brutality and alienation.[17] Melville's ideas on race are equally convoluted and ambiguous; he clearly contrasts the white and nonwhite characters, but it is hardly clear which he considers "better," or even if there is a "better."[18] Finally, and most important for us, the book is full of religious images applied to practically every character and object in it, in addition to the theologically overflowing soliloquies provided by Ahab and others and the theological ruminations of the narrator. As with the political or social implications of the book, the final or exact meaning of these images and speeches is open to interpretation, but it is clear that the book must have some theological meaning(s). I will argue for a particular meaning that is more hopeful than many have thought, but one that is anything but warmly pious or optimistic; it is dark and unorthodox enough for us to understand Melville's own evaluation that he had "written a wicked book."[19]

Just like the biblical Wisdom books or Pascal, Melville's writing is anthropocentric and experiential. Although *Moby-Dick* constantly tantalizes us with divine images applied both to the sea and to Moby Dick, "the grand god,"[20] it always anchors those images in a sea of human subjectivity and brings them back to the characters' reactions and interpretations of them, as shown vividly by the juxtaposition of the characters' reactions to "The Doubloon" that Ahab has attached to the mast: "And some certain significance lurks in all things, else all things are little worth, and the round world itself but an empty cipher, except to sell by the cartload, as they do hills about Boston, to fill up some morass in the Milky Way."[21] Nothing means just one thing, but neither is anything finally or merely subjective: Instead, every object, person, and event in the novel is imbued with layers upon layers of meanings that different humans intuit in different ways and at different times, showing their own essence and purpose more than that of the object they analyze.[22] The same dynamic may be seen in the repetition of narrative roles in the novel by more than one character: Nothing means just one thing, but neither is any one meaning fully exhaustible by just one instance of it.[23]

Just as Pascal's *Pensées* are not about God as some abstract theory but about what kind of God would be accessible to beings such as we are, so too *Moby-Dick* is not ultimately about the White Whale or God but about men's reactions to their experiences and ideas of the Whale or God. It is about why men would want to hunt the White Whale, or why they all have some unique complaint with the Deity: "So the wretched infidel gazes himself blind at the monumental white shroud that wraps all the prospect around him. And of all these things the Albino whale was the symbol. Wonder ye then at the fiery hunt?"[24] Indeed, we do not, for as Melville has created his microcosm of "Isolatoes" "from all the isles of the sea, and all the ends of the earth," there was no human reaction imaginable for them other than to lay on and pursue that maddest and most human of goals, to "lay the world's grievances before that bar from which not very many of them ever came back."[25] And although Ahab's philosophy should not be taken as identical to Melville's own, it is one that he granted "a full and proper hearing"[26] and with which he is (and wishes us to be) sympathetic.[27] Ahab's obsession is extreme, but it is utterly typical of the human condition, and that is why it can become the quest of everyone on board the *Pequod*, all of the "mongrel renegades, castaways, and cannibals,"[28] every Christian, pagan, atheist, pantheist, black, white, drunk, madman, blasphemer, buffoon, innocent, or virtuous dreamer among them.[29]

Human Nature in Melville

If any literary character recollects Pascal's image of humanity's greatness and wretchedness as a "dispossessed king," surely it would be Melville's Ahab, who is "a Khan of the plank, and a king of the sea, and a great Lord of Leviathans," while at the same time he is a "poor pegging lubber," a "mutilated," "crippled," "helpless, sad . . . insane old man."[30] Ahab himself diagnoses his condition:

> Oh, Life! Here I am, proud as a Greek god, and yet standing debtor to this blockhead for a bone to stand on! Cursed be that mortal inter-indebtedness which will not do away with ledgers. I would be as free as air; and I'm down in the whole world's books. I am so rich, I would have given bid for bid with the wealthiest Praetorian at the auction of the Roman empire (which was the world's); and yet I owe for the flesh in the tongue I brag with. By heavens! I'll get a crucible, and into it, and dissolve myself down to one small, compendious vertebra.[31]

Ahab encapsulates here all that it is to be human: mortal yet with a tantalizing concept of immortality; yearning to be free yet utterly bound;[32] knowing what physical, mental, and spiritual glory are yet painfully aware of his lack of them. Before his final, fatal confrontation with Moby Dick, Ahab again shows his worth and vulnerability as a human being: "From beneath his slouched hat Ahab dropped a tear into the sea; nor did all the Pacific contain such wealth as that one wee drop."[33] As Peleg had exclaimed earlier, "Ahab has his humanities!"[34] and one human tear is worth more than all the deadly, powerful, soulless waters of the earth. Here is a creature who is truly and completely superior to the physical world that so easily destroys him but can have no real victory over him. The world easily breaks his tiny, mortal body but not his infinite, immortal spirit, and it cannot render meaningless the meaning he has given himself, as mad and unhappy as he may be.

The number of classical, biblical, and renaissance archetypes that Ahab's character simultaneously recalls to us is staggering, and they further reveal his dual nature and the dual nature of humanity that he epitomizes. Critics have compared him to Prometheus, Narcissus,[35] Osiris,[36] Oedipus,[37] Hercules, Satan, Adam,[38] Cain,[39] the evil Israelite king Ahab, Jonah,[40] Job, (anti-)Christ, Faust, Don Quixote,[41] Manfred, Hamlet, Macbeth,[42] Lear,[43] and Edmund.[44] All of these characters share the image of overstepping some boundary, of reaching for something more than they ought, of disobeying a "natural" or God-given command and suffering for it. But the factors that make Ahab the clearest illustration of Pascal's anthropology are the timing and cause of his condition. For most of the other literary antecedents, their dispossession, their fall from grace, happens following and as a result of their overreaching hubris and defiance of boundaries. The drama of their stories is for us to watch their slow, painful, and hopefully meaningful, disintegration. But Ahab begins the novel as "branded," "dismasted," "dismembered," "stricken, blasted," "mutilated," an "ungodly, god-like man,"[45] presented with a universe that he cannot understand or accept. It is therefore not a question of how or why he got that way but how he will react to his condition.[46] His drama is for us to watch him claw his way back up to human dignity and control. He is therefore more like Job and Edmund than the others, though he is a great deal more appealing than either of these two. If we admire Job for his courage, then his submission in the end seems a little disappointing, at least when considered dramatically or aesthetically, if not morally or theologically. And while we certainly sympathize with the unfairness of the world's treatment of Edmund, his murderous treachery against the people who have done their best to minimize the harm to him seems ungrateful and spiteful, not heroic. Job and Edmund border on the "unnatural" or inhuman—one heavenly so, the other diabolically so. But Ahab is utterly "natural" and human in his situation and his reaction: He lashes out at precisely the being who harmed him—the White Whale/God—and he never relents.

Ahab is also a good deal more appealing and dogged in his outward directed quest than Lear is in his inner one, for Lear seems to postpone and avoid the pain of facing and changing himself as long as possible, while Ahab is actively and vigorously on a quest from the moment we meet him, even though his blindness to himself is every bit as willful and even more fatal than Lear's. But while we sympathize with Lear because we all make similarly foolish mistakes and reap the terrible rewards of our actions, we admire Ahab because we are all trapped in a world that we didn't make, don't understand, and can't accept, but he actually takes up a harpoon and hobbles off to do something about it, as mad and futile as that may be: "[Ahab] realizes that the Whale cannot be destroyed, that chaos and evil can never be eliminated. [But] despite this realization, Ahab continues his struggle. Value and truth cannot be achieved in any absolute sense, but in his pursuit of them, man finds salvation."[47] We are different from him only in our lesser consciousness of life and our more craven reaction to it: Most of us are content to sip "the tepid tears of orphans," or ignore "all the horrors of the half known life," while Ahab has drunk deeply of "all nature's sweet or savage impressions fresh from her own virgin, voluntary, and confiding breast," making him "one in a whole nation's census—a mighty pageant creature, formed for noble tragedies."[48] The captain of the *Pequod* clearly is wretched in his greatness, and great precisely because he is wretched. And his quest is anything but a diversion (though the trip may well be a diversion to everyone else on board, and even may have begun as such for Ishmael). For Ahab it is an act of worship, the deepest expression of the relationship he chooses to have with God, a relationship of defiance, rejection, and confrontation: "I now know thee, thou clear spirit, and I now know that thy right worship is defiance. . . . I leap with thee; I burn with thee; would fain be welded with thee; defyingly I worship thee!"[49] Ahab's quest makes his suffering into human suffering; it makes him a "personality" that objects to suffering, rather than an animal or object that unconsciously undergoes it.

Besides applying the image of a "dispossessed king" to Ahab, Melville also generalizes the image to apply to all of humanity:

> But vain to popularize profundities, and all truth is profound. Winding far down from within the very heart of this spiked Hotel de Cluny where we here stand—however grand and wonderful, now quit it;—and take your way, ye nobler, sadder souls, to those vast Roman halls of Thermes; where far beneath the fantastic towers of man's upper earth, his root of grandeur, his whole awful essence sits in bearded state; an antique buried beneath antiquities, and throned on torsoes! So with a broken throne, the great gods mock that captive king; so like a Caryatid, he patient sits, upholding on his frozen brow the piled entablatures of ages. Wind ye down there, ye prouder, sadder souls! question that proud, sad king! A family likeness! aye, he did beget ye, ye young exiled royalties; and from your grim sire only will the old State-secret come.[50]

Ahab is just the extreme, heroic, and much more insightful version of all of us; through him we now realize that we are a race of broken, conquered people, and this realization makes us even more wretched, because we now have some memory of and longing for our homeland.[51]

But just as Melville clearly sees wretchedness among the great, he finds human greatness most clearly displayed among the humble:

> Men may seem detestable as joint stock-companies and nations; knaves, fools, and murderers there may be; men may have mean and meager faces; but man, in the ideal, is so noble and so sparkling, such a grand and glowing creature. . . . [T]his august dignity I treat of, is not the dignity of kings

and robes, but that abounding dignity which has no robed investiture. Thou shalt see it shining in the arm that wields a pick or drives a spike; that democratic dignity which, on all hands, radiates without end from God; Himself! . . . [T]hou just Spirit of Equality, which hast spread one royal mantle of humanity over all my kind! . . . Thou who, in all Thy mighty earthly marchings, ever cullest Thy selectest champions from the kingly commons; bear me out in it, O God!⁵²

This is probably the closest the book will come to conventional piety or optimism, and it comes as Ishmael is contemplating human equality and humility. Ahab has focused only on the unfairness of *his* life, and his reaction is blinding and self-destructive anger, an attitude typified in his mad statement "I'd strike the sun if it insulted me."⁵³ It is usually labeled solipsism by scholars, and it is an attitude that cuts him off from other people, whom he now regards only as "wheels,"⁵⁴ "tools,"⁵⁵ or "blockhead[s]."⁵⁶ This inhuman disconnection from other people reaches three crescendos late in the book, first when Ahab levels a musket at the first mate, Starbuck; then when he brandishes the diabolical harpoon against his own crew; and finally when he refuses to help the captain of another whaling ship, the *Rachel*, search for his missing son.⁵⁷ All of these are images of violence and hatred that could be appropriately—if not effectually or healthily— directed toward Moby Dick but are instead directed at his fellow human beings, his comrades in his quest to destroy the White Whale and lay their complaints before the Deity. Although at one time Ahab had "his humanities," he has completely lost them by now, subordinated them to his hate for the White Whale/God, "horribly amputated himself from human feelings."⁵⁸ Indeed, with further tragic irony, Ahab has made himself into the very image of the cold, unfeeling, arbitrary tyrant whom he accuses God of being.⁵⁹

Ishmael, on the other hand, focuses on the common lot of all humanity, as painful and meager as this might be, and it fills him with a feeling of compassionate pride in his race, so that "over any ignominious blemish in [a man] all his fellows should run to throw their costliest robes."⁶⁰ This pride in humanity, despite their seeming undeservingness, is shown also in Ishmael's description of the ship's carpenter. Right after writing that "mankind in mass . . . seem[s] a mob of unnecessary duplicates," Ishmael immediately and categorically asserts that the carpenter "was no duplicate."⁶¹ While Ahab fits everyone interchangeably into his quest and treats them in a way that ignores their humanity and individuality, Ishmael is completely aware of everyone's uniqueness as well as their participation in a common human nature, and analyzing both of these qualities in everyone on board the *Pequod* is *his* quest. Ishmael not only appreciates others' humble greatness, he also comes to appreciate and then to love his connectedness to them, as shown in two incidents in the processing of the whale. First, there is the "monkey-rope,"[62] a rope tied between Ishmael and his friend Queequeg as the latter is lowered over the side of the ship to insert the blubber-hook into the flesh of the dead whale. It is a lifeline to assist the man who is overboard, but Ishmael comes to understand the darker implications for the man on board, who must share in the other's fate, a daunting thought that Ishmael generalizes to all human relations: "I saw that this situation of mine was the precise situation of every mortal that breathes; only, in most cases, he, one way or other, has this Siamese connexion with a plurality of other mortals."[63] Although Ishmael is at first frightened by this connectedness, another incident shows him a more positive aspect of it. As Ishmael and other crewmen dip their hands into the oily spermaceti to reliquefy it after it has partly coagulated, Ishmael drifts into dreams of complete human melding and love: "Come; let us squeeze hands all round; nay, let us all squeeze ourselves into each other; let us squeeze ourselves universally into the very milk and sperm of kindness."[64] Ishmael has learned to regard everyone with "Stoic endurance, New Testament and democratic equality in suffering and slavery, fellow-feeling and mutual help," thereby opening him up to "the emollient effect of shared suffering, of mankind full of sweet things of love and gratitude."[65] While "mortal inter-indebtedness"[66] drives Ahab mad, it fills Ishmael with joy and awe.

Melville shows the human condition as the greatness of a lost state that tantalizes and plagues us with its memory and will not leave us in the relative peace of distractions that would allow us some relief from our wretchedness: "Ahab's effort, then, is to reclaim something that man knows he has lost."[67] This concept of human nature is repeatedly shown in Melville's novel, with Ahab's consciousness of his wretchedness and the generalization of this realization to all humanity; with Ahab's superiority to the physical world, even though it can (and does) easily destroy him; and in Ishmael's discovery of the human dignity placed by God equally in all but especially noticed in the most humble.

Melville's Use of Job

Like everything else in his masterpiece, Melville's use of Scripture in *Moby-Dick* is conspicuous and overwhelming and at the same time ambiguous and elusive: "Melville was a great biblical unscriptural writer. Anything may be, indeed the rule of the reader's road is to expect it, inverted, pulled inside out, torn down, and reconstructed into its mirror opposite. In Melville's hands anything may happen to the biblical—almost certainly will."[68] This is perhaps best illustrated by the continuing debate over the most explicit use of Scripture in the novel, Father Mapple's New Bedford sermon to whalers and their families. Does Melville present it only in order to use it as "a sarcastic and sneering burlesque of Christian doctrine,"[69] or is Melville in fact expressing the "essence" of his work "through the lips of Father Mapple,"[70] and if he is, is his teaching Christian or utterly "pagan"?[71] But while the most explicit and ambiguous instance of his use of Scripture is Father Mapple's sermon on Jonah, Melville's use of the biblical Wisdom literature—especially the book of Job—more clearly coincides with his own anthropological and theological reflections.[72]

Melville's first evocation of the book of Job is in the character of Bildad, one of the ship's owners, named after one of Job's "friends." Like his namesake, he possesses a fierce but inhumane piety that takes little notice of the suffering of others: "For a pious man, especially for a Quaker, he was certainly rather hard-hearted, to say the least."[73] He lifts his face from studying the Scriptures and turns immediately to trying to pay Ishmael as little as possible for the voyage. But in the antics that follow between him and the oppositely natured Peleg, who is something of a joker and a cutup, Melville shows his typical wry humor, turning the most self-righteous character from the most sober biblical book into a figure of amusement.

Melville evokes the book of Job in the critical chapter that bears the same name as the entire novel: "Here, then, was this grey-headed, ungodly old man, chasing with curses a Job's whale round the world."[74] He signals thereby that we are to think of Moby Dick as the Leviathan from the book of Job.[75] He is anything but "a dumb brute," as the sincere but inadequate piety of Starbuck, the chief mate, labels him.[76] On the other hand, everything that Ahab says about Moby Dick is accurate, if incomplete. The White Whale is the evil that God allows (or perhaps even creates), and Moby Dick/Leviathan's existence implicates God in all the evil and suffering of the world.[77] He is, for many readers of the novel, God himself,[78] an identification Ahab puts forth, though he thinks his quest is the same regardless: "I see in him outrageous strength, with an inscrutable malice sinewing it. That inscrutable thing is chiefly what I hate; and be the white whale agent, or be the white whale principal, I will wreak that hate upon him."[79] Job could finally accept the existence of awesome, unexplainable evil and pain in the world, but Ahab cannot. Nor can he destroy it, but in the end even this goal is abandoned. At the height of his power, Ahab gives his own theology its clearest expression: "I now know thee, thou clear spirit, and I now know that thy right worship is defiance. To neither love nor reverence wilt thou be kind; and e'en for hate thou canst but kill; and all are killed."[80] Ahab cannot worship God, nor does he expect an answer from God, nor does he think he can destroy either God or God's "agent," evil; he simply defies God to do anything to him other than kill him, a prospect that in no way frightens him.[81]

Equally defiant but much less insightful is the version of Job given by Stubb, the second mate, who is as indifferent and carefree as ever. After giving his retelling of the Biblical story, Stubb responds to the objections of Flask, the ever-practical third mate, that Stubb could not hope to toss the devil overboard:

> Damn the devil, Flask; do you suppose I'm afraid of the devil? Who's afraid of him, except the old governor who daresn't catch him and put him in double-darbies, as he deserves, but lets him go about kidnapping people; aye, and signed a bond with him, that all the people the devil kidnapped, he'd roast for him? There's a governor![82]

Stubb has neither respect nor fear for God, the devil, the whale, or anything else in creation; everything is equally irrelevant and empty for him. He cannot even bend things to his own materialistic view, the way the less intelligent Flask can, for Stubb senses something more is there but chooses to dismiss it with a shrug; his ignorance is willful. After one of Ishmael's deepest reflections on human meaning, he characterizes this dismissive outlook of Stubb's as less than human, "fish-like.... always... jolly," and Ahab dismisses him as "soulless."[83] Melville has little sympathy for those who are "always jolly," and he cannot be presenting Stubb's viewpoint for anything other than ridicule as part of the pathetic absurdity of pusillanimous human pride and folly.[84] Shortly after Stubb's retelling of Job, however, Melville does present Stubb's prosaic or debased estimation of the whale's power as partially correct by quoting Job 41:7, 26–29, "Canst thou fill his skin with barbed irons? or his head with fish-spears?"[85] Even nineteenth-century technology had rendered these questions rhetorical in the opposite way that they had been for the author of Job, for men now did just those things to whales all over the world every day. But in the overall context of the novel, such an estimation of God's creation is completely inaccurate, and Melville never foresees a time when it will not be so: "However baby man may brag of his science and skill . . . yet for ever and for ever, to the crack of doom, the sea will insult and murder him."[86] Even the body of the slain whale itself is a reminder of the awful wonder of the world and the feebleness of human attempts to destroy, control, or understand it. Within a whale's carcass they find a spearhead that Ishmael speculates is over four hundred years old, meaning that generations of men have died trying to kill just this one whale, a sobering testimony to how much the "governor" of this world demands respect and fear, if not love: "*Moby-Dick*, like Job, affirms the mystery of the sacred, beyond the human capacity to comprehend."[87] It is beyond our ability to comprehend, but nothing is beyond humans' ability to ignore and disrespect, capacities epitomized in Stubb.

Closer to Job's acceptance is the position of Queequeg, the pagan harpooner who befriends Ishmael. Queequeg by no means overlooks or approves of the brutality of God's world, but he also does not question or defy it. He simply describes it in his matter-of-fact way: "Queequeg no care what god made him shark . . . wedder Fejee god or Nantucket god; but de god what made shark must be one dam Injin."[88] As we saw with Job, acceptance of evil does not mean the approval of evil. And as Job can know and trust God after all the terrible revelations of his story, Queequeg's admission of divine malice and inscrutability never keeps him from devoutly and innocently worshiping his own little god, Yojo, nor does it keep him from calmly listening to the preaching of the "Nantucket god" at the Whaleman's Chapel, nor does it keep him from being a permanent member of "the great and everlasting First Congregation of this whole worshipping world."[89] In fact, it never troubles him in the least, for he is always "entirely at his ease; preserving the utmost serenity."[90] He is "always serene in a furious world," possessed of a "wisdom . . . that saves the innocence of Ishmael."[91] Again, this is neither naivete nor pious rationalization of God's silent brutality, but rather a calm and vitalizing acceptance and awe of it.

Job is evoked again at the very end of the novel, as Ishmael refers to himself with the same verses that the four messengers in Job give after they each report their respective disasters: "And I only am escaped alone to tell thee."[92] The encounter with God in the book of Job very nearly destroys Job, physically and spiritually, but he can finally confront the voice in the whirlwind with "wise ignorance" and withdraw his demand for a divine accounting and explanation. This does not, I think, deny the legitimacy of such a request (again, the middle of the book seems a colossal waste of time if this is the message) but only brackets it as a question whose necessity and inevitability we must accept, and whose unanswerability we also must accept if we are to remain either faithful or sane. Like Queequeg's tattoos, which supposedly reveal the meaning of the universe, such a question captivates everyone but remains forever undecipherable, a "tantalization of the gods."[93] But the encounter with the White Whale/God is fatal to the captain and crew of the *Pequod*, for they continue to demand an answer up to their final breath, up to the final, spiteful swing of Tashtego's hammer that smashes and pins the taunting sea hawk to the mast and so "sink[s] to hell . . . dragg[ing] a living part of heaven along with her."[94]

Significantly, Ahab's final confrontation is not with a whirlwind descending from above but with the diabolical inversion of it, as the *Pequod* and all aboard are dragged down by a silent, "sullen" whirlpool, a "closing vortex"[95] that silences their protest forever. In a way, Melville outdoes the author of Job in his depiction of the outrageousness of faith: Not only must one accept a God who cannot offer an account of himself and his arbitrary, violent, cruel creation, one must accept a God who remains utterly silent and who jealously guards his silence by destroying those who dare to question him.[96] Significantly, though, Melville does offer us one character who can survive the encounter the way Job did, for Ishmael is preserved to learn something from the terrible voyage of the *Pequod:* "This unique salvation of Ishmael is essential to the theme of the novel. He alone of those on the *Pequod* has faced with the courage of humility the facts of his universe; he alone has learned to know woe without becoming mad."[97] In Melville's theology, suicidal defiance is certainly an understandable reaction to the pain of existence, but it is not the only or necessary reaction. Ahab's defiance has meaning not only to him but also, in a far different and life-giving way, to Ishmael: "In the Christ story, the experience of death and rebirth is expressed in one figure.... Moses and Joshua also represent the same figure, divided into two, as do ... Ahab and Ishmael. Where the experience is split, one character suffers and dies and a separate character benefits by his sacrifice."[98]

Without forcing Melville into orthodoxy with Pascal, even the Adam/Christ typology is not wholly absent from *Moby-Dick* in the figure of Queequeg. Clearly he is the antithesis to the industrialized, white characters and their rationalizing madness that is typified in Ahab: "Opposite to Queequeg, [Ahab] is a gigantic symbol of the sickness of the self, the disease of the egoist-absolutist of Christendom. If immortal health shines in the dying Queequeg, then mortal illness festers in Ahab."[99] Queequeg possesses a "simple honest heart"[100] and bears within himself the remnants of an innocent and more vital physical and spiritual state, from which the other characters have fallen much further than he.[101] He is more like Adam, more like God's original creation, than anyone else on board the ship, which is itself a microcosm of the world.[102] And without forcing Queequeg into the role of a Christ figure, it is clear that he is Christlike in many ways: "It is Queequeg, the nonwhite, non-Christian South Sea islander, who embodies Jesus' message of love when he offers to die for Ishmael if need be and divides his 'thirty dollars in silver' with him, reversing Judas' betrayal."[103] He repeatedly saves people in increasingly dramatic, yet nonchalant, scenes: first by diving overboard into the icy Atlantic waters to save the "greenhorn" who had been insulting him a moment before;[104] and then by diving into the water to carve his fellow harpooner Tashtego out of a severed whale's head in which he is trapped, sinking to the bottom, drowning in a sweet and deadly container that Melville specifically compares to a womb, a tomb, and the inner sanctum of the temple.[105] Throughout the book, his presence is redemptive to the receptive acolyte Ishmael (who refers to himself as Queequeg's "attendant or page," as well as his "wife"), starting with their first encounter: "I felt a melting in me. No more my splintered heart and maddened hand were turned against the wolfish world. This soothing savage had redeemed it."[106] By defying society and making Queequeg his friend, Ishmael is forever less of an "Isolato,"[107] for he has permanently adopted Queequeg's more wholesome and healthy state of love and acceptance.[108] Queequeg's redemption of Ishmael continues to the end of the book, as his coffin saves the narrator, who floats safely upon it after all the rest of the *Pequod*'s crew have been killed by Moby Dick: "Here in the broad watercourses, the illimitable solitudes traversed by Ahab, where God's predatory sharks and menacing hawks could have ripped this lone survivor in pieces, it is the sustaining influence of Queequeg that protects Ishmael. . . . Now in his loneliest hour Ishmael is redeemed again with the peace of that same Queequeg."[109] And as Adam and Christ remain forever incomprehensible for Pascal, so does Queequeg remain for Ishmael, who can only gaze at him in "awe," just as he gazes in amazement at the stupefied predators of God's deep at the end of the book, held at bay by some vital force still emanating from Queequeg's "immortality-preserver."[110] Ishmael has learned quite vividly the lessons of Job, and he can only gratefully accept, but not comprehend, the redemption that his Christlike friend Queequeg has brought to him.

The Inadequacy and Use of Reason in Melville

Melville of course does not give an explicit treatment of the role of reason in his novel, but he leaves hints of Ahab's and Ishmael's attitudes toward it. Ahab's quest—to destroy the White Whale/God who has insulted and maimed him—clearly comes from the heart, not from reason: "He piled upon the whale's white hump the sum of all the general rage felt by his whole race from Adam down; and then, as if his chest had been a mortar, he burst his hot heart's shell upon it."[111] But neither is his quest incompatible with reason: "Now, in his heart, Ahab had some glimpse of this, namely: all my means are sane, my motive and my object mad."[112] Nor can reason object to or change his goals, as shown by the impotency of Starbuck to stop him: "But he . . . blasted all my reason out of me!"[113] But Ahab needs reason to accomplish his goal, and Ishmael reminds us that finding "one solitary creature in the unhooped oceans of this planet"[114] might be mad, but it is not impractical. With planning and precision it could be carried out with a reasonable expectation of success, and Ishmael shows us Ahab poring over his charts and maps, using all his reason to further his mad quest. Continuing the martial image, Ishmael sees Ahab's reason as providing more firepower to his heart's artillery: "Not one jot of his great natural intellect had perished. . . . [H]is special lunacy stormed his general sanity, and carried it, and turned all its concentred cannon upon its own mad mark; . . . Ahab, to that one end, did now possess a thousand fold more potency than ever he had sanely brought to bear upon any one reasonable object."[115] Although self-destructive from a Pascalian point of view, Ahab's quest is not disordered in its relation to reason, nor can it be thought of as empty, meaningless, or inhuman. It is not a diversion but a profound realization and actualization of Ahab's vision, in which he finds purpose and dignity, though clearly not happiness.

But if Ahab begins his quest by using reason to further his heart's goal, he ends in a quite different state. When Ahab is at the height of his power, Melville seems quite deliberate in depicting him as going against reason, as attacking it in himself and in the world, the way he had attacked and overwhelmed Starbuck's at the beginning of the journey. Whereas previously he had used the tools of navigation, he now smashes the quadrant, so they henceforth have no idea where on the planet they are: "Science! Curse thee, thou vain toy; and cursed be all the things that cast man's eyes aloft to that heaven, whose live vividness but scorches him. . . . Curse thee, thou quadrant!"[116] Significantly, the diabolical Fedallah (the harpooner of Ahab's boat) sneers approvingly at Ahab's assault on reason. And like Faust, Ahab turns from science to magic, forging a supernatural harpoon to destroy his supernatural enemy, blasphemously baptizing the iron in human blood.[117] But Ahab's magical manipulations seem to be done mostly to mesmerize and control the credulous crew. For when presented with his real, divine opponent, Ahab turns to sheer willpower. As they fly against the wind into a raging typhoon, all sails torn from the masts, one of the boats smashed against the side of the ship, lightning repeatedly striking the bare masts, men hanging helplessly from the rigging, Ahab emerges on deck to shout down the fury of the storm. This time there are no incantations, just raw will and defiance: "To neither love nor reverence wilt thou be kind; and e'en for hate thou canst but kill; and all are killed. . . . I own thy speechless, placeless power; but to the last gasp of my earthquake life will dispute its unconditional, unintegral mastery in me."[118] Ahab dares God to kill him. Ahab stares down God, and God blinks. While others seek, usually unsuccessfully, to tame nature and understand God through reason, Ahab is successful at it through sheer will and the denial of reason.

But these temporary supernatural powers come at an enormous price. While Pascal's submission of reason leads to the opening up of the heart to others and to God, Ahab's attack on reason and his inhuman will shuts him off from every other human being. Immediately following his superhuman commanding of the storm, Ahab turns the harpoon against his own crew: "Ahab, unlike Lear, does not in this night of storm discover his love for his fellow wretches. . . . He commits the greater blasphemy than defiance of sun and lightning. He turns the harpoon, forged and baptized for the inhuman Whale alone, upon his own human companions."[119] Pulled from the water after nearly being killed by Moby Dick, Ahab is not grateful to his shipmates: "Begone! . . . Ahab stands alone among the millions of the peopled earth, nor gods nor men his neighbors!"[120] It is this detached, objectifying, dehumanizing treatment of others that is Ahab's evil side and his doom, not his challenging of the Deity. In the following chapters, in the most heartbreaking scenes of the book, Ahab is repeatedly tempted to abandon his mad quest by his love for Starbuck and for the little African-American cabin boy Pip: "Thou touchest my inmost centre, boy; thou art tied to me by cords woven of my heart-strings"; "Close! Stand close to me, Starbuck; let me look into a human eye; it is better than to gaze into sea or sky; better than to gaze upon God."[121] We find only now that the eloquence of the captain of the *Pequod* expresses love just as beautifully as it does hate. But Ahab manages to conquer the power of these humbling, human feelings just as he did the power of the humbling, divine storm—through sheer, inhuman will. But even this awesomely powerful will finally undoes itself, for in the end, Ahab is no longer in control: "Fool! I am the Fates' lieutenant; I act under orders."[122] Ahab has not conquered anything; he has surrendered his will, himself, and his crew to an inhuman Fate, robbing them of freedom and making them all "mechanical."[123] Unlike the infinite possibilities and freedom that Ishmael sees in an ocean voyage, Ahab's voyage is like a runaway locomotive, locked on to one path only, unstoppable and no longer under his control: "The path to my fixed purpose is laid with iron rails, whereon my soul is grooved to run. . . . Naught's an obstacle, naught's an angle to the iron way!"[124] By spurning both reason and feeling in favor of an all-powerful will, Ahab finally loses all three, dehumanizing himself and his quest into a soulless clash of forces. When Moby Dick and the *Pequod* finally collide, it might as well be a meteor crashing into a planet, for now both truly are "dumb brute[s],"[125] and both have become such by Ahab's awful, fatal choice.[126]

Ahab's madness and self-destruction come about by his exclusive focus on himself, an imploding, inhuman solipsism. But it is worth considering Pip's madness, for it comes from the opposite experience of losing himself, drifting outward and never returning. One day Pip falls overboard while they are being dragged by a stricken whale, and the boat is dragged far out of sight, leaving the frightened boy alone on the deep, where he is granted a most amazing and awful revelation:

> [T]he miser-merman, Wisdom, revealed his hoarded heaps; and among the joyous, heartless, ever-juvenile eternities, Pip saw the multitudinous, God-omnipresent, coral insects, that out of the firmament of waters heaved the colossal orbs. He saw God's foot upon the treadle of the loom, and spoke it; and therefore his shipmates called him mad.[127]

Ahab himself diagnoses the two kinds of madness in himself and Pip: "True art thou, lad, as the circumference to its centre."[128] The Manxman who sees Ahab with Pip also sees their madnesses as complementary: "There go two daft ones now.... One daft with strength, the other daft with weakness."[129] Ahab looked within and saw so much pain that no one else's pain would ever matter to him again. Pip looked outward and saw so much beauty and mystery that his own self was lost, unimportant to him from then on, dwarfed and eclipsed by the grandeur of creation.

It is here that we can bring in Ishmael as the final contrast and piece to the puzzle. As we will see in the next section of this chapter, Pip's vision is remarkably similar to one earlier granted to Ishmael, and being lost alone at sea is also similar to Ishmael's experience at the end of the novel, but Ishmael does not go mad. After his revelation, Pip refers to himself only in the third person, while Ishmael can refer to himself in both third and first person:[130] Ishmael has held on to a sense of self and particularity without falling into Ahab's solipsism. Does this healthier attitude have anything to do with a different use of reason by Ishmael? Again, the evidence would be indirect, but I think yes. It certainly has a great deal to do with something most often associated with reason—language, which otherwise seems to be depicted as a huge failure in the novel: "In *Moby-Dick* dialogue itself leaves cinders in the mouth of advocates of reason."[131] It is Ishmael's telling of his story that both keeps him sane and keeps him connected to and concerned with other people: "To survive one must turn away from the real world toward the 'thoughts and fancies' of an imaginative one.... [T]he narrator's language and the truth which lurks behind it put him in touch with other men. His self-conscious lies ... keep the heavens from falling and provide the first link in the chain of conversation which binds men together."[132] Even if he had survived, it is impossible to imagine Ahab writing anything similar to a reading world of "blockheads" or "poltroon[s]":[133] What could they ever understand of his pain or his quest? And what does Ishmael tell us in his tale? He famously tells us minute, scientific details of the physiology and habits of whales and the many steps taken to kill and process their bodies. A rational understanding of the facts and figures of whales—and by implication, the God who created Leviathans—fascinates Ishmael—not for mere profit, as with Flask; not out of habit, as with Stubb; not for family tradition, as with Starbuck; and not for an inward obsession, as with Ahab—but for an outward-directed curiosity toward God's creation that is typical of reason. In what must partly be a spoof of this scientific rigor, the diligent Ishmael has even had the measurements of a whale skeleton he saw on a South Seas island tattooed on his arm.[134] With the inquisitiveness of reason, Ishmael has avoided Ahab's solipsism, just as with his imagination and feeling he has avoided Ahab's fatalism, for Ishmael strongly asserts the power as well as the limitation of his free will: "I ply my own shuttle and weave my own destiny into these unalterable threads. . . . [A]ye, chance, free will, and necessity—no wise incompatible—all interweavingly working together."[135]

It would seem fair to say that in the characters of Ahab and Ishmael we can see a literary illustration of Melville's ideas of the role of reason in human life. By Ahab's self-destruction and Ishmael's renewal and redemption, we can see that reason is a necessary part of living a meaningful and fulfilling life, a life that investigates and embraces the mysteries of life, loves and is open to others, and understands the limitations and potentials of oneself.

Feminine Imagery in *Moby-Dick:* Beyond God the Father

Please excuse me if this section seems nearly oxymoronic: There are only two female characters in the book—Aunt Charity, who helps provision the ship, and Mrs. Hosea Hussey, at whose inn Ishmael stays in Nantucket—and both of these are left behind when the men take to sea. The book is about as masculine, indeed, phallic, as one can get. Besides the title, there is Chapter 95, "The Cassock," on the whale's enormous penis, and the overall action of the novel, in which brawny men take to sea for three years at a time to stab their harpoons into giant sea creatures, which are themselves phallic-looking. There would seem to be little room in this imagistic world for anything remotely feminine, but as usual with the novel, there is "the little lower layer,"[136] the unexpected meaning behind the obvious and misleading surface meaning. And in *Moby-Dick,* this world behind the mask is at several crucial points in the book feminine.

It is in chapter 87, "The Grand Armada," that Ishmael receives a salvific vision of creation and a reconciliation to it. Their boat has been dragged into the center of an enormous shoal of whales. In this center, they are surrounded by female and baby whales, so surrounded that they dare not attack the whales, lest the animals' sudden, violent motions swamp or crush the boat. And then they gaze down into the water:

> But far beneath this wondrous world upon the surface, another and still stranger world met our eyes as we gazed over the side. For, suspended in those watery vaults, floated the forms of the nursing mothers of the whales. . . . [A]s human infants while suckling will calmly and fixedly gaze away from the breast, as if leading two different lives at the time; and while yet drawing mortal nourishment, be still spiritually feasting upon some unearthly reminiscence;—even so did the young of these whales seem looking up towards us, but not at us. . . . Starbuck saw long coils of the umbilical cord of Madame Leviathan, by which the young cub seemed still

tethered to its dam. . . . Some of the subtlest secrets of the seas seemed divulged to us in this enchanted pond. We saw young Leviathan amours in the deep.[137]

Here is a vision of the ocean and of Leviathan far more peaceful and life-giving than either Job's or Pip's, and it is thoroughly, overwhelmingly feminine. For one of the few times in the novel, removed from the influence of Ahab's solipsistic madness and the industrialized brutality of the whaling industry, the ocean is not a cannibalistic hell that would vie with the horrors of Dante but an aquatic vision of heaven that overwhelms these men with a combination of maternal and sexual love that can never be forgotten, no matter what atrocities they go on to witness or perpetrate. It takes Ahab's self-destructive confrontation and transforms it into Job's confrontational acceptance. The scene is still confrontational, in that these men have madly journeyed halfway around the globe to ask the kinds of questions and hunt the kinds of animals that normal people think better left alone: "But as in landlessness alone resides the highest truth, shoreless, indefinite as God—so, better is it to perish in that howling infinite, than be ingloriously dashed upon the lee, even if that were safety!"[138] But their vision is also accepting, in that they put down their harpoons when the answer is unexpectedly before them and the animals they hunt as murderous monsters turn suddenly into gentle mothers and lovers. Significantly, neither the monomaniac Ahab, nor the diabolical Fedallah, nor the unconcerned Stubb, nor the shallow Flask are privy to this revelation, but only the pious Starbuck, the virtuous Queequeg, and the curious and receptive Ishmael. Only these men on board the *Pequod* possess the wisdom to see and accept the feminine side of these creatures and, by implication, of the Creator who made them.

It is explicitly the feminine side of God or nature that even Ahab is granted a momentary vision of in chapter 132, "The Symphony":

But the lovely aromas in that enchanted air did at last seem to dispel, for a moment, the cankerous thing in his soul. That glad, happy air, that winsome sky, did at last stroke and caress him; the step-mother world, so long cruel—forbidding—now threw affectionate arms round his stubborn neck, and did seem to joyously sob over him, as if over one, that however wilful and erring, she could yet find it in her heart to save and to bless.[139]

Here is that aspect of the divine that can "save and . . . bless," and it is not the stern, arbitrary God the Father whom Ahab hates and hunts throughout the rest of the novel, but rather an inconsistent "step-mother," who can be both "cruel" and "affectionate."[140] In a similar way, it is when he sees himself as a kind, loving father to Pip that Ahab almost relents in his cursed quest, for it is only then that he can briefly glimpse a world "full of the sweet things of love and gratitude."[141] But these glimpses of happiness are momentary for Ahab, because he can will himself to stop seeing them. He can wilfully ignore the goodness of God, nature, or himself. And tragically, by ignoring the goodness of these things, they become just as evil as Ahab thought they were all along: "Nor did such soothing scenes, however temporary, fail of at least as temporary an effect on Ahab. But if these secret golden keys did seem to open in him his own secret golden treasuries, yet did his breath upon them prove but tarnishing."[142]

The step-mother image is transformed into a natural, maternal image at two other important points. One is when everyone on board the *Pequod* seems granted a momentary vision of peace and joy on the deep, but ends with Ishmael's morbid rumination, "Our souls are like those orphans whose unwedded mothers die in bearing them: the secret of our paternity lies in their grave, and we must there to learn it."[143] Full knowledge of God and our origins will never be achieved in this life, for we are as separated from them as an orphan from her mother. But the final invocation of this image is certainly more hopeful. It is the last line of the novel, as the lost Ishmael, floating alone on Queequeg's coffin, is found by another ship: "It was the devious-cruising Rachel, that in her retracing search after her missing children, only found another orphan."[144] Here the mother is able to find the orphan and save him, the way the "step-mother" world could not save Ahab. And here the sadness is on both sides: The mother mourns the loss of her children, while Ishmael the orphan painfully wonders about the identity of his lost parents and mourns the loss of all his shipmates. But amid this mutual pain, they are able to offer each other some comfort and love.

It is these two haunting images together—of the dead mother and unknown father we will never know in this life and of the orphan being found unexpectedly by the grieving mother—that I think explain Ishmael's use of feminine images. In a way quite similar to the books we examined in Chapter 2, Melville powerfully gives us female, maternal images that balance or even overcome the masculine, paternal images that Christians usually associate with God. We long not for the stifling domesticity that Ishmael flees at the beginning of the novel (and, apparently, repeatedly since), nor for the judgmental, absent Father God whom Ahab seeks ineffectually and self-destructively to destroy; the stereotypical expressions of gender—either in ourselves or in our concept of God—destroy us at either extreme. Melville believes that what we long for is much more mysterious. We long for a Mother and Father we have never known but whom we desperately long to know; and we believe that, in the case of our Mother at least, she loves and accepts us, and we hope and trust that she is searching for us, just as we are searching for her. This I think is one of the strange and beautiful lessons

Ishmael has learned from Ahab's madness. God is indeed absent and frustrating, just as Ahab thought, but not like a Father whom you blame for his lack of responsibility and caring, but like a Mother who once bore you within herself and, no matter what has happened since, wants you back. Without forcing this divine Mother into conformity either with the Old Testament's Sophia or with the New Testament's Mary or Jesus,[145] it is clear that Ishmael's salvation is possible in part because of his ability to see and appreciate a feminine side to God and himself, a vision of which the monomaniac Ahab is incapable.

Conclusion: Wisdom in the Encounter with God

For the final word on Ishmael's experience of wisdom and God, I think we should look elsewhere than his physical redemption at the end of the book, since, after all, his life is not very much redeemed if he has been physically saved from the marine variety of sharks only to return to the terrestrial world of the bipedal variety.[146] Earlier in the novel, everyone in Ishmael's boat gazes down through the water to see the deepest, most life-giving secrets of God's creation. It is this vision that results in Ishmael's mental and spiritual redemption:

> And thus, though surrounded by circle upon circle of consternations and affrights, did these inscrutable creatures at the centre freely and fearlessly indulge in all peaceful concernments; yea, serenely revelled in dalliance and delight. But even so, amid the tornadoed Atlantic of my being, do I myself still for ever centrally disport in mute calm; and while ponderous planets of unwaning woe revolve round me, deep down and deep inland there I still bathe me in eternal mildness of joy.[147]

Approached with the defiance of Ahab's egoism, God's world is a silencing and annihilating vortex that drags one into its center, which is oblivion, nothingness.[148] But approached with Ishmael's innocent receptivity, his "insatiable wonder at his world,"[149] together with the simple, loving, and redemptive wisdom of his friend Queequeg, the "unwaning woe" of life becomes the storm that forever revolves around one but can never harm or change a secret, impervious center of "eternal joy," a human heart finally at peace.[150]

With this vision, Ishmael has overcome the land/sea dichotomy that drove him to sea on the first page of the novel, for he is now and forevermore both in an "enchanted pool," which is itself in the middle of the ocean, and "deep inland." Surely it is this joyous equanimity that has allowed him to return repeatedly to the sea and its "unwaning woe" even after his experiences on board the *Pequod*.[151] It also empowers and even demands that he tell his story, over and over again, so that others can also learn the truths he saw on the deep.[152] Furthermore, he has overcome and inverted the potential self-centeredness of all knowledge that he mentioned in the first chapter and that he saw epitomized throughout the novel in Ahab's solipsism—the tendency to see only the self reflected everywhere, for he no longer sees "that same image [of himself] . . . in all rivers and oceans,"[153] but he now sees the ocean within himself. The "wisdom that is woe" has been neither forgotten nor ignored, but it has become a wisdom that allows Ishmael finally to be redeemed by and reconciled to God and God's creation: "He has seen that, although the whale and the creation must remain unsolved to the last, the creation is plenteous, that it contains those radiant moments, abundant with spirit, which are redemptive. . . . [T]his response issues in the deepest kind of reconciliation with the terms of experience."[154] While this reconciliation may not be uniquely or necessarily Christian, it is nonetheless compatible with and, indeed, essential to Pascal's view of Christianity: "To become a Christian will involve not so much acceptance by the intellect . . . of a certain set of beliefs, as a surrender of the whole personality to something . . . greater than the personality itself. It will be . . . proved by the reality of the experience which the surrender will involve."[155] Ishmael's experience seems profoundly real, as fantastic as his voyage has been, for he finally has the happiness, the anchoring centeredness and rest that Pascal knew all people desperately longed for but could never achieve through self-centered and self-destructive activity but only through the wisdom of acceptance, humility, and love: "With wisdom comes inner peace, and with peace, true happiness."[156]

Notes

1. R. B. Y. Scott, *The Way of Wisdom in the Old Testament* (New York: Macmillan, 1971), 138.
2. On the composition, see G. von Rad, *Wisdom in Israel* (trans. J. D. Martin; Nashville: Abingdon Press, 1972), 207–9; Scott, *Way of Wisdom*, 147–52.
3. J. L. Crenshaw, *Old Testament Wisdom: An Introduction* (Atlanta: John Knox Press, 1981), 110.
4. R. E. Murphy, *The Tree of Life: An Exploration of Biblical Wisdom Literature* (2d ed.; Grand Rapids: Eerdmans, 1990), 45, quoting David N. Freedman.
5. Ibid., 43, quoting G. K. Chesterton.
6. Crenshaw, *Old Testament Wisdom*, 110–11.
7. Scott, *Way of Wisdom*, 161–62.
8. Murphy, *Tree of Life*, 46, quoting C. R. Seitz.
9. Ibid., 43.
10. Ibid.
11. Crenshaw, *Old Testament Wisdom*, 115.

12. E. Wiesel, *The Trial of God* (trans. M. Wiesel; New York: Schocken Books, 1979).

13. Despite his procreative activities, it has often been concluded that Melville was homosexual, and his works glorify erotic love between men; see the brief summary in M. L. Taylor, "Ishmael's (m)Other: Gender, Jesus, and God in Melville's *Moby-Dick*," *Journal of Religion* 72 (1992): 325–50, esp. 343–45, with bibliography. I cannot decide such an issue of literary history: I will just leave it as another perfect example of his rich and suggestive ambiguity that people cannot even decide on his sexual orientation.

14. For the history of the reception of Melville's work, see K. McSweeney, *Moby-Dick: Ishmael's Mighty Book* (Boston: Twayne Publishers, 1986), 13–22.

15. A. Lebowitz, *Progress into Silence: A Study of Melville's Heroes* (Bloomington: Indiana University Press, 1970), 3.

16. Read in its entirety, the novel actually contains very little suspense; as early as chapter 13, "Wheelbarrow," p. 61, we know that Queequeg will not survive; by chapter 27, "Knights and Squires," p. 108, we know the same fate awaits the rest of the crew. All references to *Moby-Dick* are to the Norton Critical Edition: *Moby-Dick* (ed. H. Hayford and H. Parker; New York: W. W. Norton, 1967). All subsequent page references are to this edition. Although we know the crew is doomed, I still will myself to believe that they might kill Moby Dick every time I read the novel.

17. Cf. R. Slotkin, "*Moby-Dick:* The American National Epic," in *Twentieth Century Interpretations of Moby-Dick: A Collection of Critical Essays* (ed. M. T. Gilmore; Englewood Cliffs, N.J.: Prentice-Hall, 1977), 25, who concludes that Ahab is "the true American hero," though one whose "quest [is] fraught with complex ironies." The very next essay in the same collection, however, concludes that it is Ishmael who is the hero, and the novel is written against Ahab as the epitome of American individualism and alienation: H. N. Smith, "The Image of Society in *Moby-Dick*," in *Twentieth Century Interpretations of Moby-Dick: A Collection of Critical Essays* (ed. M. T. Gilmore; Englewood Cliffs, N.J.: Prentice-Hall, 1977), 27–41. J. Markels, *Melville and the Politics of Identity: From* King Lear *to* Moby Dick (Urbana: University of Illinois Press, 1993), makes a similar identification.

18. For an example, see R. Zoellner, "Queequeg: The Well-Governed Shark," in *Twentieth Century Interpretations of Moby-Dick: A Collection of Critical Essays* (ed. M. T. Gilmore; Englewood Cliffs, N.J.: Prentice-Hall, 1977), 87–93.

19. Melville's letter to Hawthorne, 17 November 1851, found in the excellent material that follows the actual text in the Norton Edition, *Moby-Dick,* 566. Cf. H. A. Murray, "In Nomine Diaboli," in *Moby-Dick: Centennial Essays* (ed. T. Hillway and L. S. Mansfield; Dallas: Southern Methodist University Press, 1953), 9: "The implication is clear: all interpretations which fail to show that *Moby-Dick* is, in some sense, wicked have missed the author's avowed intention."

20. Melville, *Moby-Dick,* chap. 133, "The Chase—First Day," 448.

21. Ibid., chap. 99, "The Doubloon," 358.

22. Cf. D. S. Arnold, "'But the Draught of a Draught': Reading the Wonder of Ishmael's Telling," *Semeia* 31 (1985): 181: "But of course the reader is seized by other presentations, where he experiences, together with Ishmael, how concrete images, placed in a rich atmosphere, add on to one another, and grow to the point whereby meaning transcends mere 'factuality' and enters the realm of the symbolic.... All experience, we learn, is multiple for Ishmael."

23. This repetition is analyzed from the standpoint of compositional layers by H. Hayford, "Unnecessary Duplicates: A Key to the Writing of *Moby-Dick*," in *New Perspectives on Melville* (ed. F. Pullin; Kent, Ohio: Kent State University Press, 1978), 128–61.

24. Melville, *Moby-Dick*, chap. 42, "The Whiteness of the Whale," 170.

25. Ibid., chap. 27, "Knights and Squires," 108.

26. P. H. Reardon, "Captain Ahab's Rebellion," *Touchstone* 8 (1995): 15–18, quote from p. 15, where he continues, "Melville is not really convinced that the old sea captain is altogether wrong."

27. Cf. W. Braswell, *Melville's Religious Thought: An Essay in Interpretation* (New York: Pageant Books, 1959), 68, who believes Ahab "sounds very much like Melville."

28. Melville, *Moby-Dick*, chap. 41, "Moby Dick," 162.

29. Cf. E. M. Behnken, "The Joban Theme in Moby Dick," *The Iliff Review* 33 (1976): 42, "Melville makes the ship into a microcosm of the world. Ahab as its captain is not different in kind but only in degree from the rest of mankind. Ahab, then, provides a magnified case of the reality that is man."

30. Melville, *Moby-Dick*, chap. 30, "The Pipe," 114; chap. 36, "The Quarter-deck," 143; chap. 41, "Moby Dick," 160; chap. 29, "Enter Ahab; to Him, Stubb," 112; chap. 52, "The Albatross," 203.

31. Ibid., chap. 108, "Ahab and the Carpenter," 391–92.

32. This image is much elaborated in chapter 89, "Fast Fish and Loose Fish," and generalized there to include the whole human species.

33. Melville, *Moby-Dick*, chap. 132, "The Symphony," 443.

34. Ibid., chap. 16, "The Ship," 77.

35. The identification of J. F. Gardner, "Ishmael on Watch," *Parabola* 2 (1977): 30–39, and T. Woodson, "Ahab's Greatness: Prometheus as Narcissus," in *Critical Essays on Herman Melville's* Moby-Dick (ed. B. Higgins and H. Parker; New York: G. K. Hall, 1992), 440–55.

36. The primary identification of H. B. Franklin, *The Wake of the Gods: Melville's Mythology* (Stanford, Calif.: Stanford University Press, 1963), 72–98.

37. Hinted at by P. A. Sitney, "Ahab's Name: A Reading of 'The Symphony,'" in *Herman Melville's* Moby-Dick (ed. H. Bloom; New York: Chelsea House, 1986), 131–45, esp. 142–43.

38. Ahab's identification of himself in chap. 132, "The Symphony," 444.

39. One of the points made by J. Stampfer, "Reply to 'The Modern Job,'" *Judaism* 13 (1964): 361–63.

40. Ishmael is also compared to Jonah; see S. VanZanten Gallagher, "The Prophetic Narrator of *Moby-Dick*," *Christianity and Literature* 36 (1987): 11–25, esp. 19–20.

41. W. H. Auden, "Ahab," in *The Enchafèd Flood; or, The Romantic Iconography of the Sea* (Charlottesville: University Press of Virginia, 1950), 133–40; repr. in *Ahab* (ed. H. Bloom; New York: Chelsea House, 1991), 15–19.

42. For all the Shakespeare identifications, see L. Ziff, "Shakespeare and Melville's America," in *New Perspectives on Melville* (ed. F. Pullin; Kent, Ohio: Kent State University Press, 1978), 54–67; C. Olson, "Call Me Ishmael," in *Herman Melville's* Moby-Dick (ed. H. Bloom; New York: Chelsea House, 1986), 13–37. Bloom makes the identification with Mabeth: *Invention of the Human*, 489.

43. See C. Olson, "Ahab and his Fool," in *Twentieth Century Interpretations of Moby-Dick* (ed. M. T. Gilmore; Englewood Cliffs, N.J.: Prentice-Hall, 1977), 55–58.

44. On the identifications, see the excellent collection of essays *Ahab* (ed. H. Bloom; New York: Chelsea House, 1991), and the short discussion in Lebowitz, *Progress into Silence*, 13–14. On the parallels with Edmund, see Markels, *Melville and the Politics of Identity*.

45. Melville, *Moby-Dick*, chap. 28, "Ahab," 110; chap. 36, "The Quarter-deck," 143; chap. 37, "Sunset," 147; chap. 16, "The Ship," 77; chap. 41, "Moby Dick," 160; chap. 16, "The Ship," 76.

46. Ahab's past is left deliberately ominous, meaningful, but mysterious, by the crew's conflicting speculations on Ahab's scar: Melville, *Moby-Dick,* Chapter 28, "Ahab," 110.

47. J. Bernstein, "Herman Melville's Concept of Ultimate Reality and Meaning in *Moby-Dick,*" *Ultimate Reality and Meaning* 5 (1982): 104–17; quote from p. 116.

48. Melville, *Moby-Dick,* chap. 2, "The Carpet-Bag," 19; chap. 58, "Brit," 236; chap. 16, "The Ship," 71.

49. Ibid., chap. 119, "The Candles," 416–17.

50. Ibid., chap. 41, "Moby Dick," 161.

51. Cf. B. Cowan, "Reading Ahab," in *Ahab* (ed. H. Bloom; New York: Chelsea House, 1991), 120: "This something, roughly phrased, consists of the realization that man in his present state not only is alienated from his original kingly image but has even forgotten this alienation. The reason for both alienation and forgetting is the too great suffering attendant on the dethronement of original man."

52. Melville, *Moby-Dick,* chap. 26, "Knights and Squires," 104–5; cf. the analysis of the passage in W. Hamilton, *Melville and the Gods* (Chico, Calif.: Scholars Press, 1985), 12–13. On Pascal's compatibility with democracy, see Morris, *Making Sense of It All,* 147: "On the contrary, many people have argued that the case for democracy can be made most strongly from the perspective of a worldview in accordance with which all human beings are created with equal, eternal, and infinite value in the image of God."

53. Melville, *Moby-Dick,* chap. 36, "The Quarter-Deck," 144.

54. Ibid., chap. 37, "Sunset," 147.

55. Ibid., chap. 46, "Surmises," 183. Cf. J. T. Matteson, "The Little Lower Layer: Anxiety and the Courage to Be in *Moby-Dick,*" *Harvard Theological Review* 81 (1988): 107: "Ahab's affirmation is an assertion of pure will. It is individualism run rampant. . . . Ahab does little to affirm others. What he does affirm is his own demonic depth."

56. Melville, *Moby-Dick,* chap. 108, "Ahab and the Carpenter," 392.

57. Ibid., chap. 109, "Ahab and Starbuck in the Cabin"; chap. 119, "The Candles"; and chap. 128, "The Pequod Meets the Rachel," respectively.

58. Ibid., chap. 16, "The Ship," 77; Olson, "Ahab and his Fool," 56.

59. Cf. W. A. Young, "Leviathan in the Book of Job and *Moby-Dick,*" *Soundings* 65 (1982): 394, "His downfall is not his metaphysical challenge, but a moral deterioration which destroys the innate human tendency to act justly and with compassion. . . . In the final analysis, 'Ahab becomes an accomplice of the divine malice to which he offers the worship of defiance'" (quoting T. W. Herbert Jr., *Moby-Dick and Calvinism: A World Dismantled* [New Brunswick, N.J.: Rutgers University Press, 1977], 157).

60. Melville, *Moby-Dick,* chap. 26, "Knights and Squires," 104.

61. Ibid., chap. 107, "The Carpenter," 387.

62. Ibid., chap. 72, "The Monkey-Rope," 270–73.

63. Ibid., chap. 72, "The Monkey-Rope," 271.

64. Ibid., chap. 94, "A Squeeze of the Hand," 349.

65. H. Hayford, "'Loomings': Yarns and Figures in the Fabric," in *Critical Essays on Herman Melville's* Moby-Dick (ed. B. Higgins and H. Parker; New York: G. K. Hall, 1992), 456–69; quote from p. 464. On the democratic theme, see also N. K. Hill, "Following Ahab to Doom or 'Goberning de Shark': *Moby Dick* as Democratic Reflection," *Cross Currents* 40 (1990): 256–64; and Markels, *Melville and the Politics of Identity,* esp. 86–104, for the Hobbesian and Lockean influences on the contrast between Ahab and Ishmael. Through strange numerological manipulations, V. Sachs, "Moby Dick; or The Wale [sic] et l'écriture biblique," *Foi et Vie* 90 (1991): 81–92, arrives at the similar conclusion that the novel is an allegory for Melville's America.

66. Melville, *Moby-Dick,* chap. 108, "Ahab and the Carpenter," 392.

67. A. Kazin, "Ishmael and Ahab," *Atlantic Monthly* 198, no. 5 (November 1956): 83; repr. in *Ahab* (ed. H. Bloom; New York: Chelsea House, 1991), 28–30.

68. Edwin Cady, "'As through a Glass Eye, Darkly': The Bible in the Nineteenth-Century American Novel," in *The Bible and American Arts and Letters* (ed. G. Gunn; Philadelphia: Fortress Press, 1983), 33–55; quote from p. 38. The classic work on Melville's overall use of Scripture is N. Wright, *Melville's Use of the Bible* (Durham, N.C.: Duke University Press, 1949).

69. L. Thompson, *Melville's Quarrel with God* (Princeton, N.J.: Princeton University Press, 1952), 163.

70. D. B. Lockerbie, "The Greatest Sermon in Fiction," *Christianity Today* 8 (8 November 1963): 9–12; quote from p. 12.

71. The opinion of J. A. Holstein, "Melville's Inversion of Jonah in *Moby-Dick,*" *The Iliff Review* 42 (1985): 13–20.

72. Cf. J. Stout, "Melville's Use of the Book of Job," *Nineteenth-Century Fiction* 25 (1970): 69–70: "Both Job and Ecclesiastes . . . held special appeal for the speculative and unorthodox Melville."

73. Melville, *Moby-Dick,* chap. 16, "The Ship," 72.

74. Ibid., chap. 41, "Moby Dick," 162.

75. It of course hardly matters that Leviathan is now usually identified as a crocodile; this is clearly not what Melville has in mind.

76. Melville, *Moby-Dick,* chap. 36, "The Quarter-deck," 144.

77. Cf. Reardon, "Captain Ahab's Rebellion," 17: "So God is as responsible for evil as for good. In this line of reasoning, damnation is not a divine afterthought. God himself must be held to account for the metaphysical injustice of man's plight. Of this, Captain Ahab entertains no doubts."

78. Cf. Murray, "In Nomine Diaboli," 14: "That God is incarnate in the Whale has been perceived by Geoffrey Stone, and, as far as I know, by every other Catholic critic of Melville's work, as well as by several Protestant critics. In fact, Richard Chase has marshaled so fair a portion of the large bulk of evidence on this point that any more from me would be superfluous."

79. Melville, *Moby-Dick,* chap. 36, "The Quarter-deck," 144.

80. Ibid., chap. 119, "The Candles," 416–17. Again, this position is at least in part Melville's own, as Stout, "Melville's Use of Job," 78, points out: "It appears likely enough that he meant as his own Ahab's 'I now know thy right worship is defiance.'"

81. Cf. Behnken, "Joban Theme," 43–44: "Ahab and Job were asserting their natural right to know, to receive answers, and when they were close to the Unknowable, they became even more determined and insistent. . . . His complaints cannot be ignored until he is dead because as long as he is living, he will raise the taboo questions of existence."

82. Melville, *Moby-Dick,* chap. 73, "Stubb and Flask Kill a Right Whale," 277.

83. Ibid., chap. 114, "The Gilder," 406; chap. 133, "The Chase—First Day," 452.

84. But cf. J. A. Holstein, "Melville's Inversion of Job in *Moby-Dick,*" *The Iliff Review* 37 (1980): 13–19, esp. 14–15, who regards Stubb's interpretation as simply a less sophisticated version of Melville's own.

85. Melville, *Moby-Dick,* chap. 81, "The Pequod Meets the Virgin," 300.

86. Ibid., chap. 58, "Brit," 235; cf. M. Friedman, "The Modern Job: On Melville, Dostoevsky, and Kafka," *Judaism* 12 (1963): 440: "If *Moby-Dick* is, indeed, a celebration of the American whaling industry and of expanding American civilization, it is also, at a profounder level, a deep recognition of the tragedy of such expansion—the inevitable, tragic

limitations that are encountered by the American frontiersman, the giant industrialist, or, for that matter, modern man in all his forms since the Renaissance. These are the limits of existence, the limits of creation with which God 'taunts' Job."

87. Young, "Leviathan in the Book of Job and *Moby-Dick*," 398.
88. Melville, *Moby-Dick*, chap. 66, "The Shark Massacre," 257.
89. Ibid., chap. 18, "His Mark," 83.
90. Ibid., chap. 10, "A Bosom Friend," 52.
91. J. Baird, *Ishmael* (Baltimore: Johns Hopkins Press, 1956), 247.
92. Melville, *Moby-Dick*, epilogue, 470, quoting Job 1:14–19.
93. Ibid., chap. 110, "Queequeg in His Coffin," 399.
94. Ibid., chap. 135, "The Chase—Third Day," 469.
95. Ibid., epilogue, 470. On the image of the vortex in *Moby-Dick*, see Baird, *Ishmael*, 266–73; R. Zoellner, "Ahab's Entropism and Ishmael's Cyclicism," in *Ahab* (ed. H. Bloom; New York: Chelsea House, 1991), 104–15, esp. 112–14.
96. Though possibly even the end of Job could be read this way, as done by Behnken, "Joban Theme," 46: "God has put eternity in men's minds, and then He punishes the person who reaches out to grasp it. Both Job and Ahab know in the end that they *must* take destiny into their own hands because no loving God will take care of them" (emphasis in original). On the contrast between Ahab and Job, see Friedman, "Modern Job," 440: "Ahab contends with existence but can have no real dialogue with it. Ahab has stood his ground before Moby Dick as Job before God Who created Leviathan together with him. But Ahab lacks that experience of an answering response to his cry that gives Job back his humanity and gives meaning to his suffering."
97. C. H. Holmain, "The Reconciliation of Ishmael: *Moby-Dick* and the Book of Job," *South Atlantic Quarterly* 57 (1958): 477–90; quote from p. 490.
98. Rice, "Empathic Edgar," 59.
99. Baird, *Ishmael*, 251.
100. Melville, *Moby-Dick*, chap. 10, "A Bosom Friend," 52.
101. This is true, even if Queequeg is "only" a "well-governed shark," as per Zoellner, "Queequeg: The Well-Governed Shark," 87–93, for he does not participate in the hypocrisy and subtle viciousness of the white characters; his "sharkishness" is frank, acknowledged, and always under control.
102. Cf. W. S. Gleim, *The Meaning of* Moby-Dick (New York: Russell & Russell, 1962), 57–59, for whom Queequeg symbolizes "Religion," in a broad, vital, primitive sense.
103. Taylor, "Ishmael's (m)Other," 333.
104. Melville, *Moby-Dick*, chap. 13, "Wheelbarrow," 61.
105. Ibid., chap. 78, "Cistern and Buckets," 290. Cf. Slotkin, "American National Epic," 24–25: "But where Ahab's deeds or gifts are of death and violence, Queequeg's are of love and kindness. Ahab makes corpses out of the whales; Queequeg, rescuing the Indian Tashtego, dives into the spermy basin of the whale's head to bring a renewed and resurrected life out of that figurative womb."
106. Melville, *Moby-Dick*, chap. 47, "The Mat-Maker," 185; chap. 10, "A Bosom Friend," 54; ibid., 53.
107. Cf. Smith, "Image of Society," 39: "If society is evil, some human relationships are nevertheless good. These can be designated by the general name of brotherhood or community, and Ishmael's love for Queequeg is the most obvious example of a redeeming force brought to bear upon him in the course of action. This love exists between two men who are, so to speak, outside society—Ishmael by choice, Queequeg by birth. But to the extent

that they can cherish one another they escape from the dreadful fate of being 'isolatoes,' discrete individuals without the sustenance of membership in a human community."

108. Cf. Holmain, "Reconciliation of Ishmael," 488: "Queequeg, the cannibal harpooner, gives him the first lesson in acceptance, and he doubles his world by pledging eternal friendship with this heathen seller of shrunken heads."

109. Baird, *Ishmael*, 246–47. Cf. the opposite conclusion of Hill, "Goberning de Shark," 263, who sees the final image as hopeless: "This image of hopeless hope, like the closing image of Ishmael the lone survivor clinging to a coffin, is all the agnostic Melville can offer us. If reflection on his great tragedy results in a restorative change of course, his minimal hope will have had an effect beyond his hoping." The ending clearly is not optimistic, but neither can it accurately be characterized as hopeless. Nor is Ishmael floating the final image; his rescue as an orphan by a grieving mother is the final image.

110. Melville, *Moby-Dick*, chap. 110, "Queequeg in His Coffin," 395; chap. 127, "The Deck," 433.

111. Melville, *Moby-Dick*, chap. 41, "Moby Dick," 160.

112. Ibid., chap. 41, "Moby Dick," 161.

113. Ibid., chap. 38, "Dusk," 148.

114. Ibid., chap. 44, "The Chart," 171.

115. Ibid., chap. 41, "Moby Dick," 161.

116. Ibid., chap. 118, "The Quadrant," 412.

117. Cf. Olson, "Call Me Ishmael," 27: "Ahab is Conjur Man. He invokes his own evil world."

118. Melville, *Moby-Dick*, chap. 119, "The Candles," 416–17.

119. Olson, "Ahab and His Fool," 55.

120. Melville, *Moby-Dick*, chap. 133, "The Chase—First Day," 452.

121. Ibid., chap. 125, "The Log and Line," 428; chap. 132, "The Symphony," 444.

122. Ibid., chap. 134, "The Chase—Second Day," 459. Cf. Matteson, "Little Lower Layer," 109: "The tragedy of Ahab's radical assertion of the will is that he can govern everyone but himself."

123. Melville, *Moby-Dick*, chap. 134, "The Chase—Second Day," 459.

124. Ibid., chap. 37, "Sunset," 147.

125. Ibid., chap. 36, "The Quarter-deck," 144.

126. Cf. E. Ziarek, "'Surface Stratified on Surface': A Reading of Ahab's Allegory," *Criticism* 31 (1989): 280, "Although such allegorical reading endows Ahab's action with mad purpose, the usurpation of understanding by the performative rigor deepens further the gaps and discontinuities in the representation of the whale. Thus Ahab's monomaniac purpose fails him in a more serious way than the lost battle with the whale: instead of reenacting a meaningful scenario, which would impose intelligibility on nature, Ahab's performance increases fragmentation and epistemological confusion."

127. Melville, *Moby-Dick*, chap. 93, "The Castaway," 347.

128. Ibid., chap. 129, "The Cabin," 436. Cf. Gardner, "Ishmael on Watch," 34: "Pip represents the extreme of the 'centrifugal tendency' Melville felt in his soul. Ahab represents the extreme development of its opposite, the centripetal pull."

129. Melville, *Moby-Dick*, chap. 125, "The Log and Line," 428.

130. Cf. Sitney, "Ahab's Name," 142: "He does not, like Pip, lose the capability of saying both I and his own name, after falling into the sea. He has already lost his name and his autonarrating authority in the final chapters. The epilogue restores both to him."

131. Ibid., 143.

132. E. A. Dryden, *Melville's Thematics of Form: The Great Art of Telling the Truth* (Baltimore: Johns Hopkins Press, 1968), 105.

133. Melville, *Moby-Dick,* chap. 108, "Ahab and the Carpenter," 392; chap. 133, "The Chase—First Day," 452.

134. Ibid., chap. 102, "A Bower in the Arsacides," 376.

135. Ibid., chap. 47, "The Mat-Maker," 185.

136. Ibid., chap. 36, "The Quarter-deck," 144.

137. Ibid., chap. 87, "The Grand Armada," 325–26.

138. Ibid., chap. 23, "The Lee Shore," 97.

139. Ibid., chap. 132, "The Symphony," 443.

140. Though some have argued for maternal aspects even for Moby Dick himself; see Murray, "In Nomine Diaboli," 13; Slotkin, "American National Epic," 25. *Jaws, Jurassic Park,* and the new *Godzilla,* as well as lesser known movies such as *Deep Blue Sea,* use a similar idea to produce female or androgynous monsters who are as destructive as their male predecessors but possess the further awesome power of being able to create more killing machines.

141. Melville, *Moby-Dick,* chap. 125, "The Log and Line," 428.

142. Ibid., chap. 114, "The Gilder," 406.

143. Ibid.

144. Ibid., epilogue, 470.

145. Cf. Taylor, "Ishmael's (m)Other," 348–49: "Through Ishmael, Melville names a site on the unstable boundary between masculine and feminine, and that site is the hermaphrodite Jesus."

146. Though Melville most frequently contrasts the land and sea, on the image of sharks he sees both realms as full of them: *Moby-Dick,* chap. 64, "Stubb's Supper," 249, and chap. 65, "The Whale as a Dish," 255–56. He performs the same undoing of the land/sea dichotomy with chap. 89, "Fast Fish and Loose Fish." Cf. Arnold, "Draught of a Draught," 189: "Thus we realize this paradox, or ultimate dilemma: both land and sea become hostile to human existence."

147. Melville, *Moby-Dick,* chap. 87, "The Grand Armada," 326.

148. On the contrast between Ahab and Ishmael, cf. Young, "Leviathan in the Book of Job and *Moby-Dick,*" 394: "The lack of interaction between Ahab and Ishmael suggests that Melville intends to separate their journeys and exploit the resultant ambiguity of meaning." See also Matteson, "Little Lower Layer," 107: "Followed to its conclusion, Ahab's form of self-affirmation leads to self-destruction. . . . When Ahab affirms his demonic depth, he affirms madness and destruction. He affirms into a bottomless vortex."

149. Holmain, "Reconciliation of Ishmael," 482; cf. Arnold, "Draught of a Draught," 177: "It is surely his [Ishmael's] unquenching activity for wondering that allows him to enter the metaphysical dimensions of his quest."

150. Cf. the similar conclusions of Zoellner, "Ahab's Entropism and Ishmael's Cyclicism," 113–14: "The Grand Armada is a partial, essentially cetological resolution for Ishmael's hypo concerning the void. . . . The 'Epilogue' is the ultimate statement of the redemptive cyclicism of *Moby-Dick,* and the final repudiation of Ahab's entropism"; and Arnold, "Draught of a Draught," 185–186: "Ahab finally does not submit to transformation. Contrariwise, Ishmael, rejecting determined closure, is flexive, fluidly willing to be open to the process of perceiving experience this way, and then that, and then both, refusing to unify what essentially cannot be joined . . . it is Ishmael's identity that survives, for, unlike Ahab, he has achieved some sense of equipoise with ambiguity."

151. Cf. Arnold, "Draught of a Draught," 183: "He is compelled to return again and

again to the religious quest felt most fully only in the theater that yields the 'interlinked' terrors and wonders of God." Contra J. Stampfer, "Reply," 361, "The paradoxes remain, the awesome mystery and power of the whale, but however Biblical Melville's drama, his point of view is that of Ishmael, rather than of Isaac. Men are redeemed not by encounter, but by its avoidance." This last sentence cannot be correct: Ishmael has continued his encounter with the sea and God, but it is with a much different outlook and goal than he temporarily shared with Ahab.

152. See VanZanten Gallagher, "Prophetic Narrator," 22–23.

153. Melville, *Moby-Dick*, chap. 1, "Loomings," p. 14; cf. R. A. Sherrill, "The Career of Ishmael's Self-Transcendence," in *Herman Melville's* Moby-Dick (ed. H. Bloom; New York: Chelsea House, 1986), 76: "When all meaning appears to be relative, when the possibility of objective knowledge seems lost, it is not surprising that knowledge, for Ishmael, comes to be understood as self-projection onto what is essentially indeterminate ground. His gazing into the water reflects only his self-image: he can become Narcissus."

154. Sherrill, "Ishmael's Self-Transcendence," 94–95; cf. Stout, "Melville's Use of Job," 78: "But like Job Ishmael regains his serenity; he learns reconciliation to the world, though not an answer to the riddle of why evil and suffering exist."

155. Soltau, *Pascal*, 115.

156. From the last page of Morris, *Making Sense of It All*, 212.

6. Conclusion:
Life and Love with Wisdom of the Heart

What then have we learned from one thousand years of the biblical wisdom tradition, and from a long, narrow slice of two thousand years of Western, Christian literary tradition built upon it? Can these texts, so ancient and out-of-date in regard to science, technology, psychology, human rights—really tell us anything worthwhile about how to live our lives today in the twenty-first century? Perhaps we might want to hold on to their idea of monotheism, updated as necessary with our more optimistic views of human nature and intellect, supplementing their primitive ideas with the more enlightened and humane outlooks of feminism, democracy, and a deeper respect for individuals and for the environment. Perhaps these ancient authors did the best they could under the circumstances and limitations of their society, but let's face it, they didn't know Marx, Freud, or Darwin, so what really can they say about human nature that hasn't been overturned and rendered obsolete in the last hundred years?

If you have read this book this far, you know that the above is another fool's speech, and you can probably guess my answer to the above questions. But in case I have been too detached or coy in my analyses thus far, allow me a moment of complete honesty and bluntness here in my conclusion. All I can say to the above is, "Get a clue." Don't get me wrong; the last 150 years have left us with enormous improvements in human life for which we should be endlessly grateful. The abolition of slavery, universal suffrage, and the spread of democracy and free markets across the world were social changes that were long overdue and that were sometimes impeded by the Church and its policies; they have resulted in an inestimable reduction of human misery around the planet. Technologically, especially in the case of medicine, our lives are incomparable to those of people in the nineteenth century or before. Never mind conveniences or luxuries; just think of necessities: My family and all the other people where we live have enough to eat, we have heat throughout the winter, and almost all our children will survive to adulthood. Even if these blessings are not shared by everyone in all other countries, the reduction or eradication of many communicable diseases and the improvement of food production and distribution have resulted in significantly reduced misery for much of the planet. Two hundred years ago, my own ancestors were living in holes they had dug in the steppes of the Ukraine (unwisely having settled where there was good farmland, but no trees with which to build houses), their children and livestock huddling around them in the dark and cold, as they clutched shovels or other farm tools to use to defend themselves from the marauding packs of wolves and Cossacks that frequently swept through the area. If they survived the attacks of the lupine and human predators, they could look forward to short, lice-ridden lives in which they would bury half of their children before maturity, lose all their own teeth by forty, and die themselves from tuberculosis, cholera, or some other epidemic. None of them knew how to read or write, and their community was so isolated and insular that they almost inevitably married their cousins: no social mobility, culture, or education, and plenty of inbreeding, suffering, and death. Though I sometimes like to think of myself as a strong individual, I am very glad that I don't have to deal with such trials. I am nearly helpless every time there is a power outage or my car breaks down, so I can't imagine that I would fare very well burying a child, and I thank God for every day that I am spared that particular growing experience.

So socially, economically, and physically, my life is nearly unrecognizable from that of any of the authors we have considered, or from the lives of the hole-dwelling Paffenroths of two hundred years ago. I'm glad, and I frequently express my gratitude to God for this improvement. But as improved as our lives are now, are we so improved, even in these few areas of human existence, that our experience is qualitatively different from premodern times? I have never had to bury one of my children, but I did have to watch my mother die a slow, lingering death from cancer when I was thirteen. I thank modern medicine for reducing the amount of suffering and grief in my life, but apparently we are not yet to the point at which I can count on modern science to insulate me completely from such experiences, and I hope that no one will consider me too pessimistic if I express doubt that we will ever reach such a point. I also hope that no one will consider me deranged or primitive if I express some reservation about the potential cost of such insulation from suffering; it does not seem at all out of reach of modern science that we might soon be able to prevent cancer by finding a cancer gene and aborting fetuses that carry it.[1] So I could have been spared the anguish of my mother's death if her parents had aborted her, thereby offering me the strange option, at least in thought, of freedom from pain only by my own and her nonexistence, a sort of retroactive suicide. Thank you, modernity, but most of us find suicide in the present in order to avoid future pain a troubling enough option.

And even in terms of reduction of misery, it is clear that the modern world, for all its triumphs, will ultimately have to answer for a much more ambiguous, less satisfying record. The twentieth century was the bloodiest in history; averaged out over its hundred years of mind-numbing cruelty and violence, a hundred people an hour died at the hands of other human beings during the twentieth century. Such carnage makes it seem to me utterly absurd to call premodern times or cultures "barbaric" and ours "enlightened": What could be more barbaric than Auschwitz, Cambodia, or planes full of screaming civilians pleading for their lives being deliberately flown into buildings full of other civilians? Even "semi-legitimate" military actions such as Dresden, Hiroshima, and the holding hostage of other countries' populations through nuclear deterrence are morally questionable and hardly seem the actions of an "enlightened" mind or society. I would call the unspeakable violence of the twentieth century bestial, savage, or insane, except that such labels seem grossly unfair to animals, savages, or the mentally deranged, most all of whom are quite peaceful.

In all of this litany of evil, I am not suggesting that modernity has created evil, to be sure. Modernity did not create Hitler, but it could not prevent his appearance, and with the modern tools of mass communication, aircraft, tanks, submarines, and ballistic missiles, he was infinitely more deadly than he would have been in any previous century. What I am suggesting is that modernity's inability to eliminate evil has finally and unambiguously unmasked evil as something that is not attributable merely to base urges, mental instability, bad habits, or demonic possession, but rather to a fundamental flaw in humans that modernity tried to ignore and could never fix. Enlightenment thinkers thought that by getting rid of religion and all the other bad, old, primitive institutions and ideas of bygone centuries, we could eliminate or at least curtail human brutality. They thought that evil was something that as a species we would outgrow, the way most societies have outgrown such primitive practices as slavery, child sacrifice, and cannibalism. But instead, by its denial of sin and evil, modernity let them run amok with unbelievable power and ferocity, having also put modern weapons at their command. If so many brilliant and virtuous minds have been working for centuries to make people better through education and rationality, resulting only in an increasing level of carnage, then I for one have to express some serious doubt that the dark side of human nature will ever be illumined through merely human means.[2]

This rather depressing tour of modernity leads us back to what I think are the relevant points of the books we have been examining. We have not been examining these authors for their analyses of social, economic, or physical conditions, but rather for their insights into the more important and inescapable concept of human nature, a nature that the triumphs and failures of modernity have shown has not changed one iota over thousands of years of human history. I may not live in a hole and wield a shovel all day like my forebears, and unlike them I can read and write and I didn't marry my cousin, but it seems to me that the more important and basic problems, hopes, and fears of our lives are probably identical, or would at least be recognizable to one another. Our lives have all been filled with suffering, grief, pleasure, joy, triumph, despair, love, loneliness, sinning, and being sinned against. And for all the human beings who have ever lived, it has been in how they deal with these experiences that their lives become blessed or wretched, while it is the honest and troubling depiction of people wrestling with these experiences that makes some literature great and relevant to our lives. People who would dismiss the works we have discussed as irrelevant or dated are truly stunted either in their experience of life or in their reaction to it: "You can fail to perceive Lear's greatness, if your program does not allow for such a quality's existence. But then, who or what are you, if you lack even the dream of greatness? . . . [T]o lose Lear's greatness is also to abandon a part of our own capacity for significant emotion."[3] I've hurt enough people whom I loved and been hurt by them enough to know that there isn't a single line in *King Lear* that isn't true. There have been too many times I've wanted desperately to fit in while simultaneously wishing I didn't need to fit in, so I know there is nothing the least bit unbelievable about the narrator in *Notes from Underground*. I have enough self-destructive habits of my own, and I've known people with much worse ones, so Fyodor and Dmitri Karamazov seem to me like old, familiar, if rather unsavory, friends. For all my derision of modernity above, I've tried just as hard as Faust, Pascal, or Ivan Karamazov to reason about the universe and live my life in accordance with reason, with the same mixed and unsatisfying results. I've been ashamed of my past at the same time that I have longed for it often enough to know that I am no better adjusted than Augustine was. And I've stood alongside Job, Faust, Lear, and Ahab as we raised our fists against an indifferent, silent God often enough that I won't part company with them now.

But while my strange sense of loyalty to fictitious characters and my honesty in admitting their faults as my own are quite interesting and perhaps a little noble, I need to do something more. I may refuse to part company with these brave and doomed characters, but I would certainly like my own story to turn out better than theirs. Diagnosing the problem with human nature is an enormous and important first step, one that I suspect most people never even get to, but it is only a prelude to the infinitely more difficult task of doing something about it. While we have alluded to some of the steps that might need to be taken to live a satisfying life in this strange and frustrating world that God has given us, I would underline what I consider the most important ones here—their importance being indicated by how much they have been emphasized in the Wisdom books we have examined.

The types of behavior or attitudes encouraged by these books range from the most mundane to the most sacred, from the everyday to the cataclysmic, as we saw in the first chapter that the concept of wisdom itself ranges from mere carefulness to the highest experience of the divine itself. At the mundane level, it is striking to me how much the works we have examined extol persistence. The patience of Job in the face of his suffering is proverbial (Jas 5:11), but it is his persistent questioning that seems the more prevalent image in the book in its final form: He won't give up on God, but he also won't give up nagging and pestering God. This image of belligerent persistence continues in Faust, who first draws the Lord's attention, not for his faith, but for his constant striving, his inability to be satisfied with the easy answers that placate others; the Lord rightly believes that only a man of such deep dissatisfaction and inquisitiveness will be able to withstand the devil's temptations of transitory things that often satisfy less demanding people. Dogged persistence reaches a fatal extreme in Ahab, who should give up his mad quest, but even here, isn't there a hint of nobility and revelation? Ishmael and we never would have gotten the answers of joy and contentment if Ahab had not taken us with him halfway around the globe in a leaky ship to try to kill an animal (or God) that normal men insisted could not be killed, to ask questions that normal people hush as inappropriate. As people often tell you at training sessions, the only dumb question is the one you don't ask. To refrain from asking God whether he is just is therefore not piety but ignorance. To refrain from expressing doubt is not faith but insecurity and cowardice. And persistence reaches a different and beautiful extreme in *King Lear*, when the characters persist in loving Lear in spite of himself, in spite of all the reasons he has given them not to. To love people in spite of all their flaws, or to love God in spite of all his mystery and silence, requires an exceptional level of determination, almost stubbornness, but someone who is capable of this kind of love would truly be wise.

Another seemingly mundane mental habit that was elevated in these books higher than I expected was the practice of good memory, of holding on to memories rather than letting them slip away. It seems a damning and hellish oblivion that Fyodor Karamazov lives in, forgetting everything and everyone who isn't right in front of him. A much deeper man than Fyodor, Ahab practices a far deeper and more complex forgetfulness, holding on to the memory of Moby Dick's attack and God's injustice with monomaniac, idolatrous devotion, while willing himself to forget the sweeter things of his life—his wife, child, and the love and loyalty he once had for his crew. But the characters whom we have seen achieve real happiness and peace—Alyosha, Father Zossima, Augustine, Faust, Lear, and Ishmael—have all done so by finally embracing their pasts.[4] This is not nostalgia or a longing for the past—a false kind of memory—but the grateful acceptance that the past, as painful and imperfect as it may have been, has led them to whatever love and grace they now have. The wisdom of this holding on to the past seems clear, for regretting, denying, or forgetting the past are all ways of denying God's beneficent providence and excluding him from our lives. But the difficulty of this wise practice should probably be stressed. Don't think of beautiful sunsets, lovers' kisses, or the laughter of children; think of the worst sin you have ever committed or the most horrific tragedy you have ever witnessed, and then try thanking God for that event. That is how difficult having a good memory would be, and how tempting forgetfulness would be. But only by holding on to the past, contemplating the truth and beauty in it and to which it has led, can we experience life as a mysterious, unfolding gift from God and thank God for it.

A higher practice of wisdom whose value is praised consistently in these books is the acknowledgment of one's vulnerability and neediness before God, the "fear of the Lord" as it is called in the biblical Wisdom books. Almost every one of the male characters in these books tried to take control of his life and assert his power over other people and his independence from any higher power. Their means varied widely, but the image of masculine control and domination is as consistent as it is ugly. The Underground Man's reclusive rebellion, Fyodor's irresponsible debauchery and hoarding, Augustine's ambitious career and womanizing, Faust's alchemical and magical manipulations, Lear's emotional tyranny and manipulation, Pascal's mathematical and scientific ambitions, Ahab's mad hunt of the whale, perhaps even Job's pious sacrifices—all are the acts of "impotent rebels,"[5] of "baby man"[6] striving to deny his attachment to and powerlessness before God the Father. Only those characters who can imitate the humility and self-acknowledged weakness of Mary, Monica, and Gretchen can be saved. But this acknowledgment of weakness has a paradoxical outcome. As Pascal observed, it allows us to appreciate and understand our real greatness: When we stop trying to usurp God's power, we begin to experience our real greatness as his children and heirs. And when we stop trying to control and dictate our own lives, we can feel Ishmael's joy and surprise at every turn of our lives, as playful and happy as Lady Wisdom is with God and with the world they have created. Again, as with memory, this is probably not an easy practice at all. In almost everything we do, we assume we are controlling what happens to us, and ironically, the wisdom tradition itself tried to give people more control over their lives. But all this seeming control is really in someone else's hands, someone we love and trust but whose reasons we cannot fathom and whose final goals remain obscure. As difficult as it may be, we must stop fooling ourselves into thinking we are masters of our fates, for only then can we enjoy the path God has wisely and lovingly chosen for us, as baffling and painful as that path often is.

Turning to the higher and more positive practices of wisdom in these books, I am a little surprised at what has emerged. For a collection of books in which theodicies are so numerous and in which profound, agonizing experiences of innocent suffering abound, I would have expected ruminations on evil and justice to be much more prevalent than the praise of love that has emerged in every chapter I have written. What has come out of these books is first the necessity of love. Our state as individuals is so weakened, flawed, and vulnerable that there seems little question about our ability to satisfy or fulfill ourselves. It is the height of folly to deny that we need God and others to make our lives happy or complete: "The fear of the LORD is the beginning of wisdom" (Prov 9:10); "Love the Lord your God . . . and your neighbor as yourself" (Luke 10:27).[7] Love is as necessary to our lives as food or air, and since it feeds a higher part of ourselves, it is also much harder to achieve or maintain.

But as much as we need to love God and others, this spiritual need may well run contrary to our physical needs, as shown by the number of noble, loving characters we have seen killed in these books. The authors we have been examining were not unrealistically optimistic or sentimental in their portrayal or praise of love; except for Shakespeare, none of these guys could get a job working for Hallmark. Love is the most powerful and precious thing in our life, but that means it is the most overwhelming and the most costly: "For love is strong as death, passion fierce as the grave. Its flashes are flashes of fire, a raging flame. Many waters cannot quench love, neither can floods drown it. If one offered for love all the wealth of his house, it would be utterly scorned" (Song 8:6–7). It is wise to love, and one will be loving if one is wise, but it is just as hard to love God or people as it is to love wisdom: All require complete commitment and infinite sacrifice. It is neither insignificant nor surprising that Jesus, the most famous religious leader of all time, and Socrates, probably the most famous philosopher, were both killed by the people they loved and were trying to help. (And if one wishes to add political leaders martyred for their love of their fellows, one could note Abraham Lincoln, Mohandas Gandhi, and Martin Luther King Jr.) Wise or Christlike love exists in the shadow of the cross and embraces that suffering, but it also overwhelms the power of death.

I now see better how love and wisdom go together, more than I had first suspected. They are the closely interwoven parts—more like yin and yang than even the male/female pairing I suggested in Chapter 2—that together define the goal of human life, which is to be happy, true happiness being possible only by our serving God. It is the highest wisdom to love, for love is the service that God commands us to give him and his creatures, and only love can offer us real and eternal life with God and others: "Love never ends" (1 Cor 13:8). At the same time, it is the most ardent kind of love to pursue wisdom, for it expresses our love of God and his creation and passionately ties us to our fellow seekers of truth: "I love those who love me, and those who seek me diligently find me" (Prov 8:17); "Come to me, you that yearn for me, and be filled with my fruits" (Sir 24:19). Our yearning to understand and embrace God and his wisdom is a kind of passion, and at the same time our love of God and others is the deepest, most life-giving kind of wisdom. Although they arise from the necessity of our weakness and limitedness, wisdom and love free us to partake of God's infinity and eternity.

Holding on to the past through memory, facing the future with determination, at all times acknowledging our limitedness and vulnerability, and therefore always devoting ourselves to others and God in love—this would be a life of true wisdom, and the only kind that would bring us real happiness.

Notes

1. Thanks to Robert Kennedy for helping me to see the aptness of this example.

2. Cf. J. D. Frodsham, "Conflicting Theodicies—Some Modernist Literary Approcahes to the Problem of Evil," *Religious Traditions* 5 (1982): 36: "Until 1914 Western man was confident that evil was but a barbarous relic of the past. . . . Nevertheless, his reaction has been one of defiance rather than repentance, for the blame of these calamities is not ascribed to man himself but rather to society in general or to some particular economic system, as though man were not responsible individually and collectively for his own social organisation."

3. H. Bloom, *Shakespeare: The Invention of the Human* (New York: Riverhead Books, 1998), 512–13.

4. On memory in Augustine's *Confessions*, see M. Mendelson, "*venter animi/distentio animi:* Memory and Temporality in Augustine's *Confessions*," *Augustinian Studies* 31 (2000): 137–63.

5. F. Dostoevsky, *The Brothers Karamazov* (trans. C. Garnett; New York: Penquin Books, 1958), bk. 5, chap. 5, p. 248.

6. H. Melville, *Moby-Dick* (ed. H. Hayford and H. Parker; New York: W. W. Norton, 1967), chap. 58, "Brit," 235.

7. Cf. Matt 22:37–38; Mark 12:29–31; Lev 19:18; Deut 6:5.

Bibliography

Adam, K. *Saint Augustine: The Odyssey of His Soul.* Translated by D. J. McCann. New York: Macmillan, 1932.

Adamson, D. *Blaise Pascal: Mathematician, Physicist and Thinker about God.* New York: St. Martin's Press, 1995.

Adelman, J. Introduction to *Twentieth Century Interpretations of King Lear: A Collection of Critical Essays.* Edited by J. Adelman. Englewood Cliffs, N.J.: Prentice-Hall, 1978.

Anchor, R. "Method and Family in Goethe's *Faust:* Gretchen's Mother and the Gretchen Tragedy." *Historical Reflections* 23 (1997): 29–48.

Andrews, W. P. *Goethe's Key to Faust: A Scientific Basis for Religion and Morality and for a Solution of the Enigma of Evil.* Port Washington, N.Y.: Kennikat Press, 1913.

Arnold, D. S. "'But the Draught of a Draught': Reading the Wonder of Ishmael's Telling." *Semeia* 31 (1985): 171–93.

Auden, W. H. "Ahab." Pages 133–40 in *The Enchafèd Flood; or, The Romantic Iconography of the Sea.* Charlottesville: University Press of Virginia, 1950. Repr. pages 15–19 in *Ahab.* Edited by H. Bloom. New York: Chelsea House, 1991.

Augustine. *The Confessions of St. Augustine.* Translated by J. K. Ryan. New York: Doubleday, 1960.

———. *Soliloquies.* Translated by K. Paffenroth. Hyde Park: New City Press, 2000.

Baird, J. *Ishmael.* Baltimore: Johns Hopkins Press, 1956.

Barber, C. L. "On Christianity and the Family: Tragedy of the Sacred." Pages 117–19 in *Twentieth Century Interpretations of King Lear: A*

Collection of Critical Essays. Edited by J. Adelman. Englewood Cliffs, N.J.: Prentice-Hall, 1978.

Basney, L. "Is a Christian Perspective on Shakespeare Productive and/or Necessary?" Pages 19–35 in *Shakespeare and the Christian Tradition.* Edited by E. B. Batson. Lewiston, N.Y.: Edwin Mellen Press, 1994.

Batson, E. B., ed. *Shakespeare and the Christian Tradition.* Lewiston, N.Y.: Edwin Mellen Press, 1994.

Behnken, E. M. "The Joban Theme in Moby Dick." *The Iliff Review* 33 (1976): 37–48.

Belknap, R. L. "Memory in *The Brothers Karamazov.*" Pages 227–42 in *Dostoevsky: New Perspectives.* Edited by R. L. Jackson. Englewood Cliffs, N.J.: Prentice-Hall, 1984.

Bernstein, J. "Herman Melville's Concept of Ultimate Reality and Meaning in *Moby-Dick.*" *Ultimate Reality and Meaning* 5 (1982): 104–17.

Blackmur, R. P. "*The Brothers Karamazov:* The Grand Inquisitor and the Wine of Gladness." Pages 205–15 in *Critical Essays on Dostoevsky.* Edited by R. F. Miller. Boston: G. K. Hall, 1986.

Bloom, H., ed. *Ahab.* New York: Chelsea House, 1991.

———, ed. *Fyodor Dostoevsky's* The Brothers Karamazov. New York: Chelsea House, 1988.

———. *Shakespeare: The Invention of the Human.* New York: Riverhead Books, 1998.

———, ed. *William Shakespeare's King Lear.* New York: Chelsea House, 1987.

Boadt, L. *Reading the Old Testament: An Introduction.* New York: Paulist Press, 1984.

Booth, S. "On the Greatness of *King Lear.*" Pages 98–111 in *Twentieth Century Interpretations of King Lear: A Collection of Critical Essays.* Edited by J. Adelman. Englewood Cliffs, N.J.: Prentice-Hall, 1978.

———. "On the Greatness of *King Lear.*" Pages 57–70 in *William Shakespeare's King Lear.* Edited by H. Bloom. New York: Chelsea House, 1987.

Braswell, W. *Melville's Religious Thought: An Essay in Interpretation.* New York: Pageant Books, 1959.

Brown, J. K. *Goethe's Faust: The German Tragedy.* Ithaca, N.Y.: Cornell University Press, 1986.

Brown, P. *Augustine of Hippo: A Biography.* Berkeley: University of California Press, 1967.

Bruce, F. F. *1 and 2 Corinthians.* New Century Bible Commentary. Grand Rapids: Eerdmans, 1971.

Cady, E. "'As through a Glass Eye, Darkly': The Bible in the Nineteenth-Century American Novel." Pages 33–55 in *The Bible and American Arts and Letters.* Edited by G. Gunn. Philadelphia: Fortress Press, 1983.

Calderwood, J. L. "Creative Uncreation in *King Lear.*" Pages 121–37 in *William Shakespeare's King Lear.* Edited by H. Bloom. New York: Chelsea House, 1987.

Camp, C. V. *Wisdom and the Feminine in the Book of Proverbs.* Sheffield, U.K.: Almond Press, 1985.

Catteau, J. "The Paradox of the Legend of the Grand Inquisitor in *The Brothers Karamazov.*" Pages 243–54 in *Dostoevsky: New Perspectives.* Edited by R. L. Jackson. Englewood Cliffs, N.J.: Prentice-Hall, 1984.

Chadwick, H. *Augustine.* Oxford: Oxford University Press, 1986.

Cowan, B. "Reading Ahab." Pages 116–23 in *Ahab.* Edited by H. Bloom. New York: Chelsea House, 1991.

Crenshaw, J. L. *Old Testament Wisdom: An Introduction.* Atlanta: John Knox Press, 1981.

Danby, J. F. *Shakespeare's Doctrine of Nature: A Study of King Lear.* London: Faber & Faber, 1949.

Danson, L., ed. *On King Lear.* Princeton: Princeton University Press, 1981.

Davidson, C. "History of *King Lear* and the Problem of Belief." *Christianity and Literature* 45 (1996): 285–301.

Davidson, H. M. *The Origins of Certainty: Means and Meaning in Pascal's Pensées.* Chicago: University of Chicago Press, 1979.

Dostoevsky, F. *The Brothers Karamazov.* Translated by C. Garnett. New York: Penguin Books, 1958.

———. *Notes from Underground.* Translated by M. Ginsburg. New York: Bantam, 1974.

Dryden, E. A. *Melville's Thematics of Form: The Great Art of Telling the Truth.* Baltimore: Johns Hopkins Press, 1968.

Ehrman, B. D. *The New Testament: A Historical Introduction to the Early Christian Writings.* Oxford: Oxford University Press, 1997.

Elton, W. R. *King Lear and the Gods.* San Marino, Calif.: Huntington Library, 1968.

Fairley, B. *Goethe's Faust: Six Essays.* Oxford: Clarendon Press, 1953.

Florovsky, G. "The Quest for Religion in 19th Century Russian Literature." *Epiphany* 10/11 (1990): 43–58.

France, R. T. *The Gospel of Mark: A Commentary on the Greek Text.* Grand Rapids: Eerdmans, 2002.

Franklin, H. B. *The Wake of the Gods: Melville's Mythology.* Stanford, Calif.: Stanford University Press, 1963.

Friedman, M. "The Modern Job: On Melville, Dostoievsky, and Kafka." *Judaism* 12 (1963): 436–55.

Frodsham, J. D. "Conflicting Theodicies—Some Modernist Literary Approaches to the Problem of Evil." *Religious Traditions* 5 (1982): 24–43.

Gardner, J. F. "Ishmael on Watch." *Parabola* 2 (1977): 30–39.

George, P. "Remembering the Dead: Kierkegaard and Dostoevsky." *Modern Believing* 35 (1994): 24–31.
Gibson, A. B. *The Religion of Dostoevsky*. Philadelphia: Westminster, 1973.
Gleim, W. S. *The Meaning of Moby-Dick*. New York: Russell & Russell, 1962.
Goddard, H. C. *"King Lear."* Pages 9–43 in *William Shakespeare's King Lear*. Edited by H. Bloom. New York: Chelsea House, 1987.
Goethe, J. W. von, *Faust. Part 1*. Translated by Anna Swanwick. New York: P. F. Collier, 1909–14.
Goldberg, S. L. "On Edgar's Character." Pages 114–16 in *Twentieth Century Interpretations of King Lear: A Collection of Critical Essays*. Edited by J. Adelman. Englewood Cliffs, N.J.: Prentice-Hall, 1978.
Green, J. B. *The Gospel of Luke*. Grand Rapids: Eerdmans, 1997.
Guardini, R. *Pascal for Our Time*. Translated by B. Thompson. New York: Herder & Herder, 1966.
Hackel, S. "The Religious Dimension: Vision or Evasion? Zosima's Discourse in *The Brothers Karamazov*." Pages 139–68 in *New Essays on Dostoevsky*. Edited by M. V. Jones and G. M. Terry. Cambridge: Cambridge University Press, 1983.
Hamilton, W. *Melville and the Gods*. Chico, Calif.: Scholars Press, 1985.
Hayford, H. "'Loomings': Yarns and Figures in the Fabric." Pages 456–69 in *Critical Essays on Herman Melville's* Moby-Dick. Edited by B. Higgins and H. Parker. New York: G. K. Hall, 1992.
———. "Unnecessary Duplicates: A Key to the Writing of *Moby-Dick*." Pages 128–61 in *New Perspectives on Melville*. Edited by F. Pullin. Kent, Ohio: Kent State University Press, 1978.
Hazelton, R. *Blaise Pascal: The Genius of His Thought*. Philadelphia: Westminster Press, 1974.
Hegedus, L. "Jesus and Dostoevsky." *European Journal of Theology* 1 (1992): 49–62.
Hill, N. K. "Following Ahab to Doom or 'Goberning de Shark': *Moby Dick* as Democratic Reflection." *Cross Currents* 40 (1990): 256–64.
Holmain, C. H. "The Reconciliation of Ishmael: *Moby-Dick* and the Book of Job." *South Atlantic Quarterly* 57 (1958): 477–90.
Holquist, M. "How Sons Become Fathers." Pages 39–51 in *Fyodor Dostoevsky's* The Brothers Karamazov. New York: Chelsea House, 1988.
Holstein, J. A. "Melville's Inversion of Job in *Moby-Dick*." *The Iliff Review* 37 (1980): 13–19.
———. "Melville's Inversion of Jonah in *Moby-Dick*." *The Iliff Review* 42 (1985): 13–20.
Hubert, M. L. *Pascal's Unfinished Apology: A Study of His Plan*. New Haven: Yale University Press, 1952.
Jackson, R. L. "Aristotelian Movement and Design in Part Two of *Notes from*

the Underground." Pages 66–81 in *Dostoevsky: New Perspectives*. Edited by R. L. Jackson. Englewood Cliffs, N.J.: Prentice-Hall, 1984.

———. "The Wound and the Lamentation: Ivan's Rebellion." Pages 119–35 in *Fyodor Dostoevsky's* The Brothers Karamazov. Edited by H. Bloom. New York: Chelsea House, 1988.

Kantor, V. "Pavel Smerdyakov and Ivan Karamazov: The Problem of Temptation." Pages 189–225 in *Dostoevsky and the Christian Tradition*. Edited by G. Pattison and D. O. Thompson. Cambridge: Cambridge University Press, 2001.

Kaufman, W., ed. and trans. *Goethe's Faust*. New York: Doubleday, 1961.

Kazin, A. "Ishmael and Ahab." *Atlantic Monthly* 198, no. 5 (November 1956): 83. Repr. pages 28–30 in *Ahab*. Edited by H. Bloom. New York: Chelsea House, 1991.

Kloppenborg, J. S. *The Formation of Q: Trajectories in Ancient Wisdom Collections*. Harrisburg, Pa.: Trinity Press International, 2000.

Knights, L. C. "On the Fool." In *Twentieth Century Interpretations of King Lear: A Collection of Critical Essays*. Edited by J. Adelman. Englewood Cliffs, N.J.: Prentice-Hall, 1978.

Kolakowski, L. *God Owes Us Nothing*. Chicago: University of Chicago Press, 1995.

Kronenfeld, J. *King Lear and the Naked Truth: Rethinking the Language of Religion and Resistance*. Durham: University of North Carolina Press, 1998.

Kurrick, M. J. "The Self's Negativity." Pages 97–118 in *Fyodor Dostoevsky's* The Brothers Karamazov. Edited by H. Bloom. New York: Chelsea House, 1988.

Lao Tzu. *The Way of Lao Tzu (Tao-te ching)*. Translated by W. T. Chan. New York: Macmillan, 1963.

Lebowitz, A. *Progress into Silence: A Study of Melville's Heroes*. Bloomington: Indiana University Press, 1970.

Lockerbie, D. B. "The Greatest Sermon in Fiction." *Christianity Today* 8 (8 November 1963): 9–12.

Mack, M. "The World of *King Lear*." Pages 56–69 in *Twentieth Century Interpretations of King Lear: A Collection of Critical Essays*. Edited by J. Adelman. Englewood Cliffs, N.J.: Prentice-Hall, 1978.

Markels, J. *Melville and the Politics of Identity: From* King Lear *to* Moby Dick. Urbana: University of Illinois Press, 1993.

Marx, S. *Shakespeare and the Bible*. New York: Oxford University Press, 2000.

Matteson, J. T. "The Little Lower Layer: Anxiety and the Courage to Be in *Moby-Dick*." *Harvard Theological Review* 81 (1988): 97–116.

McFarland, T. "The Image of the Family in *King Lear*." Pages 91–118 in *On King Lear*. Edited by L. Danson. Princeton: Princeton University Press, 1981.

McSweeney, K. *Moby-Dick: Ishmael's Mighty Book.* Boston: Twayne Publishers, 1986.

Melville, H. *Moby-Dick.* Edited by H. Hayford and H. Parker. New York: W. W. Norton, 1967.

Melzer, S. E. *Discourses of the Fall: A Study of Pascal's* Pensées. Berkeley: University of California Press, 1986.

Mendelson, M. "*venter animi/distentio animi:* Memory and Temporality in Augustine's *Confessions.*" *Augustinian Studies* 31 (2000): 137–63.

Morgan, J. *The Psychological Teaching of St. Augustine.* London: Elliot Stock, 1932.

Morris, T. V. *Making Sense of It All: Pascal and the Meaning of Life.* Grand Rapids: Eerdmans, 1992.

Muir, K. "On Christian Values." Page 120 in *Twentieth Century Interpretations of King Lear: A Collection of Critical Essays.* Edited by J. Adelman. Englewood Cliffs, N.J.: Prentice-Hall, 1978.

Murphy, J. L. *Darkness and Devils: Exorcism and King Lear.* Athens: Ohio University Press, 1984.

Murphy, R. E. *The Tree of Life: An Exploration of Biblical Wisdom Literature.* 2d ed. Grand Rapids: Eerdmans, 1990.

Murray, H. A. "In Nomine Diaboli." Pages 3–21 in *Moby-Dick: Centennial Essays.* Edited by T. Hillway and L. S. Mansfield. Dallas: Southern Methodist University Press, 1953.

Nelson, R. J. *Pascal: Adversary and Advocate.* Cambridge: Harvard University Press, 1981.

Nevo, R. "On Lear and Job." Pages 120–22 in *Twentieth Century Interpretations of King Lear: A Collection of Critical Essays.* Edited by J. Adelman. Englewood Cliffs, N.J.: Prentice-Hall, 1978.

O'Donnell, J. J. *Augustine.* Boston: Twayne Publishers, 1985.

Olson, C. "Ahab and his Fool." Pages 55–58 in *Twentieth Century Interpretations of Moby-Dick: A Collection of Critical Essays.* Edited by M. T. Gilmore. Englewood Cliffs, N.J.: Prentice-Hall, 1977.

———. "Call Me Ishmael." Pages 13–37 in *Herman Melville's* Moby-Dick. Edited by H. Bloom. New York: Chelsea House, 1986.

Paffenroth, K. "Book Nine: The Emotional Heart of the *Confessions.*" In *A Reader's Guide to Augustine's Confessions.* Edited by K. Paffenroth and R. P. Kennedy. Louisville: Westminster John Knox, 2003.

———. "Paulsen on Augustine: An Incorporeal or Nonanthropomorphic God?" *Harvard Theological Review* 86 (1993): 233–35.

———. "Tears of Grief and Joy. Confessions Book 9: Chronological Sequence and Structure." *Augustinian Studies* 28 (1997): 141–54.

———. "The Testing of the Sage: 1 Kings 10:1–13 and Q 4:1–13." *The Expository Times* 107 (1996): 142–43.

Pascal, B. *Pensées.* Garden City, N.Y.: Doubleday, 1961.

———. *Pensées.* Translated by A. J. Krailsheimer. New York: Penguin, 1966.

Patrides, C. A., and J. Wittreich, eds. *The Apocalypse in English Renaissance Thought and Literature.* Ithaca, N.Y.: Cornell University Press, 1984.

Pattison, G. "Freedom's Dangerous Dialogue: Reading Dostoevsky and Kierkegaard Together." Pages 237–56 in *Dostoevsky and the Christian Tradition.* Edited by G. Pattison and D. O. Thompson. Cambridge: Cambridge University Press, 2001.

Pelikan, J. *Faust the Theologian.* New Haven: Yale University Press, 1995.

———. *Fools for Christ: Essays on the True, the Good, and the Beautiful.* Philadelphia: Fortress Press, 1955.

Pevear, R. "The Mystery of Man in Dostoevsky." *Sourozh* 66 (1996): 31–35.

Rackin, P. "On Edgar: Delusion as Resolution." Pages 123–25 in *Twentieth Century Interpretations of King Lear: A Collection of Critical Essays.* Edited by J. Adelman. Englewood Cliffs, N.J.: Prentice-Hall, 1978.

Rad, G. von, *Wisdom in Israel.* Translated by J. D. Martin. Nashville: Abingdon Press, 1972.

Reardon, P. H. "Captain Ahab's Rebellion." *Touchstone* 8 (1995): 15–18.

Rice, J. C. "The Empathic Edgar: Creativity as Redemption in *King Lear.*" *Studia Mystica* 7 (1984): 50–60.

Rosenshield, G. "Mystery and Commandment in *The Brothers Karamazov.*" *Journal of the American Academy of Religion* 62 (1994): 483–508.

Sachs, V. "Moby Dick; or The Wale [*sic*] et l'écriture biblique." *Foi et Vie* 90 (1991): 81–92.

Schwehn, M. "*King Lear* beyond Reason." *First Things* 36 (1993): 25–33.

Scott, R. B. Y. *The Way of Wisdom in the Old Testament.* New York: Macmillan, 1971.

Sealts, M. M., Jr. "Melville and the Platonic Tradition." Pages 355–76 in *Critical Essays on Herman Melville's* Moby-Dick. Edited by B. Higgins and H. Parker. New York: G. K. Hall, 1992.

Seeley, F. F. "Ivan Karamazov." Pages 115–36 in *New Essays on Dostoevsky.* Edited by M. V. Jones and G. M. Terry. Cambridge: Cambridge University Press, 1983.

Sherrill, R. A. "The Career of Ishmael's Self-Transcendence." Pages 73–95 in *Herman Melville's* Moby-Dick. Edited by H. Bloom. New York: Chelsea House, 1986.

Sitney, P. A. "Ahab's Name: A Reading of 'The Symphony.'" Pages 131–45 in *Herman Melville's* Moby-Dick. Edited by H. Bloom. New York: Chelsea House, 1986.

Skehan, P. W., and A. A. Di Lella, *The Wisdom of Ben Sira: A New Translation with Notes.* New York: Doubleday, 1987.

Slotkin, R. "*Moby-Dick:* The American National Epic." Pages 13–26 in

Twentieth Century Interpretations of Moby-Dick: A Collection of Critical Essays. Edited by M. T. Gilmore. Englewood Cliffs, N.J.: Prentice-Hall, 1977.

Smith, H. N. "The Image of Society in *Moby-Dick.*" Pages 27–41 in *Twentieth Century Interpretations of Moby-Dick: A Collection of Critical Essays.* Edited by M. T. Gilmore. Englewood Cliffs, N.J.: Prentice-Hall, 1977.

Soltau, R. H. *Pascal: The Man and the Message.* Westport, Conn.: Greenwood Press, 1970. Originally published 1927.

Stampfer, J. "Reply to 'The Modern Job.'" *Judaism* 13 (1964): 361–63.

Stout, J. "Melville's Use of the Book of Job." *Nineteenth-Century Fiction* 25 (1970): 69–83.

Sundberg, W. "The Demonic in Christian Thought." *Lutheran Quarterly* 1 (1987): 413–37.

Sutherland, S. R. "The Philosophical Dimension: Self and Freedom." Pages 169–85 in *New Essays on Dostoevsky.* Edited by M. V. Jones and G. M. Terry. Cambridge: Cambridge University Press, 1983.

Szabo, I. B. "'Robed Man of Justice': The Hermeneutics of Testimony and *King Lear.*" *Journal of Literature and Theology* 3 (1989): 331–40.

Taylor, M. L. "Ishmael's (m)Other: Gender, Jesus, and God in Melville's *Moby-Dick.*" *Journal of Religion* 72 (1992): 325–50.

Terras, V. "The Art of Fiction as a Theme in *The Brothers Karamazov.*" Pages 193–205 in *Dostoevsky: New Perspectives.* Edited by R. L. Jackson. Englewood Cliffs, N.J.: Prentice-Hall, 1984.

Thompson, L. *Melville's Quarrel with God.* Princeton, N.J.: Princeton University Press, 1952.

VanZanten Gallagher, S. "The Prophetic Narrator of *Moby-Dick.*" *Christianity and Literature* 36 (1987): 11–25.

Vetlovskaya, V. A. "Alyosha Karamazov and the Hagiographic Hero." Pages 206–26 in *Dostoevsky: New Perspectives.* Edited by R. L. Jackson. Englewood Cliffs, N.J.: Prentice-Hall, 1984.

Ward, B. K. "Christianity and the Modern Eclipse of Nature: Two Perspectives." *Journal of the American Academy of Religion* 63 (1995): 823–43.

Warren, M. J. "Quarto and Folio *King Lear* and the Interpretation of Albany and Edgar." Pages 45–56 in *William Shakespeare's King Lear.* Edited by H. Bloom. New York: Chelsea House, 1987.

Webb, D. A. "Dostoevsky and Christian Agnosticism." *The Iliff Review* 27 (1970): 31–39.

Wetsel, D. *Pascal and Disbelief: Catechesis and Conversion in the* Pensées. Washington, D.C.: Catholic University of America Press, 1994.

Whybray, R. N. *Ecclesiastes.* New Century Bible Commentary. Grand Rapids: Eerdmans, 1989.

Wiesel, E. *The Trial of God*. Translated by M. Wiesel. New York: Schocken Books, 1979.

Williams, G. W. "Petitionary Prayer in *King Lear*." *South Atlantic Quarterly* 85 (1986): 360–73.

Wittreich, J. *"Image of That Horror": History, Prophecy, and Apocalypse in King Lear*. San Marino, Calif.: Huntington Library, 1984.

———. "'Image of that Horror': The Apocalypse in *King Lear*." Pages 175–206 in *The Apocalypse in English Renaissance Thought and Literature*. Edited by C. A. Patrides and J. Wittreich. Ithaca, N.Y.: Cornell University Press, 1984.

Woodson, T. "Ahab's Greatness: Prometheus as Narcissus." Pages 440–55 in *Critical Essays on Herman Melville's* Moby-Dick. Edited by B. Higgins and H. Parker. New York: G. K. Hall, 1992.

Wright, N. *Melville's Use of the Bible*. Durham, N.C.: Duke University Press, 1949.

Young, W. A. "Leviathan in the Book of Job and *Moby-Dick*." *Soundings* 65 (1982): 388–401.

Zhitlowsky, C. "Job and Faust." Translated by P. Matenko. Pages 71–162 in *Two Studies in Yiddish Culture*. Leiden: E. J. Brill, 1968.

Ziarek, E. "'Surface Stratified on Surface': A Reading of Ahab's Allegory." *Criticism* 31 (1989): 271–86.

Ziff, L. "Shakespeare and Melville's America." Pages 54–67 in *New Perspectives on Melville*. Edited by F. Pullin. Kent, Ohio: Kent State University Press, 1978.

Ziolkowski, E. J. "Reading and Incarnation in Dostoevsky." Pages 156–70 in *Dostoevsky and the Christian Tradition*. Edited by G. Pattison and D. O. Thompson. Cambridge: Cambridge University Press, 2001.

Ziolkowski, M. "Dostoevsky and the Kenotic Tradition." Pages 31–40 in *Dostoevsky and the Christian Tradition*. Edited by G. Pattison and D. O. Thompson. Cambridge: Cambridge University Press, 2001.

Zoellner, R. "Ahab's Entropism and Ishmael's Cyclicism." Pages 104–15 in *Ahab*. Edited by H. Bloom. New York: Chelsea House, 1991.

———. "Queequeg: The Well-Governed Shark." Pages 87–93 in *Twentieth Century Interpretations of Moby-Dick: A Collection of Critical Essays*. Edited by M. T. Gilmore. Englewood Cliffs, N.J.: Prentice-Hall, 1977.

Index

1984 (Orwell), 10
Acts, book of the
  6:3   79
  6:10   79
  7:10   79
  7:22   79
Adam, K., 51, 143
Adamson, D., 99
Adelman, J., 80–83, 143, 144, 146–49
Aesop, 3
Anchor, R., 52, 143
Andrews, W. P., 51, 143
Arnold, D. S., 126, 132–33, 143
Auden, W. H., 127, 143
Augustine, xi–xiv, 11, 33, 37–42, 49, 138–40, 143
  life of, 37–40
  and reason, 40–41
  and wisdom, 40–42, 49

Baird, J., 130, 131, 143
Balthasar, Hans Urs von, 52
Barber, C. L., 80, 83, 143
Barone, Amy, xv
Barth, Karl, xii
Basney, L., 80–82, 144
Batson, E. B., 80, 144
Beckett, Samuel, 71
Behnken, E. M., 127, 129, 130, 144

Belknap, R. L., 29, 144
Ben Sira. *See* Sirach, book of
Bernstein, J., 128, 144
Bertonneau, Tom, xv
Blackmur, R. P., 28, 29, 31, 144
Bloom, Harold, 30, 31, 59, 62, 63, 70, 79–83, 127–30, 133, 142–51
Boadt, L., 27, 144
Bolles, Rick, xv
Booth, S., 79, 81, 82, 144
Braswell, W., 127, 144
Breyfogle, Todd, xv
Brothers Karamazov, The (Dostoevsky), 9, 17–26, 145
  character of Alyosha in, 17, 22, 24, 140
  character of Fyodor in, xii, 17–18, 25, 138–40
  character of Ivan in, 19–22, 138
  character of Smerdyakov in, 18
  character of Zossima in, 17, 22–26, 140
  Christ in, 20–23
  folly in, xii, 17–26
  freedom in, 20–26
  Grand Inquisitor story in, 20–22
  Karamazov family resemblance in, xiv, 18, 29
  love in, 24–26

Satan in, 21, 23
suffering in, 19–20
Brown, Brian, xiv
Brown, J. K., 51, 52, 144
Brown, P., 50, 51, 144
Bruce, F. F., 79, 144
Buddha, 78
Bultmann, Rudolf, xii

Cady, Edwin, 129, 144
Calderwood, J. L., 82, 83, 145
Camp, C. V., 50, 145
Capps, Donald, 51
Carrigan, Henry, xv
Cary, P., 51
Casino, Christine, xv
Catteau, J., 29, 145
Chadwick, H., 50, 145
Chan, W. T., 52, 147
Chase, Richard, 129
Chesterton, G. K., 125
Chevalier, J., 99
Christ
    and Adam, 93–94, 116–17
    in *The Brothers Karamazov*, 20–23
    death and resurrection of, 4, 20, 26, 141
    folly of, xiii–xiv, 54–56, 65, 77–79
    kenosis of, 23
Coleridge, Samuel Taylor, 82
Colossians, letter to the
1:9	79
1:28	79
2:3	79
2:23	79
3:16	79
4:5	79

Confessions (Augustine), xi, 38–42, 143
    pear theft in, 11
Confucius, 3
Corinthians, first letter to the
1:18–25	54
1:26–28	55
2:3–4	55
2:6	55
3:10	79
6:5	79
12:8	79
13:4	75
13:5	77
13:6	72
13:7	74
13:8	74, 141
13:11	77
15:36	71
15:42–43	71

Corinthians, second letter to the
11:23	73
11:30	55

Costanza, George, 8
Cowan, B., 128, 145
Crenshaw, J. L., 27, 50, 97, 98, 125, 145

Danby, J. F., 82, 145
Danson, L., 79, 145, 147
Dante, 8, 122
Darwin, Charles, 135
Davidson, C., 81, 145
Davidson, H. M., 99, 145
Death of a Salesman (Miller), 61
Deignan, Kathleen, xiv
DePalo, Erica, xv
Descartes, 28
Deuteronomy, book of
6:5	100, 142

DiLella, A. A., 27, 149
Dittes, J. E., 51
Doody, Jack, xiv
Dostoevsky, Fyodor, xi, xiii, xv, 7–26, 89, 106, 145
    belief in God, 19
    life of, 7
Downing, K. K., xv
Dryden, E. A., 132, 145
Durning, Robert, xiv

Earhart Foundation, xv
Ecclesiastes, book of, xiii, xvi, 3, 86–87
1:1	86
1:12	86
1:13	86
2:10–11	86
2:13–14	86
2:17	86
2:24	86

3:11	87
3:12–13	86
3:18–22	87
3:22	86
5:18–19	86
7:27	86
8:18–19	86
9:7–9	86
11:7–10	86
12:9–10	86

Ecclesiasticus. *See* Sirach, book of
Ehrman, Bart D., 145
Elton, W. R., 79, 81–83, 145
Eodice, Alex, xiv
Ephesians, letter to the

1:8	79
1:17	79
3:10	79
5:15	79

Fairley, B., 52, 145
faith
   of Dostoevsky, 19
   in Ecclesiastes, 86–87
   and the heart, 96–97
   in Job, 105–06
   in *Moby-Dick*, 115–16
   and reason, xi, xiv, 88, 94–96
Faust (Goethe), xiv, 42–47, 49, 138–40, 146
   character of Faust in, xiv, 33, 42–47, 49, 118
   character of Gretchen in, xi, xiv, 33, 45–47
   character of Mephisto in, 44–47
   Mary in, 46–47, 49
   reason in, 43–44
   suffering in, 43–44
Florovsky, G., 28–31, 145
folly, xiii
   in *The Brothers Karamazov*, 17–26
   of Christ, xiii–xiv, 53–56, 65, 77–79
   and evil, xiii, 21–22, 89
   and free will, 12, 20–22
   in Job, 104–05
   in *King Lear*, 64–65, 71–77
   necessity of, xiii, 15–16
   in *Notes from Underground*, 7–17
   personified, 34
   in Proverbs, xii, 4–7
   self–destructiveness of, 4–7
   in Sirach, 4–7
Ford, Henry, 78
France, R. T., 80, 145
Franklin, H. B., 127, 145
Freedman, David N., 125
Freedman, Jenna, xv
Freud, Sigmund, 135
Friedman, M., 129, 130, 145
Frodsham, J. D., 30, 141, 145

Gandhi, Mohandas, 141
Gardner, J. F., 127, 131, 145
Garnett, C., 27, 28
Gates, Bill, 78
Genesis, book of

1:1–31	35
1:27	87

George, P., 29, 146
Gibson, A. B., 28, 30, 31, 146
Gilmore, M. T., 126, 127, 148, 150, 151
Gleim, W. S., 130, 146
God
   faith in, 19, 86–87, 105–06, 115–16
   feminine depiction of, 121–24
   humans as image of, 23–24
   justice of, 19–20, 69–70, 103–05, 113, 139
   masculine depiction of, 33, 36–37, 39–40
Goddard, H. C., 82, 146
Goethe, J. W. von, xi, 42–47, 49, 146
Goldberg, S. L., 80, 146
Green, J. B., 52, 146
Groundhog Day, 9
Guardini, R., 98, 99, 146
Gunn, G., 129, 144

Hackel, S., 29, 30, 146
Hamilton, W., 128, 146
Hamlet (Shakespeare), 60–61, 80
Harbage, Alfred, 81
Harris, Angela, xv

Hawkins, A. H., 51
Hawthorne, Nathaniel, 126
Hayford, H., 126, 128, 146, 148
Hazelton, R., 99, 100, 146
Hefner, Hugh, 78
Hegedus, L., 27, 28, 146
Herbert, T. W. Jr., 128
Higgins, B., 127, 128, 146, 149, 151
Hill, Ian, xv
Hill, Marylu, xv
Hill, N. K., 128, 131, 146
Hillway, T., 126, 148
Hitler, 137
Holmain, C. H., 130–32, 146
Holquist, M., 28, 146
Holstein, J. A., 129, 146
Hubert, M. L., 98, 99, 146

Iago, 62
Iona College, xiv–xv

Jackson, R. L., 28–30, 144–47, 150
James, letter of
  1:5   79
  3:13   79
  3:15–16   63
  3:15–17   53
  3:17   72, 74, 79
  5:11   102, 139
Jarrell, Bob, xv
Jesus. *See* Christ.
Job, book of, xii, xiv, xvi, 3, 43, 70–71, 92–94, 101–06, 112–16, 138–40
  1:14–19   115, 130
  1:21   102
  2:10   102
  4:7   102
  11:6   102
  13:3   102
  40:4–5   104
  40:12–14   103–04
  41:7   114
  41:26–29   114
  42:5   105
  42:5–6   70
  42:6   102, 104
  42:7–8   104
  42:8   105

Jones, M. V., 29, 30, 146, 149, 150
Judas, 18, 116
Judas Priest, vii, xii
Jung, Carl, 60

Kant, Immanuel, 42
Kantor, V., 29, 30, 147
Kaufman, W., 51, 147
Kazin, A., 128, 147
Kennedy, Robert P., xv, 51, 141
King, Martin Luther Jr., 141
King Lear (Shakespeare), vii, xv, 138–40
  apocalyptic imagery of, 59–60
  character of Albany in, 64–65
  character of Cordelia in, xiv, 52, 72–74
  character of Edgar in, 74–75
  character of Edmund in, 62, 64, 109
  character of Fool in, 72–74
  character of Goneril in, 62–65
  character of Kent in, 74–75
  character of Lear in, xii, xiv, 60–62, 65–72, 75–77, 109, 118, 138–40
  character of Oswald in, 67–68
  Christianity of, 59–60
  clothing in, 66–68
  folly in, xiv, 64–65, 71–77
  love in, 71–77
  nature in, 63, 75
  plot of, 56–59
  worldly wisdom in, 62–71
Kloppenborg, J. S., 79, 147
Knights, L. C., 81–82, 147
Kolakowski, L., 98, 147
Krailsheimer, A. J., 98
Kronenfeld, J., 147
Kurosawa, Akira, 61
Kurrick, M. J., 31, 147

Lao Tzu, 48, 52, 147
Lebowitz, A., 126, 127, 147
Levenson, Jon, xv
Leviticus, book of
  19:18   100, 142
  25:23   70
Lincoln, Abraham, 141

literature
    as expressing theological truth, xi–xiv
Lockerbie, D. B., 129, 147
love
    in Augustine, 40–42
    in *The Brothers Karamazov*, 24–26
    in *Faust*, 44–47
    of God, 106
    in *King Lear*, 71–77
    and lust, 63–64, 77–79
    in *Moby-Dick*, 111–12, 116–17, 119, 122–25
    in *Notes from Underground*, 14–17
    and wisdom, 34, 36–37, 40–42, 77–79, 96–97, 124–25, 139, 141–42
Luke, gospel of

1:38	49
2:19	49
2:40	79
2:51	49
2:52	79
7:35	79
10:21	54
10:27	141
11:31	79
11:49	79

Macbeth (Shakespeare), 52, 60–61, 79
Mack, M., 83, 147
Manichees, 38–40
Mansfield, L. S., 126, 148
Mark, gospel of

6:2	79
12:29–31	142
12:30–31	100

Markels, J., 126, 127, 147
Martin, J. D., 27, 125, 149
Marx, Karl, 135
Marx, S., 80–82, 147
Mary (mother of Jesus), 46–47, 49, 77
Matenko, P., 51, 151
Matteson, J. T., 128, 131, 132, 147
Matthew, gospel of

7:24	79
10:16	79
11:19	79
11:25	54
12:42	79
13:54	79
16:8	79
21:15	79
22:37–38	142
22:37–39	100

Matthews, Alexandra, 27
McCann, D. J., 51, 142
McCutcheon, Bob, xv
McFarland, T., 79–82, 147
McMahon, Bob, xv
McSweeney, K., 126, 148
Melville, Herman, xi, xv, 88–89, 98, 106–25, 148
    life of, 106
Melzer, S. E., 98, 99, 148
Mendelson, M., 142, 148
Miller, Arthur, 61
Miller, R. F., 28, 144
Moby-Dick (Melville), 106–25, 148
    character of Ahab in, xii, 106–11, 113, 117–25, 138–40
    character of Bildad in, 113
    character of Fedallah in, 118, 122
    character of Flask in, 114, 120, 122
    character of Ishmael in, xiv, 111–12, 120–25, 140
    character of Peleg in, 108, 113
    character of Pip in, 119–20, 122
    character of Queequeg in, xiv, 115–17, 122
    character of Starbuck in, 111, 113, 117–20, 122
    character of Stubb in, 114, 120, 122
    feminine imagery in, 121–24
    free will in, 118–21, 123
    God in, xiv, 107, 109–10, 113, 115–16, 118, 120
    human nature in, 108–12
    love in, 111–12, 116–17, 119, 122–25
    reason in, 117–21
    sea in, 122, 124–25
    suffering in, xiv, 110, 113, 120
    use of Scripture in, 112–17
    whales in, 114, 120–22

the White Whale in, xiv, 107, 111, 113
Monica (Augustine's mother), xi, xiv, 33, 38–39, 41–42
Moore, Kelsey, 28
Morehead, Dan, xv
Morgan, J., 98, 148
Morris, T. V., 98, 100, 128, 133, 148
Mother Theresa, 78
Muir, K., 83, 148
Murphy, J. L., 79, 148
Murphy, R. E., xvi, 27, 49, 50, 97, 125, 148
Murray, H. A., 126, 129, 132, 148

Nelson, R. J., 98, 99, 148
Nevo, R., 80, 81, 148
Notes from Underground (Dostoevsky), 138, 140, 145
   character of Liza in, xiv, 14–17
   character of narrator in, xiv, 7–17, 20–21, 25, 138, 140
   folly in, xii, 7–17
   free will in, 12
   love in, 14–17
   reason in, 9–10
   self-interest in, 10–12

O'Boyle, Colleen, xv
O'Connor, Flannery, 62, 80
O'Donnell, J. J., 50, 148
Oedipus, 28, 61, 80
Olson, C., 127, 128, 131, 148
On the Free Choice of the Will (Augustine), 51
Ophelia, 52
Orestes, 61, 80
Orwell, George, 10
Othello (Shakespeare), 60–61
Owens, Tim, xv

Paffenroth, Charles, xvi
Paffenroth, Kim, 50, 51, 79, 143, 148
Paffenroth, Marlis, xvi
Paffenroth, Sophia, xvi
Parker, H., 126–128, 146, 148, 149, 151
Pascal, Blaise, xi, xii, xiv, 87–96, 107, 116–18, 125, 138–40, 149

Patricius (Augustine's father), 38–39, 41–42
Patrides, C. A., 79, 149, 151
Pattison, G., 28–30, 149, 151
Paul, 54–56
Pelikan, J., 29, 51, 52, 149
Pensées (Pascal), 107, 149
   human nature in, 89–92, 108–09
   idea of the heart in, 96–97
   reason in, xiv, 87–96
   use of Scripture in, 92–94
Peter, second letter of
   1:16   79
   3:15   79
Pevear, R., 29, 30, 149
Poidomani, Lina, xv
Procario-Foley, Elena, xiv
Proverbs, book of, xii–xiv, xvi, 3–7, 33–35
   1:7   6
   1:8   34
   1:20   34
   1:23   34
   3:7   6
   5:1–14   4–5
   5:22   5
   6:20   34
   7:1–27   5
   8:10–11   34
   8:13   6
   8:15–16   34
   8:17   34, 141
   8:18   34
   8:21   34
   8:22–23   35
   8:29–30   35
   8:30–31   35
   9:2–5   34
   9:10   6, 141
   9:3–18   34
   10–29   xiii
   10:1   34
   15:1   3
   15:33   6
   19:8   3
   20:13   5
   22:1   6
   23:26–28   5

23:29–35	5
24:13	3
24:30–34	5
26:13–16	5
26:18–19	6
27:6	105
27:17	105
31:2	34

Pullin, F., 126, 127, 146, 151

Q (gospel source), 53–54, 79
Qoheleth. *See* Sirach, book of

Rackin, Phyllis, 68, 81, 149
Rad, G. von, 27, 125, 149
Ran (Kurosawa), 61
Rapunzel, 52
Reardon, P. H., 127, 129, 149
reason
   in Augustine, 40–41
   in Ecclesiastes, 86–87
   and faith, xi, xiv, 88, 94–96
   in *Faust*, 43–44
   inadequacy of, xiii–xiv, 86–97, 117–21
   in *Moby-Dick*, 117–21
   in *Notes from Underground*, 9–10
   in Pascal, 87–96
Revelation, book of

5:12	79
7:12	79
13:18	79
17:9	79

Rice, J. C., 80–83, 130, 149
Richard III, 62
Robinson, Susan, xv
Rogers, Kenny, 99
Romans, letter to the

1:14	79
1:22	79
5:14	99
11:25	79
11:33	79
12:16	79
16:19	79
16:27	79

Rosenshield, G., 31, 149

Sachs, Joe, xv
Sachs, V., 128, 149
Satan
   in *The Brothers Karamazov*, 21, 23
Schindler, Dave Jr., xv
Schwehn, M., 80–82, 149
Scott, R. B. Y., xvi, 27, 97, 125, 149
Sealts, M. M. Jr., 149
Seeley, F. F., 29, 149
Seinfeld, 8
Seitz, C. R., 125
Shakespeare, William, xi, xii, 15, 56–77
Sherrill, R. A., 133, 149
Siconolfi, Matilda, 52
Sirach, book of, 3–7, 33

1:4	35
1:11	6
1:11–30	6
2:15	6
9:1–9	5
19:20	6
21:28	6
22:1–2	5
22:18–26	5
24:3	35
24:8–12	35
24:15	35
24:17	35
24:19	35, 141
24:23	35
24:28	35
24:32–33	35
27:16	6
31:24	6
31:25–31	5
37:30	3
38:1–2	5

Sitney, P. A., 127, 131, 149
Skehan, P. W., 27, 149
Slotkin, R., 126, 130, 149–50
Smith, H. N., 126, 130, 150
Snow White, 52
Socrates, 141
Soliloquies (Augustine), 40–41, 51, 143
Solomon, 86, 89, 92–94, 99
Soltau, R. H., 98, 133, 150
Song of Songs, the

8:6–7	34, 141

Sophocles, xii, 15
Srozenski, Barbara, xiv
Stampfer, J., 127, 133, 150
Stone, Geoffrey, 129
Stout, J., 129, 133, 150
suffering, xiii
   in *The Brothers Karamazov*, 19–20
   and evil, 103–06
   in *Faust*, 43–44
   in Job, xii, xiv, 101–06
   in *King Lear*, 70–72, 74–75
   in *Moby-Dick*, xiv, 110, 113, 120
Sundberg, W., 51–52, 150
Sutherland, S. R., 30, 150
Swanwick, A., 51, 146
Szabo, I. B., 150

Taoism, 48
Taylor, M. L., 126, 130, 132, 150
Terras, V., 30, 150
Terry, G. M., 29, 30, 146, 149, 150
Thompson, B., 98
Thompson, D. O., 28–30, 149, 151
Thompson, L., 129, 150
Tillich, Paul, xii
Timothy, second letter to
   3:15   79
Tipton, Glenn, xv
Travis, Scott, xv
Trial of God, The (Wiesel), 105
Troeltsch, Ernst, xii

VanZanten Gallagher, S., 127, 133, 150
Vetlovskaya, V. A., 28, 150
Villanova University, xiv–xv

Ward, B. K., 30, 150
Warren, M. J., 79, 150
Webb, D. A., 27, 29, 150
Weimer, Brian, xv
Wetsel, D., 99, 150

Whybray, R. N., 97, 150
Wiesel, Elie, 105, 126, 151
Wiesel, M., 126, 151
Williams, G. W., 151
wisdom
   as common sense, 3–7
   as Creator, 34–37
   difference between early and late, xvi, 85–86, 101
   in Ecclesiastes, 86–87
   as "fear of the Lord," 6–7, 140–41
   feminine aspects of, xiii–xiv, 33–49
   and the heart, 96–97
   and love, xiv, 34, 36–37, 40–42, 77–79, 96–97, 124–25, 139, 141–42
   and memory, 139–40
   in the New Testament, 53–56
   outside of Israel, xiii
   and persistence, 139
   personified, xi, 34–37, 40–41, 140
   in Proverbs, 3–7, 34–35
   in Q, 53–54
   relation to prudence, 1–3
   in Sirach, 3–7, 35
   as Torah, 35
Wisdom, book of, xiii, 33, 35–36
   8:5–6   36
   9:9   35
Wittreich, J., 79, 80, 82, 149, 151
Woodson, T., 127, 151
Wright, N., 129, 151

yin and yang, 48, 141–42
Young, W. A., 128, 130, 132, 151

Zhitlowsky, C., 51, 52, 151
Ziarek, E., 131, 151
Ziff, L., 127, 151
Ziolkowski, E. J., 151
Ziolkowski, M., 30, 151
Zoellner, R., 126, 130, 132, 151

www.ingramcontent.com/pod-product-compliance
Lightning Source LLC
Chambersburg PA
CBHW061838300426
44115CB00013B/2433